Sex before Sexuality

Themes in History

Sex before Sexuality

A Premodern History

Kim M. Phillips and Barry Reay

polity

Copyright © Kim M. Phillips and Barry Reay 2011

The right of Kim M. Phillips and Barry Reay to be identified as Author of this Work has been asserted in accordance with the UK Copyright, Designs and Patents Act 1988.

First published in 2011 by Polity Press

Polity Press
65 Bridge Street
Cambridge CB2 1UR, UK

Polity Press
350 Main Street
Malden, MA 02148, USA

ISBN-13: 978-0-7456-2522-5
ISBN-13: 978-0-7456-2523-2(pb)

A catalogue record for this book is available from the British Library.

Typeset in 10.5 on 12 pt Times
by Toppan Best-set Premedia Limited
Printed and bound in Great Britain by MPG Books Group Limited, Bodmin, Cornwall

The publisher has used its best endeavours to ensure that the URLs for external websites referred to in this book are correct and active at the time of going to press. However, the publisher has no responsibility for the websites and can make no guarantee that a site will remain live or that the content is or will remain appropriate.

Every effort has been made to trace all copyright holders, but if any have been inadvertently overlooked the publisher will be pleased to include any necessary credits in any subsequent reprint or edition.

For further information on Polity, visit our website: www.politybooks.com

Contents

List of Images

Acknowledgements

We would like to thank the editors at Polity Press for their patience and enthusiasm for the project; Louis Gerdelan and (eagle-eyed) Nina Attwood for expert research assistance; Lisa Bailey for help on late antique and early medieval scholarship; Erin Griffey for her art history expertise; the Faculty of Arts at the University of Auckland for the Faculty Research Development Fund which enabled one of us (Phillips) to find the time to work on the project; our Head of Department, Malcolm Campbell; Sherry Velasco and Marta Vicente for allowing us to draw on their forthcoming publications; our respective partners, Athina Tsoulis and John Bevan-Smith, for their interest and emotional support, and to John for generously compiling the index; and University of Auckland students in courses on the history of sex for enlivening our teaching experience over several years.

Introduction: Sex before Sexuality

A woman bends over a man in a woodland glen. She is elegantly dressed in a low-cut rose-coloured gown, tight around her high breasts and narrow waist, then falling in fullness over a swelling belly. Her golden hair is fashionably dressed with a pointed kerchief. She gazes to the horizon as her right hand grasps the reclining man behind his back and her left reaches boldly under his raised tunic to fondle his naked thigh, or something higher up. We notice two troubled older men at the right of the scene, one raising his eyes and gesturing with dismay. The lady's right knee is raised to the young man's chest, pinning him to the ground. As he attempts to rise we see that his hands are bound behind his back. He is a handsome youth with fleshy lips and thick curling hair and his rich blue tunic is lined with fur. At first glance he might be thought to be rising to meet the embrace of the lady, gazing at her with abandoned desire, but at last one notices the bloody object he has spat at her face – his own tongue – and the bloody trail issuing from his mouth.

This scene from the Limbourg brothers' early fifteenth-century masterpiece, the *Belles Heures*, made for Jean de France, Duc de Berry (1340–1416), illuminates the story of St Paul the Hermit. Its accompanying text briefly tells the story: 'Saint Paul, the first hermit, under the vehement persecution of Decius, saw a certain Christian bound to a pleasurable place (*inter amena ligatus*), and caressed by an impure woman. Whereupon he bit off his tongue and spat in her face. To escape the anguish of temptation he [Paul] fled from Rome.'[1] *The Golden Legend* (*c.* 1260) explains in a little more detail that the unfortunate youth was one of two Christians tortured for their faith under Roman rule in the later third century; the first covered in honey and left to be stung to death by bees, hornets and wasps, the second 'laid upon a downy bed in a pleasant place . . . bound down with ropes entwined with flowers', and accosted by a 'very beautiful but totally depraved young woman'. Feeling his flesh responding in spite of himself, the youth repelled her in the only way left to him.[2]

St Paul the Hermit (not to be confused with St Paul the Apostle) is a minor figure in Christian hagiography and reasons for including his life in the *Belles Heures* are unclear. Most likely it gains a place simply to provide a vivid moment between the image cycles from the lives of the better-known figures St Jerome (who wrote Paul's hagiography) and St Anthony (who succeeded Paul as a pioneer among Christian hermits and is likely the second of the two older observers in the image in question). The book's owner, the Duc de Berry, younger brother of King Charles V (d. 1382) and uncle of Charles VI (d. 1422), was an important political figure of his day but is now mainly remembered for his lavish patronage of the arts. His sexual interests and preferences have also been subject to recent scholarly interest. Some art historians have suggested, taking their cues from hints in medieval texts, that he might have been 'homosexual'. Michael Camille has argued instead that his desire for bodies should be seen in relationship to his connoisseurship of images and things.[3] Living in an age when, as we will document at length in the present book, 'homosexuality', 'heterosexuality' and the other sexual categories familiar to us did not yet exist and women, youths and children were available for the possession of more powerful men, Jean took delight in the faces and bodies of lower-ranking androgynous young males in a manner congruent with the pleasure he took in the books and *objets* made for him by the greatest artists of his day. This pleasure, moreover, could sit happily alongside his apparent taste for very young or lower-class women.

What lessons or pleasures might the scene of *St Paul the Hermit Sees a Christian Tempted* have offered its owner? As a medieval Christian, Jean may have read it straight: that is, as an illustration of the temptations of the flesh and the virtues of carnal renunciation. All sexual response was understood in Jean's day and for several preceding centuries to be tainted to some extent with sin. The seductive *femme fatale* was a recurrent trope of Christian literature on sin – figured most prominently in the first woman, Eve, and her role in the fall of humankind – and the seductive woman of this scene could be sister to the 'dancing girls' seen tormenting the daydreaming St Jerome a few folios earlier.[4] Alternatively, the near helplessness of the man when provoked by the beautiful 'depraved' woman may have roused masculine sympathy. The sexually forward or dominant woman was familiar to readers of courtly literature and viewers of

Image 1. *Paul the Hermit Sees a Christian Tempted*, The Belles Heures of Jean de France, Duc de Berry, Herman, Paul and Jean de Limbourg (Franco-Netherlandish, active in France by 1399–1416), French, 1405–1408/1409. Tempera and gold leaf on vellum. Single leaf, 23.8 × 27 cm. The Metropolitan Museum of Art, The Cloisters Collection, 1954 (54.1.1). Image © The Metropolitan Museum of Art.

secular art.[5] The assertive woman of the *Belles Heures* reminds fifteenth-century viewers that women – in this pre-heterosexual erotic
regime – allegedly felt lust more powerfully than men and as such
were objects of at once phobic and ardent imaginings. Clothed and
in control, she poses an erotic alternative to the naked tortured
figures of virgin martyrs seen elsewhere in the book.[6] Indeed in the
hermit scene the roles are reversed: it is the male victim, bound and
assaulted, who has no escape except through brutal action on his own
body. The woman's cold gaze to the horizon, meanwhile, gives clear
indication (according to the visual codes of medieval art) that in this
case she is not in love.[7] Yet perhaps the youth's response is more
complex than fear or revulsion. As Brigitte Buettner reminds us in
her short but scintillating reading of the image, 'for medieval people
all bodily fluids, including semen, were considered to be a form of
bleeding'.[8] The youth's bleeding tongue is, by implication, a form of
ejaculation. Another reading could pick up on Jean's apparently
homoerotic inclinations (even if these were not his sole sexual tastes)
and see amusing connotations in the handsome youth's violent rejection of the temptress.

There are layers of looking: one hermit watches the couple, the
other looks to the heavens, the man directs his gaze at the woman,
the reader views the scene, and the temptress stares past both
the young man and the reader. Are there layers of touching too? The
woman fondles the young man, the painter caresses the page to
fashion the scene, and perhaps the book's owner, the Duc, is drawn
to touch the beautiful painting. Voyeurism and touch: is this piece of
religious art sexual?

None of these interpretations is necessarily more 'true' than any
other. What the scene can do is alert us to a few of the many strands
to premodern sexual cultures, warn us against singular or premature
interpretations, and illuminate the highly visible and often explicit
nature of premodern erotic representation. As we will argue near the
end of this volume, the modern discourse of 'pornography' is not very
helpful to us in interpreting premodern erotic images, yet sex was
very much 'on-scene'.

In his glittering exposition of male same-sex erotics in the early
modern Arab-Islamic world, Khaled El-Rouayheb has explained
the ways in which a society that seemed to have so many of the com-
ponents or strands that comprise the thing called homosexuality
never combined them in this sexual formation – the concept of homosexuality was available to that world only in the twentieth century.
Outsiders who have navigated that culture have been puzzled by its
perceived proscription of homosexual acts while simultaneously cel-

ebrating male beauty and the close male bonds that could tempt such breaches. Yet there was no contradiction. Much like the ancient Greeks, Ottoman literature distinguished commendable, chaste infatuation with youthful, male beauty from baser, carnal longing. The former, expressed in a whole genre of poetry, was aesthetic appreciation; the latter was the lust that might result in sexual contact. Anal intercourse was the male–male act that was severely proscribed but other sexual contact between males that did not involve intercourse was treated less seriously.[9]

In many respects this regime is reminiscent of sexual cultures in Classical Athens, but with a clearer prohibition on anal penetration. Scholarly debates endure on the question of whether Athenians and indeed other Greeks condoned most forms of consensual male–male sexual contact provided they respected broader social hierarchies including age, status and citizenship, or instead celebrated only chaste love between men and were more morally dubious about penetration.[10] Despite ongoing controversy, it appears that in both the early modern Ottoman and ancient Athenian contexts the active and passive in the sex act were conceived differently. Those prone to committing sodomy exhibited moral failure rather than sexual pathology in ways that will become familiar from the pages below.

In the premodern West, sex accommodated what we would term homosexual desire, in fact that desire was part of a culture that actively encouraged homosociality (strong bonds between men) and the homoerotic (representation of female–female and male–male desires). There are certainly behaviour and desires that prefigure what we would term heterosexual: opposite-sex courtship, the centrality of marriage and married reproduction, and male dominance. Shakespeare and other playwrights repeatedly take us through the various stages of man meets woman, man marries woman, and so on. So why should we hesitate to use the word 'heterosexuality' to describe premodern desires? Because the desires we have to deal with are different to those associated with conventional heterosexuality today.[11]

Critics once interpreted early modern drama in terms of heterosexual courtship and marriage. But for the sixteenth century and the first half of the seventeenth century, as Jean Howard has put it, the 'heterosexual marriage plot was carried out, literally, by a man and a boy actor'.[12] The Cleopatra who in 1606 referred, self-referentially, to 'Some squeaking Cleopatra boy . . . / I' th' posture of a whore' was indeed a boy.[13] The sexual permutations are bewildering when one thinks of the scenarios of early modern drama with boys playing women who cross-dress as men in pursuit of women who are really boy actors.[14] When two female characters dressed as boys fall in love with each other – as happens in John Lyly's *Gallathea* (1592) – did spectators focus on the male actors or the female characters? It is a question that has certainly divided modern critics.[15]

Stephen Orgel has explained premodern fears of what could happen when men watched boys playing female roles in the theatre. They might lust after the woman being played by the boy, but they might also yearn for the boy beneath the woman's clothing. When female actors replaced the boys in the later seventeenth century, the layers of lusting could be reversed. Although Orgel is more interested in the male-to-male erotics involved in these desires, the point really is that male wants were focused on both males and females, and the sexual identity of the spectator (as we would see it) was as unstable as the actor's. It is what Orgel refers to as 'an undifferentiated sexuality, a sexuality that does not distinguish men from women and reduces men to women'.[16] English drama indicates that both boys and women were objects of sexual desire for early modern men; and Alan Sinfield has isolated dramatic moments of the appeal of sexual ambivalence.[17] We certainly know that this was the case in Italy, where a boy's lack of beard, youth and beauty, and perceived passivity put him in the same category as a woman.[18] We are a long way from conventional modern heterosexuality. A similar point can be made for women: they might lust after the boy who they knew was beneath the clothing or be seduced by the surface woman. There is copious evidence of female homoerotics on the early modern stage.[19] Life could imitate art. The depositions relating to the marriage of two women in England in 1680 revealed that the woman who had assumed male identity during the ceremony had sometimes courted 'his' bride in woman's apparel, pretending to be a man in disguise![20]

The respective erotics of the premodern and modern are very different. Michael Rocke has explained the essential distinction between the sexual cultures of Renaissance Italy and the modern West as one of gender versus sex: in Renaissance Italy it was not 'the biological sex of one's partners in erotic pleasures that significantly distinguished and classified individuals, but rather the extent to which their sexual behaviour conformed to culturally determined gender roles'.[21]

This was a society, we need to remind ourselves, that could seriously consider copulation with demons and reflect upon the nature of the bodies, genitals, fluids and pleasures involved in such sexual transactions.[22] The demons in *Malleus Maleficarum* (1486–7) demonstrate remarkable erotic and gender versatility, able (as a succubus) to remove the semen from a man in order (as an incubus) to impregnate a woman. Their seed can mingle with the semen of a woman's husband if they follow marital congress. There are claims that men had witnessed demons 'performing such acts with their wives, though they thought them not to be demons but men'. And demons can pass seed from one to another between human transfer. 'It could happen that in place of one succubus demon another one receives the seed from him and makes himself an incubus in his place,' write the *Malleus*'s authors, though they do not explain how this male-to-male transfer might occur.[23] (These demons were what moderns might term aficionados of bisexual multi-partnered sex.)

The premodern dildo or statue with penis that emits fake semen in the form of milk or fluid to heighten its user's sexual passion – both mentioned in pornography and surviving as actual artefact – demonstrates at least some sexual dissonance between premodern and modern.[24] Such things are not quite what we have in mind when we think of modern heterosexuality. As Valerie Traub once put it, we will find neither heterosexuals nor homosexuals in the contemporary sense in the premodern world.[25]

The nineteenth century has a special place in the making of Western sex. The terms 'heterosexual', 'homosexual', 'lesbian', 'bisexual', 'sadist', 'masochist' – indeed 'sexuality' itself – all date from that period and are to be found in the works of those who came to be called the sexologists, those who made a scientific study of sexual behaviour.[26] Following the great Michel Foucault, Arnold Davidson has argued that the nineteenth century saw an epistemological or conceptual shift, with the emergence of 'new structures of knowledge' and 'a new style of reasoning'. The 'science of sexuality', he writes, 'made it possible, even inevitable, for us to become preoccupied with our true sexuality. Thus our existence became a sexistence, saturated with the promises and threats of sexuality.'[27] Both the word 'sexuality' and our sense of it date from the nineteenth century: 1879 according to the *Oxford English Dictionary*.[28]

In the period dealt with in this book, *c.* 1100–1800, there was sex but no sexuality. That is, modern preoccupations with the centrality of sexual habits, tastes or preferences (what are often termed 'orientations', 'identities') to one's *true* or *inner* self were yet to emerge. In a discussion of the much-printed, premodern medical text *Aristotle's Master-piece* (1684), Roy Porter explained its difference from modern sexology. *Aristotle's Master-piece* was not concerned with sexual identity, desire or perversion; it conveyed 'no notion that sexual activity involves problems inherent to the psyche and expressive of unconscious predicaments of the self'.[29]

If one person whips another in the modern West that act will reveal – however ritualistically – something of the sexuality of those involved, based on the biological sex of the flogger and flogged. It will be evidence of either heterosexual or homosexual sex and a declaration of the participant's sadism or masochism. But no such assumptions can be made of the premodern period, where, as Niklaus Largier has charted in some detail, flagellation was either an aesthetic religious act or a means of enabling the flow of blood and increasing bodily heat to facilitate female sexual pleasure or male erection.[30] When a nun in *Venus in the Cloister* (1725) scourges herself to discipline her immoderate desires, the joke is that it merely increases them: 'For thou must know that these Sorts of Exercises, far from extinguishing those Flames that consumed her, had on the contrary increased them more and more.'[31] Lawrence Stone misapprehended the cultural context when he referred to an episode of adultery, whipping and group sex in Norwich in the 1700s as a 'flagellant sex ring' and to what he termed the participants' 'psychosexual preoccupations'.[32] Neither description applies to the premodern period. Davidson has provided the telling comparison between a seventeenth-century medical treatise on the use of flogging to facilitate erection, and late nineteenth-century descriptions of masochism. The former, it was believed, involved a physiological (humoral) response to the stimulation of the blood; the latter was an expression of sexuality. The difference between the two was the difference between a physical and a psychological act, between therapy and identity.[33]

It is true that the authors of *A Treatise on the Use of Flogging in Venereal Affairs* (1718) hinted at those who derived rather too much pleasure from the act, the man 'who the more Stripes he received, was the more violently hurried to Coition . . . it was a Question which he desired most, the blows or the Act itself . . . a rare Instance of a Man who went with an equal pace to Pleasure and Pain'.[34] And there is a tantalizing reference to 'the Hanging-lechers', practising, presumably, a version of what is now termed erotic asphyxiation but based then on the logic of manipulation of the blood-flow.[35] Yet while the authors disagreed on the precise bodily architecture of the blood's flow, they were agreed that the predominant response was physiological, a matter of the stimulation of the blood, with heat transferred to the 'Organs of Generation'.[36] The flogging cure could be abused by those whose appetites and practices were excessive – 'for the Continuation of their ungovernable Lusts, and a Repetition of the same filthy Enjoyments' – but was also available for men whose flagging desire rendered them unable to perform their marital duty and to women who wanted to improve their fertility ('*Women too*, are raised and inflam'd by Strokes to a more easy Conception').[37]

We argue that historians of premodern sex will be constantly blocked in their understanding if they use terms and concepts applicable to sexuality since the late nineteenth century. The key words qualified in successive chapters – heterosexual, homosexual, lesbian, pornography – are products of a particular historical moment – modernity – and are best reserved for it. There is nothing at all revolutionary or exceptional about our analysis, although readers will see that it runs counter to the assumptions (assumed is the most accurate description) of many historians. If one attempts to understand the past on its own terms and to refuse to see sex and sexuality as somehow excluded from historical specificity, and if so much about our world is different from that of Athens in the fourth century BCE, or France in the twelfth century, or England in the seventeenth century, we should not be surprised to find a fundamentally different sexual regime there as well. Sex, as so many others have also argued, is a historical construct.

However, our approach could be said to run counter to one recent turn in sexuality studies. Though certainly sympathetic to Madhavi Menon's desire to avoid 'progressive chronology' and sharing her antipathy to teleology, we are puzzled by her claim that the separation between past and present in the history of sex is unavoidably a privileging of heterosexuality: what she terms 'hetero-time'.[38] Nothing could be further from our project. We are not historians who 'invest in a progressive chronology according to which the stable present becomes the point from which to map an unstable past (whose instability is fixed under the mark of its pastness)'.[39] (Indeed the most recent book by one of us has been primarily concerned with the instabilities of modern sexualities.[40]) Nor are we convinced of the wisdom – quite the opposite – of embracing an approach (what Menon calls homohistory) in which 'the past is not different from us, but rather coeval with the present and, ultimately, indistinguishable from it'.[41] We do not embrace 'an understanding of sexuality bound not to historical specificity but rather to rhetorical dexterity', where postmodern and premodern Shakespeare are indistinguishable.[42] Nor would we support Menon's endorsement of a recent collection of essays 'that takes seriously the condition of being out of time.... As long as queer Renaissance scholarship is tied *to* fixed time, it will also remained confined *by* it.'[43] For us, the historical context is all-important.

For others we will not have gone far enough in our deconstruction. Peter Cryle has argued that post-sexological (modern) meanings of desire, orgasm and a sexual act distort our understandings of their *ancien régime* approximations.[44] They, like our focused-upon heterosexual, homosexual, lesbian and pornographic, are subject to his 'distancing ... from the overweening assumptions of modern sexual knowledge'.[45] Yet even he cannot avoid using the very words whose cultural meanings he unpicks: 'My point, put most broadly, is that there was in eighteenth-century France a discursive order of pleasures and *desires* [our emphasis] other than the one that dominates our time.'[46]

In a way, medieval and early modern sex is more difficult to accommodate to the 'variation' model of sexual histories that we advocate than the sexual cultures of non-Western and classical societies have proved. It is not always as dramatically different from or unfamiliar to current Western sensibilities as Arab-Islamic or ancient Athenian sex. In some respects, premodern sexual norms share similarities with current Western ones. Monogamous marriage involving a man and a woman was a central institution of premodern sexual cultures, and to a large extent it still is. The Catholic Church is still headed by a celibate male priesthood and condemns same-sex sex, while sometimes practising it. Homosexual and lesbian cultures are arguably no more stable or easy to define than premodern patterns of relationships between men and between women.

Yet our appraisal, based on years of reading and analysis within the field, is that premodern sexual cultures were significantly different from modern or indeed postmodern ones and we misrepresent them if we emphasize historical continuities and enduring patterns of sexual identity. Surface likenesses, we believe, should not be read as samenesses.

We are intrigued by subtle as well as drastic differences between sexual cultures. The first chapter, 'Sin', explores the processes by which erotic desire and arousal in themselves – even within marriage or in the absence of a sexual act – came to be attainted as sinful from the beginning of the Christian era to the Reformation. It also seeks to show the inconsistencies in this message and its frequent disavowal. We begin by examining the problem of desire because it was so central to teachings on sex, especially during the medieval millennium, that any attempt to comprehend premodern eros is impossible without it. Before the modern 'invention' of sexuality, erotic acts and desires were comprehended as species of sin, not as outworkings of an aspect of one's innermost self.

The second chapter discusses the deceptively familiar contours of what we call 'Before Heterosexuality'. Romantic love was celebrated but (at least in the medieval era) thought possible only within a social elite. Desire and sexual activity could be licit outside of marriage but only with the expectation of an imminent wedding. Women were widely believed to be more sexually voracious than men, with the consequence that non-consent was hard to argue in rape cases and feminine fickleness and perfidy were articles of truth. Women had to orgasm to conceive. Male dominance was taken for granted and forceful sex could be celebrated even in courtly literature. Adultery was subject to both official and popular repression and the figure of the male cuckold was a reliable trope of risible masculinity. 'Unnatural' sex acts were as illicit within as outside of marriage.

The case for variation is easier to make in our other chapters. The third chapter, 'Between Men', embraces the diverse range of close or intimate relationships between men – often but not always erotic – expressed in premodern discourses.[47] Encompassing 'sodomy' (which did not initially or always refer to same-sex acts), active–passive relations, friendship and effeminacy, and often compatible with desire for women, premodern same-sex love and sex between men cannot be satisfactorily described by our term 'homosexuality'.

In the fourth chapter we come to similar conclusions about relationships 'between women', but insist that these must be examined in their own right and not only in conjunction with those 'between men'. 'Sodomy' could apply to sex between women, especially (though not only) where a phallic substitute was employed. Masculine behaviour and even male impersonation were regular means by which female–female desire was 'rendered intelligible'. Intensely affective relations or 'particular friendships' between women, especially in convents, deserve a place in this history even if we avoid the unanswerable question of whether erotic acts occurred, partly because they came under suspicion by contemporaries but also given current debates about where to draw the lines around the 'sexual'. Visionary writing further blurs the boundaries by expressing female desires for the feminine Divine. From the sixteenth century with the 'Renaissance of Lesbianism' new expressions of intimacy between women emerged, with the tribade, female husband, the secular friend and the Sapphist. We argue that comprehending such diversity of intimacy between women is limited by application of the label 'lesbian', though as in our chapter on men we demonstrate that exclusively homoerotic desires are indicated by the records on certain women.

Our final chapter seeks to explore sexually explicit art and literature in a time 'before pornography'. We examine the potential meanings and uses of the bawdy carvings, illuminations and ribald literature which proliferated in medieval and early modern cultures and whose purpose was only peripherally, if at all, to arouse.

We end with an epilogue that connects the premodern and modern worlds by setting out to sea. What did Europeans find when they ventured into new worlds such as the islands of the Pacific in the eighteenth and nineteenth centuries, and how far did these newly viewed erotic cultures cause upheaval in the worlds of the observers? We suggest, on the basis of the premodern cultures documented in our study, that Europeans found such features as sexual excess and homoeroticism less startling than some recent commentators have suggested. If one of our aims is to challenge simplistic notions of premodern 'heteronormativity' (an assumption that 'heterosexual' desires and practices are the norm) and sexual constraint, then, we hope the encounter of old and new sexual worlds will be found to be one aspect of sexual histories that needs rethinking.

The title of this book, *Sex before Sexuality*, is deliberately provocative, and not everyone will approve. 'Sexuality' possesses a range of meanings, common in both popular and academic usage. Anna Clark, who (contrary to Cryle) uses the term 'desire' as a heuristic device to link her general history of European sex, characterizes sexuality 'in its widest sense as the desires, relationships, acts, and identities concerned with sexual behavior', before she notes the complex relationship between these elements.[48] Another helpfully broad definition is offered by Ruth Mazo Karras in her survey of medieval sexuality: it 'refers to the whole realm of human erotic experience. Sexuality is the universe of meanings that people place on sex acts, rather than the acts themselves.'[49] This formulation has wide applicability, and it is not our intention to prohibit it; on the contrary the present authors have often used 'sexuality' or 'sexualities' in something like this meaning (though not excluding sex acts) in their own writings on premodern sexual histories.[50] In the present book, as already intimated, we prefer a more chronologically precise application. If Peter Stearns's title 'Sexuality before modern times' was taken literally it would – for us – be an oxymoron.[51] '"Sexuality"', Jeffrey Weeks observes, 'is a "fictional unity", that once did not exist, and at some time in the future may not exist again.'[52]

When *Before Sexuality* (1990), an important early collection of essays on ancient sex, proclaimed that sexuality is particular to modernity, a number of classical and medieval scholars raised objections, arguing that they had evidence for primary sexual preferences among ancient and medieval people.[53] The opposition by some to constructionist approaches to sexual histories, the idea that sexual desires, practices and the concepts associated with them are subject to fundamental variation across time, seems to have derived at least in part from the 'acts versus identities' debates of the 1980s and 1990s, stemming from Foucault's infamous passage in the first volume of his *The History of Sexuality* (1978):

> As defined by the ancient civil or canonical codes, sodomy was a cat-
> egory of forbidden acts; their perpetrator was nothing more than the

juridical subject of them. The nineteenth-century homosexual became
a personage, a past, a case history, and a childhood, in addition to
being a type of life, a life form, and a morphology. . . . The sodomite had
been a temporary aberration; the homosexual was now a species.[54]

Although focused on the shift from 'sodomite' to 'homosexual', this
passage inspired a broader opposition of premodern and modern
sexual discourses: where the former knew only of 'acts', the latter
came to conceive of 'identities'. For many, the opposition of 'acts
and identities' seemed to imply that to endorse a constructionist
approach, inevitably influenced by Foucault, was to deny the possibility of sexual preferences or orientations – towards one's own sex, the
'opposite' sex, or something else. David Halperin subjects this reading
to strong critique, arguing that Foucault was making a narrow, discursive point rather than attempting a grand narrative of historical
change. The *legal* ('ancient civil or canonical codes') category of
the sodomite gave way to the *psychiatric* category of homosexual.
Moreover, as other classicists have argued, ancient figures such as
the Greek *kinaidos* and Roman *cinaedus* are indicative of past
conceptions of sexual dispositions, subjectivities, character – not
merely acts.[55]

Like Halperin, we do not view sexual histories in the black and
white of 'acts versus identities'. It is not that no one ever had particular sexual leanings before nineteenth-century sexologists identified
them for us; rather that ancient and other premodern dispositions
were of their own time (we hesitate around the blunt term 'identities',
in its common modern sense of self-image, or perception of coherent
individuality or selfhood).[56] Peoples of past cultures, including
those of medieval and early modern Europe, do indeed show sexual
preferences (for example, some men preferred to take the passive
role in sex with other men; some women preferred to live as men in
what may have been erotic relationships with other women). Our
consistent point is that use of the terms 'homosexual', 'lesbian' and
'heterosexual' as substantives is not particularly helpful, though for
stylistic reasons they are sometimes useful as adjectives. Premodern
people lived without our familiar sexual categories and should not
be forced to occupy them retrospectively. It is hard work to try to
comprehend and describe the special nature of premodern sexual
cultures, and often we lack suitable vocabulary to describe the patterns we observe. That intellectual challenge is a large part of the
reason we find sexual histories enduringly fascinating.

If 'sexuality' is a problematic term, 'sex' is arguably little better. It
dates to the late fourteenth century in English as a term for the differences of male and female (deriving from classical Latin *sexus*).

That is how it is used in *Aristotle's Master-piece* (1684).[57] In our title, however, sex is, in part, short for 'sexual intercourse', which is attested in English (along with other forms such as 'sexual commerce') only from the mid-eighteenth century.[58] The Cambridge University Press English translation of the first edition of *Malleus Maleficarum* (1486–7) writes of demons practising 'the most revolting sexual acts' and, in various contexts, refers to what is rendered in English as 'the sexual act'. This translation is not unreasonable but the terms used are modern. The original Latin refers to 'actus venerei', 'actum venereum' and 'carnalia facta'.[59] The candid memoirs of the eighteenth-century excise officer John Cannon, brought to the attention of historians by Tim Hitchcock, never refer to sex when describing what we would call his sexual encounters. He writes of 'carnality', feeling 'privities', 'emission', 'copulation', 'pleasure', 'will and pleasure', 'kissing and toying', 'close familiarity' and 'caressing'.[60] Our term 'sex', however, refers not only to sexual acts as such, but also (indeed, more often) to their representation in written and visual discourses and their relationship to broader moral, political and aesthetic concerns.

Throughout our book we warn against using modern terms for premodern erotic phenomena, so may be taken to task for our use of 'sex'. In our own defence, we say only that *coitus, concubitus* or *l'acte vénérien* do not have a winning ring, and sex has the additional advantage over those alternatives of alluding to the penumbra of erotic phenomena (such as desire, arousal, connotation, representation, imagination) as well as the physical act or (as Cryle would have it) *action* itself.[61] It would be unwise to aim for total semantic purity when we try to write such history. The best we can do is be aware of our language and justify usages as far as we can.

We could also debate the extent to which contemporary postmodern sexual cultures could be said to be 'after sexuality'. When Weeks states that '[s]exuality pinned you down like a butterfly on the table', his use of tense seems auspicious.[62] For him, 'sexuality' already belongs in the past. While reactionary political and religious movements have urgently sought to reaffirm sexual categories (ironically, they uphold the relatively new species of heterosexual, homosexual, and so on, rather than the older, more fluid models we partially chronicle here), other popular movements of our digitalized, globalized world have entered an era of 'post-sexuality'. According to one observer in contemporary Denmark, sexual identities are disappearing: 'Many people with strong same-sex sexual interests are beginning to think and speak of themselves in terms of *taste*. Thus, they do not see themselves as possessing a gay, lesbian, or queer identity.'[63] We will leave assessment of the current state of sex to social scientists, but if our exploration of the unstable and sometimes surprising world of pre-modern sex helps commentators to see the unexpected in the present then so much the better.

Our geographic and chronological focus is on the countries of 'Western' Europe (thus excluding areas covered by the Eastern Orthodox churches) from around 1100 to around 1800, although the first chapter paints some of the ideological backdrop by stretching back to the beginning of Christianity and subsequent chapters include a small amount of early medieval material. As the reader will discover, it would stretch credulity to claim that ours is a neglected period, yet it is sometimes underestimated in the history of sex. Véronique Mottier's _Sexuality: A Very Short Introduction_ (2008) would not have been quite so short had she not effectively jumped from sex in the ancient world to nineteenth-century sexology.[64] Stearns's world history of sex mysteriously fades between 1450 and 1750.[65]

We deal only with Christian subjects; the sexual histories of Jewish and Islamic premodern communities will need their own historians. Early modern European colonies in the Americas merit brief mention, but they too deserve specialized study. By no means do we aim for an encyclopaedic study of premodern sexualities. Rather, we seek to illuminate what we perceive to be some of the dominant themes in that history. As a contributor to the 'Themes in History' series, our study is heavily dependent on the specialized works of previous scholars who have trawled the archives, manuscripts, early editions and visual artefacts of premodern cultures. Our reading has been wide but we make no claims to being comprehensive; our focus is on scholarship that has seemed particularly illuminating to our range of interests.

One claim which we may make to originality is in the combination of medieval and early modern material. This is the first such study of premodern sex, essay collections excluded. The traditional period divide around 1500 (though often these days closer to 1550) is here breached much more than is usual. Of course, we acknowledge the significant changes that the early to mid-sixteenth century witnessed, especially the Protestant Reformation (and its Catholic counterpart), new world colonialism, state formation, population growth, rise of print culture and greater interest in classical sources, and we try at all times to be alert to chronological as well as geographic specificity. We would be alarmed if readers took our example as licence to draw conclusions about, say, thirteenth-century Germany on the basis of an example from seventeenth-century Spain! Moreover, chronology does influence the structure of the majority of our chapters more than the term 'premodern' might imply. 'Sin' follows a flexible narrative from early Christian through to Reformation times. 'Between Women' and 'Before Pornography' treat medieval material as prior to and in many respects distinct from developments in the sixteenth century and later. 'Before Heterosexuality' and 'Between Men' move more freely between the conventional periods, yet only where similarities and correspondences between eras warrant it.

For all that did change between the high medieval period and end of the early modern era, much remained constant. On relations between men and women, we find continuities in, for instance, the centrality of marriage and the 'reproductive matrix' to sexual presumptions and practice; views of premarital erotic activity as tolerable when constituting a part of courtship leading to marriage; and conceptions of the body which frequently elided anatomical differences of male and female yet which reiterated the belief in women's stronger desire. In respect to relations between men, 'sodomy' retained a flexibility of definition from early Christian times to the eighteenth century, potentially referring to a wide range of acts which could make one 'an enemy of God', even while gradually becoming more associated with acts between men; erotic encounters between men were often a product of opportunity as much as preference, not always an alternative to the sexual pursuit of women so much as continuous with it; and age-structured relationships and affective or passionate friendships were recurring forms of male homoaffectivity across our period. At times the main difference between medieval and early modern contexts seems to be the abundance of sources for the latter relative to the former.

By no means do we wish to imply chronological homogeneity in premodern sexual histories, but by spanning the traditional period divide we hope to draw attention to features that remain constant as well as those that obviously change. The authors (one a medievalist, the other a specialist in both early modern and modern social and cultural histories) have learned a great deal from sharing and comparing material through the collaborative process of writing and hope that readers will have a similar experience.

1

Sin

If ancient Greeks and Romans were concerned with the social and political implications of their sex acts, modern westerners have become obsessed with desire's objects. 'The West has been largely preoccupied *with whom* people had sex, the ancients with the question of excess or over-indulgence, activity and passivity.'[1] However, another sexual preoccupation is the problem of desire itself. In promoting the ideal of sexual abstinence, Catholic Christianity parted company with its parent, Judaism, and younger sibling, Islam, and had more in common with Hinduism and Buddhism.[2] In Christianity sexual desire became linked to sin – *hamartia* in the Greek of the New Testament, a metaphorical use of an ancient archery term meaning 'to miss the mark'. The experiences of desire, arousal and sexual acts caused a Christian soul to be diverted from its path to God; they entailed estrangement from the divine.

We begin our study of sex in premodern western cultures with a study of sexual sin because we recognize the centrality of Christian morality to medieval and early modern erotic sensibilities. Before sexuality, carnal arousal and 'venereal' acts were intimately connected with spiritual status and eternal fate. The medieval Christian view of the impact of carnality on spirituality has sometimes been viewed, especially under the influence of Michel Foucault, as a crucial stage in the formation of modern subjectivities. In Foucault's account, in the wake of the codification of the sacrament of penance in 1215,

confession became one of the West's most highly valued techniques for producing truth. We have since become a singularly confessing society. The confession has spread its effects far and wide. It plays a part in justice, medicine, education, family relationships, and love relations, in the most ordinary affairs of everyday life, and in the most solemn rites; one confesses one's crimes, one's sins, one's thoughts and desires, one's illnesses and troubles. . . . Western man has become a confessing animal.[3]

Foucault elsewhere quoted a conversation with Peter Brown, who claimed that sexuality in the early Christian centuries became 'the seismograph of our subjectivity'. 'It is a fact,' continues Foucault, 'a mysterious fact, that [in] this indefinite spiral of truth and reality in the self sexuality has been of major importance since the first centuries of our era.'[4] We have no wish to trace long genealogies in this fashion. Anxieties about spiritual readiness for eternity seem to us to be of a quite different order from modern psychological preoccupations with the truth of the self in a mortal body. In keeping with our assertion of the special modernity of sexuality we ask what constituted the sexual assumptions, the ubiquitous messages (spoken or unspoken), the continual whispering on sex which formed the background noise of premodern lives? In subsequent chapters we grapple with understanding medieval and early modern sex in the absence of the currently dominant concepts and categories – heterosexuality, homosexuality, lesbianism, pornography – but for now we stay with a concept with which premodern people were entirely familiar. Thus acknowledging their moral preoccupations, we confront the question of how sexual acts and desires became impediments to a higher experience of the divine and imperilling to the immortal soul.

Premodern Christian cultures linked sex to sin in two ways. One took as its starting point the category of lechery as one of the seven deadly sins (developed and enumerated by theologians beginning in the fourth century), and marked specific lecherous acts on a scale of illicitness.[5] Taking it as read that marital sex for procreation or to fulfil the conjugal debt was a venial, excusable sin rather than a mortal one (more on this below), by the thirteenth century theologians had worked out a hierarchy of lust. The number and order of sexual sins varied from author to author, but most ranged from fornication (sex between an unmarried man and woman) as the least serious brand of lechery to the 'vice against nature' as the worst. A common ranking ran thus: fornication, adultery, incest, violation or debauchery, abduction-rape (*raptus*) and the 'vice against nature' (which generally encompassed all acts which could not result in procreation, including use of contraceptives, masturbation, anal or oral sex, same-sex practices and bestiality).[6]

The habit of weighing the gravity of sexual sins could have startling results. In early fifteenth-century Italy, Bernadino of Siena preached that '[i]t is better for a wife to permit herself to copulate with her own father in a natural way than with her husband against nature'. Similarly, 'It is bad for a man to have intercourse with his own mother, but it is much worse for him to have intercourse with his wife against nature.'[7] Canonists taught that wives who consented to their husbands' demands to sin against nature committed mortal sin just as the men did. Better for a wife to let herself be killed or that her husband commit adultery or shame himself with a mule.[8] Even if Bernadino's message was intended more in the spirit of hyperbole than literal teaching, the example illustrates a hierarchy of sexual sin somewhat alien to modern thinking. In addition to teachings on the seven deadly sins, the Ten Commandments offered basic sexual ethics with the prohibition of adultery (often rendered in more general terms as 'unchastity' by medieval preachers) and coveting a neighbour's wife.[9] In delineating the line between licit and taboo sex the Christian tradition derives mainly from ancient Hebrew strictures against behaviours potentially detrimental to the patriarchal family, such as adultery, same-sex acts, incest and non-procreative sex.[10]

However, in splitting away from Jewish origins early Christians had also added a harder dimension to their concept of sexual sin. In Foucault's ominous words, 'Christianity proposed a new type of experience of oneself as a sexual being.'[11] Influenced in part by classical ideals of restraint but more by ambitions internal to the development of the religion itself, authoritative Christian writers developed the theory that the very act of sexual arousal was tainted by sin. More emphatically, they asserted that to be married was inferior to being celibate. The ideal of a celibate priesthood arose from this theory, although before the twelfth century many Catholic priests continued to keep wives or concubines. Throughout the 1,500 years of Catholic hegemony the vast majority of laypeople paid little attention to the celibate ideal and had a decided tendency to flout the rules against lechery.

This chapter will focus not on the sevenfold mortal sin of lechery but on the teaching that fused all sexual desire with sin, and argue that, far from being static, Christian thinking on eros evolved slowly and was continually broken. Jean-Louis Flandrin and Pierre J. Payer have suggested that Christian doctrine on sex was formed by the earliest authors of Scripture and hardly changed in its essence between the first and twentieth centuries.[12] Some authoritative accounts of late-antique asceticism paint broad brush-strokes of a sexual landscape transformed by the sixth century and, by implication, entrenched thereafter.[13] We argue instead for a narrative of discontinuity and failure. Efforts to cast sex as sinful were repeatedly fractured – by disagreement, dissent and considerations of gender. Theologians could rarely agree on the precise relationship of sin and desire; priests and laity alike persisted in marrying or flouting sexual strictures; and men's and women's sexual histories have never been the same. The Christian inventions of sexual sin and the figure of the virgin were strongly gendered. It was far more radical to enforce chastity on men than women, and the male virgin was a much more astounding figure than its feminine counterpart. In this chapter we start by sketching a mostly conventional picture of concupiscence, in its narrow sense of sinfully libidinous desire or lust, in the lives and thoughts of premodern Europeans, but then show how recent scholarship has cracked that image apart. To do this, we need to go back to the beginning.

The gospels of 'Mark', 'Matthew', 'Luke' and 'John' were written *c.* 70–95 CE following the bloody 'Jewish War' against the Roman occupiers of Palestine (66–70 CE) by Jewish rebels who followed the teachings of Jesus, a seditious Jew and faith healer who had been executed by the Romans with the assistance of Jewish leaders a generation earlier.[14] In the words of Elaine Pagels, the New Testament gospels are 'wartime literature'.[15] Their purpose was to promote the teachings of a particular minority Jewish sect which believed the end of the world was nigh. Warnings about required sexual behaviour form a small part of the four canonical gospels' warnings of apocalypse. Most enigmatic was this passage from Matthew: 'there are eunuchs who have been so from birth, and there are eunuchs who have been made eunuchs by men, and there are eunuchs who have made themselves eunuchs for the sake of heaven. He who is able to receive this, let him receive it.'[16] More explicitly condemnatory of lust was the extension of adultery to 'every one who looks at a woman lustfully'; such a man was an 'adulterer in his heart'.[17] To these scattered sexual references we can add some traditional condemnations of fornication and adultery, but it is impossible to say that sex is a major theme of the four gospels.[18] Stronger messages were contained in the letters of Paul, writing in the 50s of the first century CE, and whose message to the Christian community at Corinth made an overwhelmingly enduring impact on sexual ethics. In expectation of the imminent coming of the kingdom, Paul recommends harnessing energies in a manner best for each individual. It is best not to marry, but better to marry than to burn with passion.[19]

Other New Testament books reflected the Jewish tradition of high praise for the married state and procreative family life, and several texts denouncing the celibate message were ascribed to Paul in following centuries.[20] Sexual asceticism, or abstinence, was uncommon but not unknown in the Jewish and gentile worlds where the followers of Christ were attempting to gain a footing. A Jewish sect known as the Essenes, who lived in caves by the Dead Sea from around the second century BCE to the first century CE, practised total poverty and celibacy (non-marriage) in a manner similar to the early Christian monastic groups which would develop from the early fourth century.[21] Roman religion and culture held some respect for virgins, with the all-female vestal virgins occupying an especially sacred position.[22] Both ancient Greek and Roman cultures possessed the notion that sexual restraint was indicative of personal nobility. The Stoic philosophy, which would reach its height of popularity among Roman aristocrats in the first and second centuries CE, held some echoes of early Christian asceticism in advocating the restraint of bodily passions.[23] As the new religion gained more converts among gentile communities (with their ancient traditions on chastity, moderation and self-control [*sophrosyne*]) than Jewish ones, the message of sexual renunciation took hold more firmly than it might otherwise have done.[24]

Not all have been convinced. Kathy Gaca has rejected the notion that Stoicism advocated sexual renunciation and refutes the possibility that the philosophy had direct influence on early Christian sexual theory.[25] Debate continues over the extent to which Christians revolutionized or merely intensified the ideal of sexual abstinence; what we can say is they had particular motives for developing it and that it gained a pre-eminence in the new religion's ethical code that it had not possessed among its pagan or Jewish forebears.[26] Christianity's success relied in part on the moral example of its leaders; 'the conjunction of self-abnegation and tenacity was revered by Christians'.[27] Although Christians were more interested in martyrdom than sexual purity between the second and fourth centuries, all began to change when Christianity received approval by Constantine I in 313, and became the official religion of the Roman Empire in 391. In 320 Roman legal provisions against celibacy were lifted and in 325 the Council of Nicaea ordered clerics to abstain from sex, marriage and keeping concubines.[28] By the fourth and early fifth centuries Christians were looking for a new badge of heroism, and found it in sexual renunciation. The Christian quest for distinctiveness turned from death to sex.

In *c.* 384 Jerome told the Roman virgin Eustochium to avoid the houses of noble married women: 'you must learn a holy pride; know that you are better than they'.[29] Christians were positioned as the dominant religious group and their energies turned to the formation of hierarchies among themselves. The message of familial renunciation expressed in the gospels and by Paul became the rallying cry of the new ascetics. Yet with the end of the world no longer in sight, motivations for rejecting sexual activity, marriage and child-bearing had changed. Sexual renunciation, it was argued, was essential to individual Christian freedom.[30] Without it one would be caught in the toils of marital and parental obligations, and the turmoil of desire itself. Casting off such bonds allowed Christian men and women to preserve their energies for devotion. 'Ascetics' (the Greek *ascesis* means 'exercise'), those who subjected their bodies to strict dietary, sexual and other forms of physical discipline, were literally 'athletes' of God.[31] Yet abstinence had more than practical appeal. To remain virginal or, at second best, to adopt celibacy was to approach a state akin to that known by Adam and Eve before the Fall, indeed to come close to angels. If some human beings were akin to angels, then it was a short step to arguing that virgins and celibates were fundamentally superior to married Christians. 'The human body remained for Jerome a darkened forest, filled with the roaring of wild beasts, that could be controlled only by rigid codes of diet and by the strict avoidance of occasions for sexual attraction.'[32] It pained him that many priests continued to marry, but he likened such men to weaker soldiers in an army which also contained more powerful warriors. In contending against Jovinian, a former monk who argued that the married state was equal to celibacy, Jerome took Paul's assertion that 'it is good for a man not to touch a woman' and elaborated upon it:

> If it is good not to touch a woman, it is bad to touch one: for there is no opposite to goodness but badness. . . . Just as though one were to lay it down: 'It is good to feed on wheaten bread' . . . and yet, to prevent a person pressed by hunger from devouring cow-dung, I may allow him to eat barley. Does it follow that the wheat will not have its peculiar purity if barley is preferred to excrement?[33]

Jerome was an extremist who met much opposition.[34] Yet Jovinian's alternative was even more thoroughly condemned and his writings destroyed; ironically, his argument is preserved only in quotation by his adversary.

Most historians of sexual desire in late antique thought argue that the Church found a more acceptable opponent to Jerome in the Bishop of Hippo – Augustine (345–430) – who had given up the Manichaean tendencies of his youth, his struggles with lust and his family life with a beloved concubine, in return for orthodoxy, celibacy and power.[35] Marriage was good for three reasons, argued Augustine: because it produced offspring, because it diverted lust into the relatively safe channel of monogamy, and because it was indissoluble.[36] Augustine's argument was, in its essence, a return to the compromise position or 'durable double standard' elaborated by Clement of

Alexandria and others in the mid-second century: Christian marriage is good but second-best to celibacy.[37] However, Augustine recognized some of the weaknesses of Clement's argument and developed a new account of lust.[38] To accommodate his requirement that desire be supplanted by will, Clement had advocated that a husband overcome the desire he felt for his wife and to approach the conjugal act without lust, so that children might be begotten by a 'reverent, disciplined act of will'.[39] Augustine found this unfeasible. In desire, but especially at the moment of orgasm, the mind is so overtaken by passion that 'there is an almost total extinction of mental alertness'.[40] In that moment the inferior bodily appetites overwhelmed the superior mental will, in a chaotic inversion of proper hierarchies that mirrored the Fall. In committing the original sin, which was a sin of disobedience, the correct hierarchy was catastrophically inverted, so that the Beast commanded the Woman, who in turn commanded the Man, and all were disobedient to God the Father. Orgasm, Augustine argued, was a perpetual reminder and re-enactment of original sin, with the superior, masculine principle of mental will turned on its head and made to obey the inferior, feminine principle of bodily appetite. It was desire – *concupiscence* – which contained the sin, not the act itself. The tendency to experience desire or libido was transmitted through semen: thus Christ, the sole human to be conceived without semen, was the only person without libido. Adam and Eve would have committed no sin when they had sex in Paradise, as they could control their genitals just as if they were lifting a finger. Yet humanity, in its post-lapsarian state (that is, after the Fall), could never achieve such control, despite Clement's hopes. Thus, in the conventional account that we present for the time being, Augustine managed to resolve the long-standing tensions and contradictions inherent in the Christian tradition on sex. He affirmed the good of marriage even while asserting and explaining the essential taint inherent in sex. We are all conceived in sin.

The fifth and sixth centuries saw further fundamental contributions to theories of lust. Augustine's contemporary, the monk John Cassian (*c.* 360–435), refined the theories of desire and purity in a monastic regime espousing a six-step scale of chastity, culminating in the pure monk's freedom from sexual temptations and responses (even while asleep). If his mind is so purified of lust he can avoid even nocturnal emissions, as achieved by the aptly named exemplar Serenus. One has gained victory over the flesh, though the process might take six months of careful management of diet, emotions and conversation and in the end require reduction in fluid intake and the strapping of lead plates to the genitals.[41]

Image 2. Eve takes the fruit from the Tree of Knowledge at the urging of the serpent, and Adam is tempted to do the same. The 'Original Sin' of disobeying God's command (Genesis 3) was interpreted sexually by many medieval theologians, such as St Augustine (d. 430), who argued that post-Fall sexual desires were a mirror and reminder of humanity's Fall. Late medieval art typically depicted the serpent as female, emphasizing woman's role as temptress. Hugo van der Goes, *Diptychon mit Sündenfall und Erlösung (Beweinung Christi)*. 1479. Kunsthistorisches Museum, Vienna.

Monks might henceforth seek ways to achieve ultimate sexual purity, but matters would always be more vexed for married Christian laypeople. Pope Gregory the Great (r. 590–604) advised that married people might engage in sex if they wanted children but any pleasure they experienced (which he acknowledged as inevitable) would always be sinful ('this lawful mingling of spouses cannot be done without pleasures of the flesh'). The sin was minor and could be remedied with regular prayer, but a stain was temporarily cast over the soul. After sex, a Christian should wash before entering church or receiving communion.[42]

Near the end of his important study, Peter Brown supplies a post-apocalyptic image:

> In Augustine's piercing vision, the Roman city and the walls of the married household within it . . . were now washed by a dark current of sexual shame. Adam's shame knew no frontiers. All men and women must feel it. All ancient boundaries crumbled beneath the weight of the sadness that he had brought upon mankind. City and countryside, Roman and barbarian cultures, carefully groomed members of the upper classes and ordinary Christians, ascetics in the shimmering desert and married couples in the cities – all had been touched by the same bitter flood of a discordant sexuality. All mankind belonged to one single city of the doomed.[43]

While Brown is too subtle to argue that this vision became hegemonic in its effects on all Christians, its placement at the conventional turning point between the 'late antique' and 'early medieval' eras could lead one to that kind of interpretation. Yet the relationship between sin and desire continued to be quarrelled over, flouted and even ignored down through the centuries of the premodern era. Thus cracks appear in our history of concupiscence. The conventional history we have presented up to this point begins to fracture. We do wrong in casting Augustine in the role of chief ascetic advocate, argue Kate Cooper and Conrad Leyser, because in doing so we fail to notice the ironical tone of some of his key passages on sex. Augustine (they say) was dubious about the mania for individual self-control fostered by the writings of Cassian and (especially) Jerome because of the potential rift it could open up 'between radical ascetics and the less fiercely committed Christian majority'.[44] Indeed he ridiculed the claims of ascetic 'triumphalists' by allusion to the freakish acts of street performers who could swallow and regurgitate all manner of objects, imitate the sounds of birds and beasts, induce sweat or tears at will, or even fart with such control that they seemed to be singing

out of their anuses.[45] Far from regarding desire's chief danger as
its force, he bemoaned its unpredictability. Impotence was man's
chief erotic enemy. ('Sometimes, [desire] abandons the eager lover,
and desire cools off in the body while it is at boiling point in the
mind.'[46]) 'More emphatically even than the involuntary erection,
sexual failure spoke to the true condition of humanity after the
Fall.'[47] Furthermore, argues Leyser in a longer study, in the fifth and
sixth centuries Augustine was not the hegemonic figure of ecclesiastical authority he has often been taken for. To the contrary, at that
time 'Augustine was a figure of controversy and not without a reader-
ship, but his writings were often condemned and his thought not
necessarily a predominant influence even on those who invoked his
authority'.[48] In a still more radically revisionist reading of patristic
texts, Virginia Burrus argues that these are *counter*-erotic rather
than *anti*-erotic, and that early Christian hagiography is awash with
imagery of seduction, caresses and divine *jouissance* (joy or bliss,
especially sexual) in which pleasure is all the more intense for being
restrained.[49]

Contrary to the model posited by Foucault and Brown, sex did not
necessarily become the measure of subjectivity or Christian morality.
Cooper and Leyser cite as chief witness Faustus, Bishop of Riez in
Southern Gaul (now Provence), who in the 470s turned to the 'ancient
language of [masculine] social relations' (the footman to the master,
rower to the helmsman, attendant to bishop or soldier to his com-
mander) to describe the Christian's relationship with God. 'It is the
austere power of the *patronus*, with its implicit threat of violence,
which best serves to delineate the Deity's ultimately benevolent, yet
awesome and inescapable authority, while the cowering uncertainty
of the *servus* embodies the Christian's existential condition.'[50] Despite
what one might assume from reading Augustine, in Faustus's vision
of the Christian condition there is not a flaccid member in sight; the
preferred metaphor for obedience was social rather than sexual.

The construction of sinful sex was continually fractured by gender
as well as by dissent. Burrus and Mathew Kuefler have reconceived
early Church history as a moment when masculinity itself was transformed. Burrus reads the triumph of the Nicene conception of the
Trinity (325) as a turning point in the history of masculinity, a moment
when it was 'conceived anew, in terms that heightened the claims of
patriarchal authority while also cutting manhood loose from its traditional fleshly and familial moorings'.[51] Kuefler similarly argues for
a paradigm shift in manliness but locates it more broadly in the
Roman Empire of the third to fifth centuries. Christian writers 'moved
a previously subordinated masculinity into position as a hegemonic
masculinity', sidelining the Roman pagan ideal of a military, political,

paternal and sexually potent manliness and instating the pacific, contemplative, ascetic man in its place, yet transformed the old ideal of the warrior into a new model of the 'soldier of Christ' (*miles Christi*). Thus 'a man's daily fight against sin and temptation might take on cosmic significance'.[52] Sexual desire was only one among the possible temptations and sins against which a man must strive (others included luxury, anger and pride), and these various forms of softness (*mollitia*) stood in opposition to the manliness (*virtus*) which was his constant goal. The pacifism of the new religion required men to abjure violence, but the role of the *miles Christi* doing daily battle against the devil was ever open to him. This reinvention of the Roman warrior ethic not only strengthened the image of the Christian, it helped save masculinity. 'Here was a masculine image that could no longer be threatened with a sinking into effeminacy by the collapse of Roman borders and the invasion of foreign troops, because it did not depend on outside variables such as these but on the integrity of interior borders.' Celibacy represented the manly life, while marriage and family relations were effeminizing.[53]

This was, however, truly a man's battle. No woman martyr of late antiquity was described as a 'soldier of Christ', though many were praised for their fortitude and courage.[54] Even as they reinvented masculinity, Christian men sought to reassert their 'masculine privilege'. Kuefler suggests that the apparently incongruous victory of the Catholic orthodox position which asserted the superiority of virginity and celibacy while condoning procreative sex within marriage, over the more logically consistent position of some eastern groups such as the Montanists and Manichaeans which argued for the illicitness of all sexual and marital relationships, and advocated forms of sexual equality, can be put down to enduring male desire for patriarchal authority. So long as marriage was permitted, the role of husband and patriarch remained available (if inferior, from a theological viewpoint, to the role of celibate monk or priest) and helped maintain the principle of masculine authority over women and children.[55] The earliest Christians appear, to some extent, to have possessed an ideal of gender ambiguity, at least to the point that women could aspire to manliness, but this contributed more inconsistencies than clear messages on the status of women in debates of Jerome, Augustine and others and was in part co-opted in the celibate ideal which adapted the ancient figure of the eunuch and remade him as monk.[56] Kuefler thus distances himself from a mostly older tradition of feminist history which found gender liberation for women in early Christianity and allies himself instead with scholars who find little of encouragement for women in patristic doctrine exhorting women to overcome the essential weaknesses of their femininity.

Cooper's approach is a little different and highlights the symbolic power of the young female virgin. The image of the virgin Thecla, sitting at her window and listening to the evangelist Paul, comes in Christian imagery to replace the older dominant figure of the garrulous elderly woman. 'The continent heroine is essentially not a speaker but a listener. . . . If falsehoods were associated with the uncontrolled speech of old women, the rapt listening of feminine youth and purity were linked to the truth.' The noble, beautiful, young virgin listening to the apostle thus becomes 'an overarching metaphor for the Christian mission'.[57] To Roman writers the figure of the unmarried daughter already conveyed innocence, trust and family loyalty in a way other family members – sons especially – could not.

> Her power, at times a force to be reckoned with, existed only insofar as it harnessed the perceived moral authority of this bond of loyalty. It lent to the daughter's virginity a sacred aura. Married, a daughter stood for a family's compromise with the dynastic needs of other families, its concession to them of heirs. Unmarried, the virgin stood as a symbol of all that was uncompromised and unmixed in affiliation, and thus by extension of all that was true.[58]

Christian imagery drew also on ancient pagan symbolism of the virgin as keeper of the sacred hearth. The figure of the virtuous wife was by no means eradicated by the Christian maiden: Cooper explores Christian reinventions of the chaste *matrona* in late antique Rome.[59] But the power of the image of the feminine virgin would prevail right down to the Reformation and beyond.[60] The ancient cultural value of the female virgin – social and economic as much as spiritual – was thus magnified and remade in the Christian feminine virgin. Her power was most fully expressed in the Virgin Mary, whose cult dominated Catholic Christianity from the eleventh century on, and the many female virgin martyrs of Christian mythology whose *vitae* tell of tortures and bodily mutilation that are at once virginity's bodily opposite (the flesh is torn but chastity left intact) and its parallel (wounds miraculously heal and physical wholeness is restored).[61] A number of early medieval hagiographies, the veracity of which is always open to question, tell of nuns who inflicted severe disfigurement on themselves, some even cutting off their own noses, to repel the advances of rapists who threatened their sacred virgin state.[62]

The figure of the *male* virgin in Christian imagery has been much less explored. If a female virgin's body expressed the wholeness and unity of the Church, what symbolic function can a male virgin's hold? John Arnold distinguishes male chastity, where desire is a constant threat, from male virginity, where desire is extinguished entirely, and emphasizes labour and struggle as constant motifs of male chastity and virginity narratives.[63]

If we consider late antique and medieval societies in much broader terms, floating down from the rarefied air of patristic theologians and clerical polemicists to touch the ground of everyday living, we encounter an entirely different sexual realm. Moving north and west from its Mediterranean seed-bed, Christianity was taken into regions with vastly different cultural traditions from those which had prevailed in Mediterranean antiquity. As the Romans withdrew from north-western Europe during the fourth and fifth centuries their place was taken by waves of migrants from the east and north-east.[64] They were traditionally non-literate societies, but from the late fifth century began to set down in writing the law codes which had previously been transmitted orally.[65] These codes offer no evidence of highly developed cultures of male same-sex love, sexual partnerships based on political hierarchies, institutionalized prostitution or philosophical admiration for restraint of the bodily appetites, such as prevailed in Mediterranean antiquity. Germanic societies were small-scale rural communities based around pragmatic marriages and extended family groupings. Women were treated as items for exchange, with marriages based on mutual consent third-best to those based on bride-purchase or abduction. While premarital sex was largely condemned for both men and women, adultery was usually only punished when perpetrated by a woman. Female adultery was feared because of its impact on patriarchal lineages, and was punishable by death. These were societies which valued kinship groups and child-bearing highly. Marriages were made by consummation, cohabitation and the wish to engender children. In the *Laws of the Salian Franks* attributed to the Merovingian King Clovis I (written *c.* 507–11) the killing of a pregnant woman was punished more harshly even than killing a young male, while lower penalties adhered to killing older women past the age of child-bearing.[66] Charlemagne's law code of the early ninth century made penalties for full castration of a man more severe than for any other kind of maiming, including cutting off hands, feet, eye-gouging or cutting off an ear or nose.[67] This could be taken to imply that a man's sexual and fertile function were more highly prized than other elements of physical ability. Polygyny (taking more than one wife) and divorce were permitted, thus increasing a man's chance of fathering children (although polygyny ceased to be common by the late sixth century, with the rising influence of Christian ethics, and men generally had more latitude in divorce than women did), and bastardy was often tolerated. There were strict regulations against incest.

Despite the fact that western Europe retained strong Roman influences in law and mores even after Roman withdrawal and Germanic immigration, the sexual codes which prevailed among Germanic groups were based not in the abstract philosophical principles of virtuous restraint and self-control, such as existed in ancient Greco-Roman high culture and were passed on to Christianity. Nor were they based in a notion of the primacy of the freedom of elite men and their prerogative to behave as they wished. Rather, the code was essentially a pragmatic one, derived from the centrality of the clan in ensuring individual survival. Pairing men and women in marriage, securing the birth of healthy children, and maintaining masculine control through subjugation of women and protection of the patrilineal line – these were the concerns which shaped sexual codes in early medieval western Europe. Christian missionaries had to make their Christian message appealing in this environment. Jerome's thorough-going condemnation of all sexual activity or Augustine's highly elaborate explanation of how all sexual desire was tainted by sin had limited relevance.

In sixth-century Gaul Bishop Caesarius of Arles preached about the perils involving the battle for chastity, the dangers of consorting with women, the necessity for both women *and* men to retain their virginities until marriage (clearly a radical concept), and the need for men to seek sex with their wives only for procreation, not pleasure.[68] His message was taken as excessively austere and frankly bizarre. He was not always a popular speaker, condemned both by those in authority (three times accused of treason, tried and sent into exile, alienated by local nobility and his fellow clergymen) and by his popular audience. On one occasion he was obliged to lock the doors of his church to prevent his disgusted congregation from walking out.[69] It is possible that the bishop was considered something of an eccentric among early Gallic clergy, whose surviving sermons paid virtually no attention to sex among the laity. Of the seventy-six surviving fifth-century sermons of the so-called 'Eusebius Gallicanus' collection, for example, only two sermons make mention of sexual conduct, and both instances are no more than passing references to adultery.[70]

The sexual body continued to provide powerful metaphors in monastic (rather than lay) contexts, but in sometimes unexpected ways. In *c.* 820 Hraban Maur, Abbot of the Carolingian monastery of Fulda, asked, 'What is the Word if not semen?' In his elaborate metaphor, Christian preachers are receptacles for God's semen, and preachers inseminate other men through the ejaculate of speech: the priestly mouth is akin to phallus, the (male monastic) congregation becomes a fecund uterus which conceives 'the Word' through ears which serve as vaginas, and 'men impregnat[e] other men through the agency of the Word'.[71] One could call it queer, but that would only diminish the marvellous strangeness of Hraban's piece.

Foucault's vision of sexual histories depended in part upon a sense of the all-pervasive dominance of the confessional in Christians' experiences of what it was to be sexual.

> Confession, the examination of conscience, all of the insistence on the secrets and the importance of the flesh, was not simply a means of forbidding sex or of pushing it as far as possible from consciousness, it was a way of placing sexuality at the heart of existence and of connecting salvation to the mastery of sexuality's obscure movements. Sex was, in Christian societies, that which had to be examined, watched over, confessed and transformed into discourse.[72]

This is an exaggeration. Until the requirement for annual universal confession from 1215, confession of sin by the laity was irregular at best. '[T]he practice of confession, outside monasteries, and other than as immediate preparation for death, was nothing like universal before the thirteenth century.'[73] 'Penitentials' – works which offered priests guides to the types and nature of sins and the suitable forms of penance to impose in each case – developed first in Ireland in the sixth century, but their practical utility is hard to determine.[74] Sexual offences constituted an important component of the handbooks – between 24 per cent and 45 per cent of all canons in a representative sample as presented by Payer.[75] While premarital sex among the laymen and -women was largely overlooked, illicit practices within marriage, incest, same-sex acts, bestiality, masturbation and seminal emissions were all common themes. In contrast, contraception as such, prostitution and rape are not touched on.[76]

Payer's position is that the handbooks were used in confessional practice given their widespread presence in western Europe from the sixth to tenth centuries: 'They were practical handbooks which would have had no conceivable raison d'être aside from their functional utility in the administration of private penance. If they had not reflected the reality of human behaviour, this functional utility would have been lost.'[77] This may be so, but we really do not know. R. D. Fulk suggests that the severity of certain penances indicates that the penitentials did not deal with everyday sins and seem designed to prescribe penances for new types of sins that priests might not have faced before.[78] While lay confession spread strongly and rapidly after 1215, necessitating the better education of priests in order to help them fulfil their new duty, lay Christians were still not required to confess more than once a year.[79]

Clerical marriage and concubinage may have been condemned in the fourth century but Anne Llewellyn Barstow and others have demonstrated that they remained common and openly practised even in the mid-twelfth century.[80] Bishop Roger of Salisbury, chancellor and chief justiciar to Henry I of England (r. 1100–35), to take one prominent example, lived in open and licit marriage with his aristocratic wife and their son became King Stephen's chancellor.[81] The reformers associated with Popes Leo IX (r. 1049–54) and Gregory VII (r. 1073–85, after whom the reforms are generally named) worked hard finally to abolish priests' marriages, technically known as Nicolaitism, as part of their efforts to affirm priestly purity and pre-eminence. Peter Damian was foremost among rhetoricians vilifying priests' wives:

> And now, let me speak to you, you charmers of clerics, nasty tidbits of the devil, expulsion from paradise, venom of the mind, sword that kills souls, poison in the drink, toxin in the food, source of sinning and occasion of damnation. I am talking to you, you female branch of the ancient enemy, hoopoes, screech owls, nighthawks, she-wolves, leeches, calling without ceasing 'Give, give.'[82]

Peter rationalized his condemnation by emphasizing the pollution of the sexually active priest. 'If Almighty God himself refuses to accept sacrifice from your hands, whom do you think you are in presuming to thrust them upon him against his will? "The sacrifice of the unclean is abhorrent to the Lord" [Proverbs 15.8].'[83] Hands polluted by sexual contact were not fit to perform this sacrament. A sexually active priest was not in a state of purity and defiled the altar. Around the 1230s Jacques de Vitry expressed the connection between married priests and pollution in a sermon for lay audiences: 'A priest took his concubine with him to the house of an honest woman, and at night asked where a bed had been prepared for them. The hostess showed them the privy, and declared they could sleep nowhere else.'[84] There may also have been a more practical, economic objection to priests' marriages: that is, that Church property would be passed on to priest's children on the death of their fathers, thus causing the impoverishment of the Church. Clerical marriage was finally prohibited in 1123.[85]

The Gregorian Reforms have in traditional historiography been viewed as a time of vibrancy, cleansing and renewal in the western Church, but while motives for pressing for change may have been largely theological and political they created a new, much more austere, sexual and gender regime. Thus recent feminist and queer historians have rejected the positive interpretation of the era and argued that it ushered in an age of profound anti-feminism and sexual control.[86] Dyan Elliott has made a compelling case for the priest's wife as a 'spectre' haunting the Catholic Church.[87] Through collective and encouraged amnesia the western Church made these women – who must have numbered in their thousands – disappear. Through a similar conjuring trick the impression that sexual purity has always been a chief concern of the Church and its congregations has gained sway. The priest's wife is a spectre, but so is the married priest.

C. N. L. Brooke found among English clergy that after about 1130 the number with children began to decline,[88] yet full celibacy was never achieved and many priests were discontented with the ruling. Nancy Partner shows how the English chronicler Henry of Huntingdon (*c.* 1080–1160), himself a married priest, was 'sore and irritable on the subject of clerical marriage', and the imposition of celibacy provoked near riots in some Italian and French contexts.[89] The Italian Franciscan chronicler Salimbene de Adam complained in the mid-thirteenth century that he had seen priests 'devoting themselves wholly to usury [charging interest on loans] and gaining property, so that they could give it to their bastards', and others running taverns 'with the whole house filled with bastard children, and they sleep with their whore during the night and rise up to say mass the next day'.[90] When Eudes Rigaud, Archbishop of Rouen, undertook visitations among the monasteries and parishes of his archdiocese from 1248 to 1269, he was regularly confronted with rumours or cases of sexual misconduct among monks, nuns and priests. Many entries tell of incontinent priests in sexual relationships with local women (single, married, servants, elderly; some were the priest's own nieces, some the local seigneur's wife).[91] Some seem to have had multiple partners, such as the priest at Mesnil-David, who 'has his children at home and a concubine elsewhere'; 'two women fell upon each other in his house; they fought with each other and because one was fond of roses the other cut down the rose bushes'.[92] Eudes found that the prior of Ouville was a drunkard who did not remain in the cloister even one day in every five, but wanders around and 'because of his inebriety, he sometimes lies out in the fields; he attends festivities, drinking bouts and banquets given by layfolk; he is incontinent and his relations with a certain woman in Grainville and with the lady of Routot are subjects of scandal; there is also a certain Agnes in Rouen'.[93] Nuns were not immune from scandal: fornicating, facilitating vice, providing abortifacients and bearing children.[94]

While parishioners had cohabiting and incontinent priests in their midst (and perhaps heard rumours of monks and nuns in nearby foundations) it must have been difficult to accept the notion of sex's sinful taint. Jennifer Thibodeaux has convincingly argued that the conduct of the priests in Eudes' Norman archdiocese should be read in terms of conflicting masculinities rather than of clerical failure. When they gambled, frequented taverns, threw off clerical garb, bore weapons, kept concubines and fathered children they maintained a masculine aura in the eyes of their parishioners that might have been lost had they held themselves to the reformist model.[95] Only sexually active men are real men. Even 'simple fornication', generally referring to sexual activity by unmarried persons, was widely viewed as non-sinful before and even after the enforcement of clerical celibacy. In early medieval penitential literature 'the subject of sexual intercourse between two unmarried lay persons is virtually ignored'.[96] Bartholomew of Exeter's penitential of the twelfth century and John Bromyard's *Summa praedicantium* of the fourteenth century indicated that many congregants believed that fornication was either a minor sin or not sinful at all, while one version of Peter the Chanter's *Verbum abbreviatum* complained about 'certain stupid priests' who saw the act as no more than a venial sin.[97] The casual attitude which many laypeople, and some clerics, held regarding premarital sex and even adultery is mirrored in medieval literature, where sex between young, unmarried men and women is treated as a subject for humour, pleasure and mischief, not for shock and condemnation.[98]

Widespread illiteracy and ignorance of Christian doctrine provided a still broader barrier to the impact of patristic polemics. Lay Christians did not, as a rule, read the Latin compositions of theologians. 'The Bible' was a far from stable text down to the Reformation, and only universities, monasteries and some royal courts would have been likely to possess whole collections of Scripture. Preachers might have copies of certain books (the Gospels, Psalms and Proverbs among the more popular), but even parish priests might have access only to collections of scriptural extracts. None of the sixty-four parish churches controlled by the monastery of St Sernin in Toulouse in the mid-thirteenth century possessed a Bible.[99] Fragments of evidence for medieval popular religion indicate that many medieval Europeans had the slimmest grasp on even the most basic Christian concepts. Christina of Markyate, daughter of ambitious Anglo-Saxon burghers who aimed to marry her to a Norman nobleman in *c*. 1110, resisted familial pressure and resolved to become a nun. Despite her piety and desire to dedicate her virginity to Christ, however, her knowledge of Scripture was limited. When presented with pro-marriage arguments about the sacrament of marriage, scriptural imagery of the husband and wife as 'one flesh', the conjugal debt, obedience to parents and the hope of salvation for mothers as well as virgins, Christina replies, 'I am ignorant of the scriptures which you have quoted.'[100] A thirteenth-century *exemplum* by the German Cistercian Caesarius of Heisterbach attempts to illustrate the potential for corrupt clerics to exploit lay confusion about sexual teachings. A priest heard the confession of one of his parishioners at the close of Lent, who 'confessed that he had not kept apart from his wife during the sacred season'. The priest reprimanded him, telling him 'this holy time was set apart for the very purpose of exercising prayer, fasting, continence and other good works', and fined the man eighteen denarii. Another parishioner followed, and when questioned said that he had kept apart from his wife all during Lent. 'The priest said, "You have done very wrong in keeping away from your wife for so long; she might have conceived a child, and continence has made that impossible." The man was terrified, as is the way with simple folk, and asked what he must do to atone for his fault.' The wicked priest once more asked for eighteen denarii.[101] The Church hierarchy was not necessarily nonchalant about lay ignorance, and from 1215 onwards made repeated efforts to improve the education of both priests and their parishioners, yet as late as 1518 a Spanish man interrogated by the Inquisition admitted that he could not say the Credo or Salve Regina. He could recite the Ave Maria (in Latin, that is), but stumbled over the Pater Noster. Although he confessed and received the sacrament each year he was found to be ignorant of the Ten Commandments, the Articles of Faith, the seven deadly sins and the five senses. He was unsure whether pride, envy, lust, murder or slander were sins, yet asserted vigorously that 'God preserve us, theft was a very great sin.'[102] While one should not necessarily read any of these sources at face value, they indicate a possible disconnect between official teaching on sexual sin and lay concerns.

Lest we conclude that the Church's teaching on sin and desire had limited impact on laypeople, let us note a few examples to the contrary. Unfortunately we cannot know what penitents generally told their parish priests in confession. Narrative sources, though, can sometimes give a hint of the moral quandaries facing medieval laypeople. Many of these pertain to women. Guibert of Nogent in his memoir gives an account of his parents' troubled marriage, which for three years remained unconsummated. His pious mother as a girl 'had learned to be terrified of sin', and dreaded 'some of some sort of blow from on high'.[103] An early thirteenth-century English 'letter on virginity' paints marriage, sex, pregnancy and child-rearing in tones of unspeakable horror, neatly tying together the distortion of soul entailed by sexual activity with the distortion of body wrought by birth:

> By God, woman, even if it were not at all for the love of God, or for the hope of heaven, or for the fear of hell, you should avoid this act above all things. . . . For as St Paul says, every sin that is committed is outside the body except this one alone . . . [this sin] disfigures you and

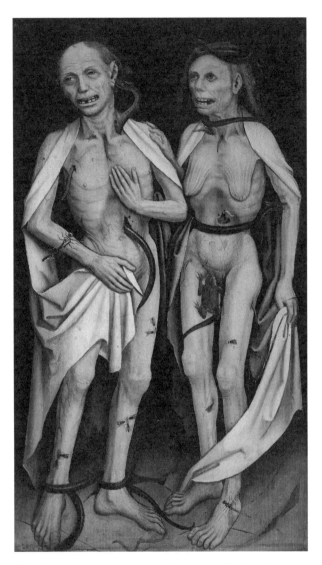

Image 3. This image depicts rotting, cadaverous flesh as the reverse image of youthful sex and love. As a *memento mori*, it draws its lay owner's attention to the effects of carnal desire on the immortal soul. *Les Amants Trépassés*. 1470. Oil on panel, 62.5 × 40 cm. Musée de l'Œuvre Notre Dame de Strasbourg. Photo Musées de la Ville de Strasbourg, M. Bertola.

dishonours your body, defiles your soul and makes you guilty in God's sight, and pollutes your flesh too.[104]

Several late medieval hagiographies tell of pious maidens who narrowly escaped marriage (for example, Christina of Markyate and Catherine of Siena), or who married under duress or out of filial obedience and later persuaded their husbands to adopt lives of chastity (such as Marie d'Oignies and Birgitta of Sweden).[105] Some accounts of their lives or their own writings employ imagery that powerfully reinforce the association of sex and dirt. The devil tempted the teenage Catherine of Siena with 'vile pictures of men and women behaving loosely before her mind, and foul figures before her eyes, and obscene words to her ears, shameless crowds dancing around her, howling and sniggering and inviting her to join them'.[106] Birgitta of Sweden, who persuaded her husband to join her in pre-coital prayers to help ward off concupiscence in the marital act,[107] later experienced a revelation in which the deceased Queen Giovanna of Naples, notorious for her sexual affairs, appears 'spattered with semen and dirt', while a voice exclaims, 'This is an ape who sniffs at her own stinking buttocks.' In a subsequent vision Giovanna sits naked on a beam, smeared in human excrement.[108] Margery Kempe (*c.* 1373–*c.* 1440), a laywoman whose life is described as the first English autobiography, tells of how she came to regret her erotic longings and the pleasures she took in marital sex ('Alas that ever I sinned! It is full merry in Heaven!'). She tried for years before persuading her husband to adopt chastity, and 'paying the debt of matrimony was so abominable to her that she would rather, she thought, have eaten and drunk the ooze and muck in the gutter than consent to intercourse, except out of obedience'.[109]

Throughout this chapter we have emphasized the discontent, dissent and failures that continually disrupted messages on the sinfulness of sexual pleasure. A recurring problem for the Catholic Church was that some Christian groups found the compromises of the orthodox position untenable. Not all were content to live with the ambiguity which made procreative marital sex licit yet sinful and subordinate to continence. 'Heretical' groups, including the Manichaeans, Bogomils, Patarines and Cathars, declared marital sex indefensible, locating procreation and sex acts among the things of a world created by Satan, necessary for renunciation in order to attain the purity of the spiritual realm created by God. Twelfth-century churchmen on the offensive against Cathars reaffirmed that marital procreative sex always involved a 'certain excitement, a certain itching, a certain pleasure' and was therefore sinful, but, contrary to the Cathar position, it was not a mortal but a 'very small venial sin'.[110] In the thirteenth century canonists explored ways that a man's 'too ardent' love for his wife could turn the venial sin of his procreative sex into mortal sin, yet prominent scholars, including Albertus Magnus and Thomas Aquinas, explored the possibility that delight in sex might be sin-free.[111] By the sixteenth century many Catholic authors renounced the view that marital procreative sex was venially sinful and some even advocated sex in marriage not only for providing children but for health benefits and for pleasure.[112] Catholic theologian John Major (d. 1550) said that having sex for pleasure within marriage was no more sinful than 'to eat a handsome apple for the pleasure of it'.[113] This was at odds, however, with the Council of Trent (1545–63), which upheld older conservative tradition.

The Protestant Reformers struck the death-knell for the theory of sexual pleasure as necessarily sinful, though even their position was not entirely straightforward.[114] Martin Luther agreed with St Augustine on the essential connection of desire and original sin and John Calvin insisted that post-lapsarian marriage was quite unlike the sinless unions of the Garden of Eden; indeed the majority of Protestant writers refused to absolve marital sex entirely of sin. Yet the prevailing view was that marriage was so good it overcame the essential moral impurity of sexual desire. Certain individuals and sects went further and denied any sinful component to marital desire. The greatest point of difference between Catholics and Protestants was on the status of marriage. Protestants decried the Catholic paradox which touted marriage as a sacrament while reviling all sexual desire; the Reformers denied marriage's status as a sacrament even while elevating it above celibacy as the best way to live a Christian life. Protestants furthermore denied that clerical celibacy was required by Scripture, found it contrary to the belief in salvation by faith alone, and thought it impractical for the vast majority given the power of natural sexual urges. Priests, monks and nuns were denounced as sexual hypocrites and, famously, Luther gave up his vows to marry a former nun, Katherine von Bora. Marriage, now a commandment rather than a dubious sacrament, took centre stage in the Christian life with Protestants urged to enjoy chaste marital sex within the 'holy household' of reformed marriage. Even so, sex retained its taint. While Reformers softened the ancient stance on the sinfulness of sexual pleasure in marriage, they upheld moral prohibitions on any form of extra-marital acts and urged married couples to try not to enjoy themselves too much. In the sixteenth century Christendom became deeply divided on questions of licit pleasure within sexual relations, yet for both sides the problem of desire remained.

Foucault's assertion that Christian confession was a way of placing sexuality at the 'heart of existence' is hard to reconcile with the shifting, unstable terrain of premodern teaching on carnal sin. Indeed, it feels uncomfortably close to Arnold Davidson's statement, quoted in our Introduction, that the late nineteenth-century science of sexuality made it not only possible but inevitable for us to become absorbed by questions of the merging of sexuality and self.[115] Erotic desire constituted a significant problem for Christian thinkers, but it was one among many deep problems. Obedience and poverty were difficult demands placed on monastics along with celibacy. Sex within marriage for the purpose of procreation was sinful, but only venially so. All other venereal acts were mortal sins, but 'lechery' was only one of seven deadly sins. Do we view requirements to confess to envy, wrath, pride, accidie, greed or avarice as keys to premodern subjectivities? Before sexuality, sex was of tremendous interest to Christian thinking and desire was perceived by many as potentially hazardous to the immortal soul, but it does not provide a distant mirror through which we might view modern subjectivities.

2

Before Heterosexuality

The power of heterosexuality resides in a strange combination of ubiquity and invisibility. Heterosexuality has maintained a hidden power in traditional ways of viewing the past. It has a history, many histories, but they have remained hidden because the category has been taken for granted. Historians have assumed that heterosexuality has always been and that it is only homosexuality that has been constructed. When Eve Kosofsky Sedgwick observed that 'heterosexuality has been permitted to masquerade so fully as History itself – when it has not presented itself as the totality of Romance', she merely touched on the problem, for even she was accepting a sexual category that did not exist, at least not in its present form.[1] Generations of historians have imposed heterosexual assumptions on the past, and, as they have done so, unconsciously helped to construct the heterosexuality of their own society – just as the early wave of gay historians were more cannily using the past to construct their identities.

This kind of presumptive history is so embedded in the historiography that it affects even the most astute commentators. In medieval studies, Allen J. Frantzen and Carolyn Dinshaw are among distinguished scholars who speak of 'heterosexuality' even while eschewing 'homosexuality'.[2] Louise M. Sylvester examines the construction of heterosexuality through medieval romance and fabliaux but consistently draws parallels between medieval texts and *modern* heterosexuality.[3] For the early modern, Susan Lanser discusses the intricacies of representations of the eighteenth-century 'homoerotic female body' but then ignores all complexity in positioning this body against a 'sustained' 'heterosexuality' and 'normalized' 'heterosexual desire'.[4] Elizabeth Wahl's account of Enlightenment 'female intimacy' deliberately uses that term to avoid subscribing to the modern binary of hetero/homo. She acknowledges sexual fluidity and the possibility that 'desire and practice might not even necessarily coincide': 'I do not view marriage as an absolute heterosexual category that cancels the possibility of homoerotic attachments but as a discursive category in which heterosexuality is strongly linked to reproductive sexuality but not to sexual identity per se.'[5] Yet eight pages later, she is situating her early modern, female same-sex desire within a 'framework of hetero-sexual teleology' and referring, still in a premodern context, to a model of phallocentric heterosexuality and containment within a 'nar-rative of heterosexual conversion'.[6]

Homosexuality is modified but heterosexuality survives. Paul Hammond is aware that he cannot assume a homosexuality in the period before homosexuality – indeed indicates that it would fore-close his very inquiry into male homoeroticism.[7] However, his analytic caution does not extend to heterosexuality for he also writes of 'textual spaces for homoerotic pleasure within works which prin-cipally satisfy homosocial and heterosexual interests'.[8] In other words, although he has banished homosexuality in favour of the homoerotic, 'heterosexual' endures as hegemony. Similarly, nearly all the chapters in the recent collection *Queer Renaissance Historiography* (2009) deal with same-sex desires in their queering.[9] Only one deals with what it calls 'heterosexuality', and refers, even more anachronistically, to John Milton's 'heteronormativity'.[10] Arguably, if homosexuality is no longer applicable as a taxonomic guide to premodern desires and actions, heterosexuality has outlived its usefulness. Just as (as we will see) we can no longer refer blithely to homosexuality before the modern period, we should not assume premodern heterosexuality, the other side of the modern sexual currency. We need new words for premodern sexualities.

Jonathan Ned Katz has argued that the word 'heterosexuality' is only 'one historically specific way of organizing the sexes and their pleasures', and, accordingly, has divided the past into several phases, all of which he terms examples of non-heterosexual societies.[11] Although Katz attempted but a cursory engagement with the histori-cal periods that he has identified and the medieval millennium forms a gaping lacuna in his survey, his framework is useful to think with. The challenge lies in such historical moments, in handling those instants without imposing modern notions upon desires and forma-tions that were almost certainly vastly different. Our concepts of heterosexual desire do not describe what has occurred throughout most of western history. Historians have been quick to demonstrate the constructed nature of *homo*sexuality but reluctant to grasp that *hetero*sexuality is also made.

In other words, one of the great problems with the history of heterosexuality is that we all think we know what it is. Whole generations of historians, art historians and literary critics have just assumed that the desires and actions of those in the past are expressions of the same sexual impulses and frameworks that we have today. As we write this last chapter, Stanley Wells's new book, *Shakespeare, Sex & Love* (2010), has appeared, writing of early modern 'heterosexual activity', 'homosexuality' and an earl who was 'what we would now term bisexual' – and this by a leading Shakespearean scholar.[12] The simple purpose of this chapter is to suggest that it may not be quite as simple as this. When we find familiarity, we should not assume that what we have is exactly the same as the ordering of desires in our own modern society.[13]

Some medievalists and early modernists have begun to challenge these assumptions. Michael Camille, as we noted in the Introduction, has argued that the wealthy French art collector Jean, Duc de Berry (1340–1416), can be classified as neither homosexual nor heterosexual and that his contemporaries were critical not of his attraction to both males and females but to the fact that they were lower-class males and females, his social inferiors.[14] James A. Schultz writes that we must be prepared to recognize that the cultures we are dealing with may actually have seen bodies differently from the way in which most of us see them today. Neither homosexuality nor heterosexuality adequately describes medieval desire. We tend to tell men from women by anatomical sex difference and to desire accordingly, but in the medieval world, while the sex of the desired body mattered, it was not of the obsessive concern that it is today. It was often hard to tell from descriptions of desire whether the object of desire was a man or a woman. Some early modern imagery of female desire for an attractive male also sounds little different to males describing desirable females. In one early modern ballad, the male object of desire for a love-sick virgin has beautiful eyes, lovely brown locks, honey smiles, youth, rose blushes, coyness, and silence – all archetypal, ideal female attributes.[15] Schultz describes the phenomenon as heterosexuality before heterosexuality, but the point is that our concepts of heterosexual and homosexual desire do not adequately describe that culture.[16] Karma Lochrie has invented the word 'heterosyncrasies' to resist the application of the term 'heterosexual' in discussions of the middle ages.[17] Rebecca Ann Bach contrasts what she terms the homosocial imaginary of the Renaissance with the heterosexual imaginary of modern society.[18] Patricia Simons has argued that the conventional binary of hetero/homo is of little use in interpreting Renaissance portraits. Male portraits varied from the naked virility of Agnolo di Cosimo's *Andrea Doria as Neptune* (*c.* 1553) to Giovanni

Antonio Boltraffio's (to us) androgynous and beautiful *Portrait of a Youth* (*c.* 1490s), sometimes seen by moderns as a woman. Like the masculinities that they represented, the erotics of such portraiture were 'multilayered'. 'Male sexuality was performed across a wider spectrum of sensualities than modern standards usually allow.'[19]

One theme strongly emerging from these studies is of the more fluid nature of attraction and arousal. Clear differentiation of sexes was not necessarily an erotic ideal, and male beauty was often celebrated in terms that may appear femininizing to modern eyes. Premodern erotics allowed for appreciation of beautiful males, though sometimes the results were homoerotic (as with the Duc de Berry) and at others not (when the gaze was female). Still, dominant models of what constituted attraction and desire required a male and female partner, even when (as in Schultz's examples) the couple resembled each other. We noted that we need new words for premodern sexualities, but in Schultz's exemplary study the useful words turn out not to be new coinages ('heterosex', 'heterosyncrasies', 'pre-heterosexuality', 'opposite-sex desire') but old ones: *minne* and *liebe*. 'I insist on "love" because . . . despite its imprecision, it is the closest to the medieval terms and does not automatically and inevitably arrange the material according to a modern conceptual framework, as "sexuality" or "desire" would do.'[20]

There is not much that can make a sexual historian blush, but 'love' just might do it. Sexual historians may no longer be termed 'perverts', but 'love' historians run the risk of being dismissed as unnecessarily euphemistic. Yet love is as complex and worthy of our serious attention as any other aspect of eros. This may be particularly true of medieval culture, which possessed a rich and diverse vocabulary on the theme. The chief Latin words for 'love' included *caritas* (selfless love), *dilectio* (admiration and high esteem), *amicitia* (friendship), *affectio* (affection), *cupiditas* (desire, often but not always sexual) and, most importantly, *amor* (romantic love or passion, encompassing *caritas* and *cupiditas*).[21] Scholars do not agree on how best to translate these into modern English but the point is that love was flexible and multi-stranded. Constant Mews has observed that the female author of a collection of twelfth-century French love letters employs *dilectio*, which has connotations of selfless and spiritual love, almost as often as *amor* in her letters to her lover, whereas he uses *amor* much more often. 'His vocabulary reflects a perception, dominant in masculine writing, that love for a woman has little to do with the love enjoined by scripture. She does not see any antithesis between passionate and spiritual love.'[22] Mews's identification of the authors as

Heloise and Peter Abelard has been challenged but the sentiments do match the couple's assertions in their authenticated letters, where Heloise is noticeably frustrated with Abelard's reduction of their past affair to a mere matter of lust.[23]

One way to make study of premodern love intellectually respectable is to add the modifier 'courtly'. *Amour courtois* was first coined by Gaston Paris in 1881 and ever since has been the subject of a vast scholarly literature.[24] Schultz's Middle High German poets speak of *minne* and sometimes *liebe* (where French and Latin counterparts wrote about *amor*), which are somewhat different phenomena from modern 'desire'. The lover and beloved are always male and female, though the female can take the lover role and the male the beloved, but in Schultz's view this is not 'heterosexuality' as we know it, partly because courtliness rather than sex difference is the chief cause of love and partly because love's operations are different. The lover does not feel a yearning originating somewhere within – in sex hormones, drive, or orientation, for example; rather the courtly and attractive aspects of the beloved enter the eyes of the lover and render him or her helpless.[25] The lover is, in a sense, invaded by love, so our conventional term 'object of desire' for the beloved does not fit. Indeed, we could add, the active and passive of 'lover' and 'beloved' seem inapt.

Pairs of knights could also express ardent affection but the scholarly debates about whether these passions might represent homosexuality, according to Schultz, miss the point. Close companions such as Iwein and Gawein of Arthurian literature or Richard the Lionheart and Philip Augustus may have seemed homoerotic to medieval observers but this was of no great consequence. '[B]efore homosexuality, sex between men may have been both more common and less significant. Because gender norms are upheld and attractions to women are by no means precluded, relations with men don't seem to matter.' What is more important, at least when thinking about thirteenth-century German literature, is that Iwein and Gawein are not in love.[26] *Minne* and *liebe* are unaffected. If we take Andreas Capellanus's word for it, the Latin *amor* works similarly: 'The main point to be noted about love is that it can only exist between persons of different sex. Between two males or between two females it can claim no place.'[27] But let us not be too hasty. The example of the knight Galehaut's love for Lancelot in the Old French *Prose Lancelot* troubles any notion that medieval *amor* is safely heterosexual. 'As many scholars have noted (though drawing different conclusions), the language and codes of *fin'amor* are used to describe Galehaut's love.'[28]

In Tracy Adams's reading of love in Old French literature, it is the tension inherent in *amor* (the good emotion, *caritas*, mixed with the

Image 4. The assertive female figure and the action of shooting her male target represent medieval courtly ideas of love as a force acting upon the helpless lover. According to artistic conventions based on medieval optical theories, the mutual gaze represents a form of touch between the lovers and seems to indicate that the passion was mutual. *Coffret* (Minnekästchen), Germany, Upper Rhineland, 1325–1350. Oak, inlay, and tempera; wrought-iron mounts. Overall: 12.1 × 27.3 × 16.5 cm. The Metropolitan Museum of Art, Rogers Fund and The Cloisters Collection, by exchange, 1950 (50. 141). Image © The Metropolitan Museum of Art.

bad, *cupiditas*) which informs presentations of love affairs in later twelfth-century French romances. *Amor* is beneficial socially and personally, but potentially destructive if not properly harnessed. '[A]mor is not presented as an ideal: it is presented rather as a problem to be wrestled into a useful form.'[29] Adams does not explore whether *amor* could be used except for love between a nobleman and noblewoman, so some questions remain about its relation to the history of sexualities. Also, in contrast to Schultz, who insists that the sinful *concupiscence* of theologians is not the same as the morally neutral *delectas* of medical authors, that both are separate from *minne* and none should be translated as 'desire', she seeks meeting points between the presentation of love in theological, medical and romantic discourses, emphasizing love as a problem not only in Augustinian theology but also in medicalized theories of lovesickness. 'Love is a psychosomatic malady for physicians.' Her point that the texts we call 'romance literature' were often, in the twelfth century, written by clergymen trained in monastic and cathedral schools reminds us of the artificiality of separating discourses on love according to modern scholarly categories of genre.[30] Additionally, where Schultz is adamant that *minne* does not arise within the lover but is the result of the image of the beloved entering his/her eyes, Adams in discussing *amor* refers to 'urges' and Barbara Rosenwein's 'hydraulic' model of medieval emotions: 'the emotions are like great liquids within each person, heaving and frothing, eager to be out'.[31] It seems unlikely, if possible, that the explanation for the different perceptions lies in the specific contexts each examines (Schultz on thirteenth-century Germany, Adams on later twelfth-century France); more likely the disparity lies in scholarly points of view. It will require specialists in these fields to resolve or develop these tensions of analysis. We find them interesting and valuable for the challenges they raise in breaking assumptions about premodern heterosexualities.

One of the recurrent questions of courtly love scholarship, alongside recurring perplexity over the relationship of the ideal to real life in medieval courts, and whether *fin'amors* elevated women or degraded them, is whether it could refer to married relationships or only adulterous ones. Gaston Paris, C. S. Lewis and others argued for the latter, influenced by the adulterous relationship of Lancelot and Guinevere and Andreas Capellanus's assertion that marital affection (*maritalis affectio*) should not be confused with *amor* because lovers give themselves freely to one another whereas married couples are bound by the conjugal debt.[32] The view has been roundly refuted, and it remains necessary to analyse the place of marriage in premodern sexual regimes.[33] Sedgwick's earlier-referenced lament about heterosexuality's disguise 'under its institutional pseudonyms such as Inheritance, Marriage, Dynasty, Family, Domesticity, and Population' does not undo the need to re-examine marriage within the history of sex.[34]

One of the predominant (and recognizable) aspects of premodern sex was its strong focus on married or procreative intercourse. The highly disruptive demons in *Malleus Maleficarum* (1486–7) demonstrate this preoccupation by the very nature of their evil doing. Their work is either that of procreation, extracting semen and inseminating to breed an evil progeny, or aimed to disrupt marriage and cause infertility and impotence.[35]

Historians accept the centrality of marriage and the 'reproductive matrix' within premodern culture.[36] In Chapter 1 we saw how late antique and medieval theologians developed a sexual ethics based on the distinction between procreative conjugal sex (a venial sin) and all other sexual acts (mortal sins). Ruth Mazo Karras structures her survey of medieval sexualities around the opposition of chastity and marriage.[37] Katherine Crawford's survey of premodern European sex starts with marriage and the family, what she calls 'the nexus of the sexual'.[38] Thomas Foster's recent study of eighteenth-century American sex begins with a discussion of the absolute centrality of marriage to concepts of American manhood.[39] The theme of Edward Behrend-Martínez's study of impotency trials in the Basque area of early modern Spain is the importance of marital sex to that society and the manner in which (functioning) sex maintained matrimony.[40] The range of exemplars is practically endless.

We need not revisit in detail the clerical medieval position on marital sex, but it is worth reminding oneself of the importance of sex for marital affection. Drawing on Paul (1 Cor. 7: 1–5), medieval theologians acknowledged the necessity of paying the 'conjugal debt'. It was so important, said Jean Gerson (1363–1429), that while you should avoid paying it in public, 'if one knows the other is in a state of dangerous desire, one is obliged to seek out a secret nook and pay the debt'. Berthold of Freiburg added that a spouse must accede to urgent requests to pay the conjugal debt even if they are 'in a holy place'.[41] The doctrine of *maritalis affectio*, combined with the requirement for consent, encouraged married couples to maintain a loving sexual relationship throughout their marriage.[42] Sex was important too in the very making of marriage. When the Catholic Church first codified its rules of marriage with the *Decretals* of Gratian (*c.* 1140) it made sexual consummation essential to indissoluble marriage. Canon lawyers quickly discerned that this made the marriage of Joseph and Mary invalid, according to the theology of the Virgin's

Image 5. This painting was commissioned by a Bergamo wool merchant
to commemorate his son's marriage. The conjugal ties that bind the
couple are foregrounded in the joined hands, the nuptial ring and the yoke
that Cupid uses to bind the couple. The richness of the wife's clothing and
jewellery indicate her standing. One art historian has described the
painting as a visual inventory of the bride's wealth and the groom's future.
Lorenzo Lotto, *Signor Marsilio Cassotti and his Wife, Faustina*. 1523. Oil on
canvas. Prado, Madrid. Bridgeman Art Library.

perpetual virginity, and Pope Alexander III (r. 1159–81) ruled for the
opinion of Peter Lombard (d. 1160) and Parisian theologians who
stated that consummation was only necessary to confirm a marriage
where promises had been made in the future tense ('I *will* take
you . . .'). Marriage vows in the present tense ('I take you . . .') sufficed
for full marriage.[43] However, some married couples pursued chastity
even within marriage so we should not be too quick to equate 'pre-
heterosexuality' with marriage.[44] One could be married but asexual.

A large part of the business of the Church courts – the records of
which supply most of our information about sexual activity among
the laity in premodern Europe – was devoted to managing the sexual
relations of laypeople. More than sixty per cent of suits heard in
the London ecclesiastical commissary courts between 1470 and 1516

concerned sexual offences, namely fornication, adultery, pimping and prostitution; furthermore the defamation suits that took up the second greatest amount of court time frequently concerned sexual slanders.[45] Adultery was the courts' prime sexual concern, followed by fornication, pimping (bawdry) and prostitution.[46] In fourteenth-century Rochester the consistory courts heard more fornication than adultery cases, but the latter seem to have earned harsher punishments.[47] Somewhat surprisingly, the English records that have merited extensive study (notably London and York) pay almost no attention to same-sex relations.[48] In late medieval Bruges, Ghent and the Holy Roman Empire Church courts were similarly inattentive to same-sex acts, even though secular courts were subjecting them to increasing persecution.[49] We should not assume that it was only the officials of the Church who were concerned to bring sexual offences to court. Although Church courts employed summoners, the system was heavily dependent on neighbours and gossips to identify alleged offenders and report them to court officials.[50] Local communities happily took on the role of sexual policing. While this may be interpreted in terms of disputes, grievances and vendettas between individuals, it has also been suggested that urban communities feared that divine wrath could entail 'collective disaster'; an earthquake on 21 May 1382 just preceded a London ordinance of May and June of that year outlining penalties for the city's 'bawds, strumpets, adulterers, adulteresses, incontinent clergy and scolds'.[51]

Extra-marital sex, as such court records indicate, was at once illicit and ubiquitous. Although the modern-day editor of a tale from Renaissance Florence has outlined the obstacles against the adultery of elite women in that society (the presence of spying servants and neighbours, social conditioning, fear of 'loss of dowry and expulsion from the household'), it still remains the case that the story, by Lorenzo de' Medici no less, assumed the sexual availability of the younger brides of jealous older husbands.[52] The novellas of the seventeenth-century Madrid writer María de Zayas are stories of noble (and fake noble) courtship, marriage and adultery. Their dramatis personae include mistresses, gigolos and lovers, as well as husbands, wives and the unmarried. They are tales of honour and lack of honour, deception, seduction, extreme cruelty, violence and horrible revenge. They are about marriage, though a fractured and threatened marriage. They deal with love and its vicissitudes, but it is primarily adulterous love. Remove adultery from these narratives of handsome men and beautiful women and the novellas would disintegrate.[53]

The supposedly celibate clergy were not immune either: 'If today clerics were locked up in monasteries because of adultery, few of them would walk in the streets.'[54] Priests also feature in Joanne Ferraro's study of illicit sex in the Venetian Republic.[55]

Although the English conduct books urged marital chastity, adultery and fear of adultery were important themes of popular ballad literature.[56] By the seventeenth century a wide range of source material indicates that English adultery was commonplace and increasingly public due to the impact of print.[57] Adultery was a recurring theme of dramatic plot and sub-plot. The upside-down world in Richard Brome's play *The Antipodes* (1640), where gender roles are reversed, has merchants' wives who trade 'Beyond seas, while their husbands cuckold them/ At home.'

> What, do you laugh that there is cuckold-making
> In the Antipodes? I tell you sir,
> It is not so abhorr'd here as 'tis held . . .[58]

'The extent of the extra-marital promiscuity in this play is remarkable,' a modern critic has observed of Brome's *A Mad Couple Well Match'd* (1653). In this play, adapted by Aphra Behn as *The Debauchee* (1677), 'no one is sexually innocent'.[59] A man who remained faithful to his wife was a curiosity:

> Impossible! I wou'd not have you so degenerate from the true gallantry of your Sex, and Age, to be a constant husband. O how vile a sound it has! a young Lord and constant to his Wife! Not for the World, wou'd I be that Woman, that shou'd be guilty of making you so strange a Monster.[60]

In the cities, even in this premodern period, anonymous sex was always a possibility.[61] It is interesting that the worldly-wise, female character in the pornographic *The School of Venus* (1680) associated marriage with sexual freedom because potential pregnancy was not a threatening badge of dishonour: 'the Husband is the Cloak for all, and the Gallants children sit at his fire side without any expences to him that got them, so that this security make them Fuck without fear, and enjoy one another the more freely'.[62]

Any study of premodern marital and extra-marital sex must acknowledge the basic marriage structures of that society. Essentially, there were two European patterns which applied at least from the fourteenth century on: the north-western pattern (as in England), where both partners married at about the same age, in their twenties; and the southern European pattern found in Italy and Spain, where the man was older, in his thirties, and the woman younger, often in her teens.[63] The former was associated with greater relative freedom for both males and females, although this did not translate to gender equality. The latter encouraged male freedom in the form of sodomy and resort to female prostitutes, but allowed less freedom for women.[64]

Historians argue about the degree of sexual freedom before marriage. Crawford writes that 'most Europeans lived much of their lives in considerable sexual denial'.[65] But this is debatable. Sex before marriage in England occurred and was even tolerated – though often within the framework of intention to marry.[66] Either marriage would be promised or agreed upon and sexual intercourse would commence, or couples would have sex, with the spoken or unspoken assumption that the couple would get married if the result was pregnancy. We know that in early modern England from 20 to 25 per cent of brides were pregnant when they entered the church, and that in some parishes the figure was as high as 30 or even 50 per cent.[67] While statistical data are not available for the period before the parish registers of baptisms, marriages and deaths were instituted in 1538, a good range of anecdotal evidence gathered from medieval ecclesiastical court records also suggests that young women had sex with boyfriends on the assumption that marriage would follow.[68]

That the promise of marriage was not invariably honoured is evident from the recurring cases of illegitimacy found, for example, in the early modern English court records. Yet here too the matrix of marriage was evident: '[He] hath kept my company in the way of love, or as a suitor for the space of three years last past . . . as often times attempted me, hastily affirming and declaring that he would marry me.'[69] Another way to read such evidence is to place it back within the context of legal disputes. Female litigants could insist that their male partners had promised to marry them before they agreed to sex as part of the narrative they presented to court. In York in 1417 Margaret Barker made such an argument in trying to enforce a claim of marriage against fellow servant John Waryngton.[70] Premarital sex was also a common experience in fourteenth- and early fifteenth-century Normandy, where 'fornication itself was not necessarily a bar to marriage and was sometimes an integral part of the process by which marriages or other stable unions came to be formed. . . . [S]exual activity can be best viewed as an accepted part of courtship.'[71]

The premarital sexual regime in early modern Spain was remarkably similar – apart from its more pronounced preoccupation with honour and loss of virginity.[72] There, as Renato Barahona summarizes, 'courtship was no idle or gratuitous endeavour for pleasure's sake alone; courtship activity was directed at marriage'.[73] The broken promise of marriage was a leitmotif of the prose of María de Zayas. He 'gave me his word to marry me, and I gave him possession of my body and my soul, believing that in that way I could hold him more securely to his promise. That night passed more quickly than ever, for it was followed by the day of my great misfortune.'[74] 'For women, there's no bond like marriage. . . . Once she loves you, it'll be easy for you, by promising marriage, to enjoy her.'[75] 'Don Fernando, being astute, knew that doña Juana would never surrender herself to him except in marriage, so he pretended to want just that. That is what he told everyone who might repeat it to her, especially her maids, whenever he spoke with them.'[76] Such were the recurring refrains of love gone awry. Marriage, explained one narrator, 'is the prize men offer in order to sugarcoat the bitter pill of their deception'.[77] Although de Zayas's message was the wrongs that men did to women, her scenarios of promised marriage, the sexual relations that followed such negotiations, and the omnipresent threat of the breach of such agreements should hold no surprises for those familiar with premodern sexual culture.

There is also growing evidence of a tolerance of sexual activity other than sexual intercourse. It has been argued that the second half of the eighteenth century saw a privileging of sexual intercourse, a shift towards a penetrative sexual culture. Before that, references to kissing, mutual fondling and groping suggest that many unmarried couples may well have limited their sexual activity within that frame, and that intercourse may not have had the centrality in people's desires that it had in modern sexual cultures.[78]

In north-western Europe, where men and women often did not marry until their late teens or twenties, the sexes commonly worked and socialized in mixed company. Even in the great households of the medieval aristocracy there was little emphasis on strict sexual segregation, although interaction was monitored by the presence of elders and chaperones. In fields and towns of later medieval and early modern England unmarried men and women regularly worked alongside one another.[79] The diaries of those at the middling levels in early modern England convey the impression of a world where there were numerous opportunities for the sexes to meet; where networks of friends, brothers and sisters, servants and apprentices interacted and interceded on one another's behalf; where young people talked of love and marriage and sent and received love letters.[80] In Italy and Spain such interactions were probably much less likely, although the domestic closeting of women did not mean that they were not sexually accessible, as the cases of illicit sex with family members and priests in early modern Venice attest.[81]

Early modern foreign observers were struck by the abandon with which English men kissed women in public.[82] (The English, for their part, were horrified by the manner in which French men kissed one another.[83]) Yet, as we have already noted of later medieval London, this was not a world without rules. The community was an important locus of restraint and control upon the sexual behaviour of the unmarried. Courting couples came under neighbourhood scrutiny, as

is clear from the number of witnesses able to comment on the courtship practices and liaisons of those who appeared before the courts.
There was a framework of moral vigilance and comment.[84] Charivaris
– an early modern public shaming ritual aimed at rebellious women
and based on the assumption that a woman who wore the breeches
was likely to seek extra-marital sex – were merely a dramatic version
of such vigilance. A man beaten by his wife was also a man cuckolded.[85] Yet charivaris were part of a 'wide and flexible' repertoire of
mockery which included individual acts of insult involving crudely
constructed pudenda and horn motifs as well as folk drama and
libels.[86] Such sexual mockery included cases like the woman who
erected a stage in her backyard to act out the infidelities of nearby
residents, and those who threw dildos and 'merkins' over their neighbour's wall with the intention of defaming.[87]

Amy Froide has pointed out that at least a third of early modern
English women were single; in some of the towns the proportion was
even higher. Around a fifth of the population never married. Why,
she asks, is marriage seen as the normative state?[88] Yet it seems pretty
clear that normative premodern sex was indeed organized around the
spiritual and social institution of marriage. Monogamous and fertile
marriage provided the organizing concept for sexual desire and activity. As we have stressed repeatedly, this is not the same as arguing for
premodern 'heterosexuality', as the latter is organized primarily by
sexual object choice and requires its opposite, 'homosexuality', for
definition. We have seen also that constructions of normative marital
sexualities were inflected by cultural differences, notably in the variation between 'north-western' and 'Mediterranean' regimes, and by
gender. In England as in Italy greater emphasis was placed on the
sexual honour of women than men – though this is not to deny
notions of male sexual probity, the power of other non-sexual deter-
miners of a woman's reputation, or the complex ways in which social
position, of women as well as men, could override a breach in moral
conduct.[89] However, as Laura Gowing has written, 'the force with
which women's unchastity was imagined, ridiculed and proscribed
made for a culture in which the possibilities of dishonour seem almost
to erase those of honour'.[90] Men, it was true, were labelled 'whore-
monger' or 'whoremaster'.[91] Yet there was no real male equivalent to
the (loosely defined) 'whore'.[92] The men who were mocked as cuckolds were derided for their lack of control over their wives; the primary
focus of ridicule was the cuckold rather than the male adulterer.[93]

Ideas about the body and the physiological bases for sexual pleasure
at once supported and complicated social restrictions on women's

sexual agency. Thomas Laqueur has proposed a basic division between what he has described as a pre-Enlightenment 'one-sex/flesh' perception of the body and the post-Enlightenment 'two-sex/flesh model'. Before the late eighteenth century, a woman was portrayed in the medical texts as a man with sex organs inverted: the vagina was an interior penis, the ovaries were testicles. Male and female were the same sex with different genders. The rigid, modern two-sex correlation between gender and sex, male and female as different sexes with different genitals, as 'organically one or the other of two incommensurable sexes', was not part of the premodern mindset.[94] The eighteenth century, according to the argument, effected the modern framework of two sexes and two genders, where women and men have different bodies and gender corresponds to this anatomical difference. A 'two-seed' model of reproduction accompanied the one-sex model. Women's orgasms were necessary for conception, as both women and men produced an essential seed; hence there was a stress on female pleasure and on foreplay as a means of achieving this arousal. But in the late seventeenth and early eighteenth centuries, women's bodies were reconceptualized as primarily passive vessels designed for man's pleasure and their active reproductive drive. Female sexual pleasure, despite the sixteenth-century 'discovery' of the clitoris, was no longer so imperative.[95]

Of course, there has been considerable debate about premodern European bodily configurations and theories of reproduction and the timing, extent and nature of the representations identified so influentially by Laqueur.[96] Medievalists have repeatedly pointed out the primacy of 'complexion' theory, in which hotness and dryness defines the biological male and wetness and coldness creates the female. 'Heat ... was the most fundamental physical difference between the sexes and a cause of many other differences' (including quantity of facial and body hair and women's menstruation). 'The general belief was that the coldest man was still warmer than the warmest woman.'[97] How could a 'cold' woman take greater pleasure in sex than a 'hot' man? Medieval scholars wondered about this too and devised an ingenious answer. A woman (cold and wet) was like a damp branch. It was difficult to make her catch fire but once she did she burned hot and long. A man, by implication, was mere kindling – quick to catch alight and quick to burn out.[98]

The modern distinction between biological 'sex' and cultural 'gender' can be misleading when interpreting medieval medical writing, which found continuity between physical characteristics and personal traits. Women's coldness and wetness entailed a 'softness' which made them apt for learning, in the eyes of some, or prone to inconstancy and a kind of weak impressionability.[99] Furthermore, some medieval authors made explicit and detailed comparisons of male and female bodies, such as the author of an English version of the widely circulating 'Trotula' text who argued for five 'diversities' between man and woman: baldness/not baldness; beards/smooth faces; 'little warts'/long hanging breasts; penis and testicles/'bele chose' or 'wicket' (gate); and internal absence/uterus. Monica Green suggests that it is ultimately unhelpful to seek a 'grand thesis of sexual difference'.[100]

In her discussion of eighteenth-century erotica, Karen Harvey has argued for a less schematic history of the body, identifying cultural continuities, variations and inconsistencies (even in the same text). The models of one-sex and two-sex, one-seed and two-seed, if we should persist in calling them models, overlapped and interacted.[101] Male and female bodies 'were imagined as distinctive and commensurable, as both different and the same'.[102] 'In fact, the early-modern sexually voracious woman and the desexualized, domesticated woman who supposedly took her place appeared alongside one another.'[103]

Nonetheless, we can still think of a culture with a powerful recognition of the strength of female desire.[104] *Aristotle's Master-piece* (1684) posited that women

> have greater pleasure, and receive more content than a Man: for since by Nature much delight accompanies the ejection of the Seed, by breaking forth of the swelling Spirit, and the stiffness of the Nerves, in which case the operation of the Womans part is double, the suffering both ways, even by ejection and reception, whereby she is more recreated and delighted in the Venereal Act.[105]

This belief was regularly put into the service of a persistent and ubiquitous misogyny. Women, as Anthony Fletcher has expressed it, were perceived as 'possessing a powerful and potentially destructive sexuality which made them naturally lascivious, predatory and, most serious of all, once their desire was fully aroused, insatiable'.[106]

Garthine Walker has argued that the languages of sex that stressed male activity and female complicity made it extremely difficult for women to demonstrate or even describe rape. It was a culture in which sexual submission was interpreted as consent. As she puts it, 'there was no popular language of sexual non-consent upon which women could draw'.[107]

Sex must therefore be seen in the context of power. We can see the logic of subordination at its most objectionable in the situation of some female servants, what Kristina Straub has called 'a long history of love and hate'.[108] Servants dominate a chapter on sexual coercion and violence in a study of lawsuits over loss of virginity (*estupro*) in the Basque area of early modern Spain, where a third of the victims in these suits were women in service.[109] The sexual access of domestic servants seems to have been taken for granted by married masters as well as by their sons and their friends. A London master actually said this to his maid in 1605: 'he had the use of her at his pleasure, saying thou art my servant and I may do with thee what I please'.[110] An eighteenth-century French servant resisted her master's advances at first but stated that 'since he was her master she was obliged to consent'.[111] It was an unfortunate part of the institution of service, so central to premodern households. 'Hungry Dogs will eat dirty Puddings' was the metaphorical advice given to seventeenth-century kitchen maids as a warning against sexual predation.[112] Gowing has charted the complex ways in which premodern English women nego-tiated a sexual culture that simultaneously acknowledged female desire while privileging feminine passivity.[113] Where there were slaves – in the Chesapeake and Caribbean, for example – the assumptions of sexual possession were even more marked.[114]

Yet let us not presume that premodern households uniformly exploited female servants and other dependants. Although some late medieval English evidence exists of girls coerced into commercial sex, procured for rape or abused by their masters while living away from the natal home, apprenticeship indentures and court records also depict such young women as protected by their masters and mistresses acting *in loco parentis*. English apprenticeship indentures illustrate a sexual double standard: where male apprentices were warned against visiting brothels or fornicating with his master's wife or daughter, females were enjoined not to engage in any sexual activ-ity at all.[115]

We should not ascribe a passive role to women. Bernard Capp has outlined the various ways in which early modern Englishwomen negotiated a place in a society that seemed always to subordinate or contain them.[116] Women who felt that they had no other recourse against men who had wronged them could use gossip. The domestic servant Margaret Knowsley took this gamble in 1625 when the min-ister Stephen Jerome sexually assaulted her. Steven Hindle has traced the networks of gossip as Knowsley publicized her employer's attempted rape: she talked to women while hay making, walking in the streets and fields, and knitting at the fireside; she even told her midwife as she went into labour. Others relayed her allegations – in agreement and denial – as they talked to neighbours and argued in the churchyard. But it was a risky means of retribution. Knowsley was prosecuted for slander and sentenced to a public shaming and whipping.[117]

Gowing has shown that patriarchal power depended on the agency of women as well as men: particular women were granted authority (the married and the orderly); others were excluded (the single and disorderly).[118] The conduct books were fully aware that many women did not adhere to the ideal, that there were women who stood up to their husbands. In the wider world of European popular literature female characters were frequently portrayed as strong and rebellious.[119]

Elizabeth Foyster has argued that by basing itself so strongly on control of female sexuality, by being defined essentially in terms of mastery of its 'other', premodern masculinity was an anxious masculinity, all too easily threatened or undermined by the words and actions of women. Men were continually worried about the potential adultery of their wives, and the sexual honour of their daughters. And if the woman did stray, the implications for manliness were immense. Cuckold was the name given to such a man, based on the word cuckoo, a bird that lays its eggs in other birds' nests. A cuckold (the man who is the victim of the cuckoo) had lost authority, for it was assumed that if he had had any control his wife would not have wandered in the first place. There are many ballads along the lines of the woman wearing the trousers in a relationship, or, in premodern terms, the breeches, thus rendering her husband effeminate. A cuckold had also demonstrated his lack of sexual prowess: if he had been able to sexually satisfy his wife, she would not have been tempted to adultery. Such a man's manliness was therefore seriously compromised.[120] The double bind was that jealousy was equally unmanning: 'Observed all the time by friends and neighbours, men walked a tightrope between losing control of their wives, and showing excessive concern for their chastity which could be labelled as jealousy.'[121]

Licit and admired modes of premodern sex were at once similar to and intriguingly different from modern heterosexual regimes. Passionate love between men and women was exalted in medieval literature even if cautioned by theologians, but such love was only possible within a courtly milieu. It usually (not always) presumed male and female partners, but courtly appearance was more important than sexual dimorphism in creating attraction. In life as well as literature, love which crossed boundaries including rank and religion was subject to strong taboos. Premodern Europeans, and indeed early modern Americans, followed a sexual regime structured by the expectation of fertile monogamous marriage. This allowed for quite a strong degree of toleration for premarital sexual activity between men and women, up to but also including penetrative sex, provided legitimate matrimony was the predictable outcome. Adultery troubled courts and communities more than fornication did, and same-sex activity did not greatly disturb the marital paradigm. As we will see in the next chapter, anxieties about sodomy applied in particular contexts (notably medieval monasteries and the most ambitious civic regimes), and in certain discourses of political or religious defamation. Premodern scientific and medical theories about male and female bodies constructed a strong emphasis on female orgasm as essential for conception which chimed with wider cultural beliefs in women's greater lust and pleasure in sex.

Although a focus on marriage and reproduction implies men and women having sex, Schultz has warned against assuming that this was heterosexuality as we would understand it.[122] The fact that in Italy a rapist might be forced to marry his unmarried victim is an indication that we are talking about different sexual worlds.[123] Heterosexuality today is not tied to or equated with reproduction; indeed it is more likely to be linked to the avoidance of it.[124] Nor does the fact that Renaissance men and women had sex with each other tell us anything about their sexual identity. In the modern heterosexual framework, oral sex between husband and wife would be seen as not widely different to sexual intercourse. In the premodern regime, the latter (intercourse) was permissible for reproductive purposes but the former (oral sex) was on par with sodomy, and rape was a lesser sin given that it could result in pregnancy. There was no privileging of opposite-sex interaction as something intrinsically good in itself.[125] Schultz has also argued that when historians look back on premodern marriages and assume them heterosexual, they are in fact mistaking gender power for heterosexual choice; sex between husband and wife could have more to do with subordination to male power and/or desire to have children than with 'inherent desires for the other sex'.[126] 'Marriage, marital bed, sex, reproduction: here we are again at the heart of our Renaissance discourse of adult masculine identity,' Guido Ruggiero observes.[127] But when he refers repeatedly to 'sexual identity', indeed 'heterosexual identity', he mistakes obsession with fertility for heterosexuality.[128]

The well-known case of John/Eleanor Rykener, apprehended in women's dress and accused of committing 'that detestable, unmentionable, and ignominious vice' with another man in late fourteenth-century London, unsettles any assumptions about premodern sex. As Ruth Mazo Karras and David Lorezno Boyd point out, he does not easily fit modern sexual categories such as 'homosexual' but the medieval authorities who heard his case seemed not to know how to label him either. Available vocabulary for 'prostitute' (e.g. *meretrix*, 'common woman') was not used in his trial records, and neither was 'sodomite'. Karras and Boyd argue that it was Rykener's gender transgression that most troubled the court. They are too wise to hazard any suggestions about his own sexual preferences or proclivities, yet their claim that 'all his sexual encounters with men were for money, while those with women were not', could be taken as evidence of his 'heterosexuality'.[129] In fact, the record of his case is not at all clear on this point. Not every man who is mentioned among his sexual partners is noted as having paid him. Conversely, it is possible that some of the 'many' nuns, married and other women recorded in his sexual history did give him money for sex.[130]

Rebecca Ann Bach's case study of the poet John Donne argues that while, superficially, modern-day (heterosexual) observers might claim him as one of theirs because of his love poetry, his privileging of close male friendships, obsession with his soul rather than his self, and belief in the corrosive effects of lust and sin rather than the benefits of sex (orgasm was, after all, known as the little death) indicate a rather different sexual regime.[131]

Donne and his society understood desire not in terms of the self and personality but in terms of the blood. Sex was humoral rather than psychological.[132] A man's lust could be the result of his humoral disposition.[133] Surfeit of seed and thus heat in the womb was thought to cause immoderate desire in women.[134] Lesel Dawson has contrasted modern obsessive love with premodern lovesickness or melancholy. The former, when it is explained, is seen as psychiatric disturbance; the latter always had a *physiological* component. Love-sickness – not a modern term – was humoral, a medical matter, 'a dangerous physical illness'.[135] The cure was release of seed (male or female) or the letting of blood. Indeed allied sexual complaints – green sickness (the so-called sickness of virgins), suffocation of the mother (hysteria or 'the mother') and uterine fury – female afflictions – were likewise explained as humoral imbalance.[136] Edward Jorden's *A Briefe Discourse of a Disease Called the Suffocation of the Mother* (1603) wrote that 'the want of due and monethly evacuation, or the want of the benefit of marriage in such as have beene accustomed or are apt thereunto, breeds a congestion of humors about that part, which increasing or corrupting in the place, causeth this disease. And therefore we do observe that maidens and widowes are most subiect thereunto'.[137] Though sexual intercourse or marriage were among the recommended cures for such maladies, so too was the use of scent to lure the womb back into its natural position.[138] We remain somewhat remote from the various erotic elements of modern heterosexuality. Future reflections on premodern sexual histories will only advance by deeper consideration of specific cultural contexts, closer attention to contemporary language and abandonment of the term 'heterosexualities'.

3

Between Men

Nowhere is the difference between modern and premodern sexual worlds clearer than when we explore male same-sex attractions. The majority of historians of sex concur that in the premodern world there was homosexual behaviour without the homosexual identity that is taken for granted in modern and postmodern times. A variety of studies have described the ways in which medieval and early modern poetry, drama and prose created 'textual spaces . . . in which homoerotic desire could be articulated and homosexual relations imagined'.[1] Male-to-male sexual interaction was something that all men might engage in. It was part of being sexual. That is not to say that all aspects of homosexual activity were acceptable in the medieval or early modern period (as we will see, anal penetration and other varieties of 'sodomy' often carried severe penalties), but those who engaged in such sexual practices were rarely seen as a different species of person. David Halperin has argued that rather than assuming a single history of homosexuality, it is useful to consider a variety of categories or sites for the location of what he terms *pre-homosexual* discourses or patterns in the period leading up to the nineteenth and twentieth centuries, after which homosexuality was actually used as a word and became more closely related to what we mean by the term.[2] Sodomy, friendship and effeminacy, while possessing a range of connotations that were not always sexual, provide three such 'sites' of pre-homosexual meanings in premodern cultures.

There is a tendency for discussions of male homosexuality to merge with discussions of the crime of sodomy and for both to focus on male-to-male anal sex. But this is highly misleading. 'Sodomy' as defined by religion and law included a range of condemned practices, 'a way to encompass a multitude of sins with a minimum of signs', as one critic has cleverly expressed it.[3] In ancient and early medieval writings, 'Sodomites' (from the destruction of Sodom and Gomorrah in Genesis 18–19) were comprehended as enemies of God and the Christian religion.[4] Sodomy was a theological category, alongside and analogous to 'blasphemy'. The Hebrew Bible and other Rabbinic writings tended to interpret the crime as some combination of 'pride, greed, luxury and inhospitality'.[5] In early Christian teaching, including works by Jerome and Ambrose, Sodomites were condemned for clusters of sinful behaviours that gradually came to include sexual sins, though not necessarily male–male acts; when early authors such as St Augustine made explicit mention of attempted rape of the angels by the men of Sodom, this nefarious act was indicative of their generalized depravity rather than standing as 'the Sodomitic sin' itself. Penitential texts of the seventh to twelfth centuries, furthermore, were less than clear about the implications of the nature of that sin. Peter Damian, castigating lascivious priests in 1049, was one of the first to use the abstract noun *sodomia* and limit its meaning to men's sexual sins, specifically self-pollution (masturbation), mutual masturbation, intercourse between the thighs and anal intercourse.[6] Later medieval theologians found *sodomia* helpful when discoursing on the non-reproductive 'vice against nature'. Aquinas counts 'sodomy' ('copulation with undue sex, male with male or female with female, as the Apostle states [Romans 1.27]') third on a list of ways to commit unnatural 'vice'.[7] Many later medieval authors went further, making 'the vice against nature' and 'sodomy' synonymous. *Fasciculus Morum*, a fourteenth-century preacher's handbook, called 'the fifth and last branch of lechery... the diabolical sin against nature, called sodomy'.[8]

Well into the late medieval and early modern periods sodomy was often unhelpfully described as 'that unspeakable sin' or 'that unmentionable vice'. 'I hardly dare speak of this vile and horrible sin, and especially in our France', Jean Benedicti wrote in 1610.[9] As the account of the Earl of Castlehaven's 1631 trial expressed it, 'the *crimen sodomiticum ...* is of so abominable and vile a nature (that as the indictment truly expresses it, *crimen inter Christianos non nominandum*), it is a crime not to be named among Christians'.[10] Now and then, the descriptions corresponded to anticipated denotations, though with a somewhat wider range of infraction. Peter of Abano wrote in the fourteenth century of 'those who exercise the wicked act of sodomy [*sodomiticum*] by rubbing the penis with the hand; others by rubbing between the thighs of boys, which is what most do these days; and others by making friction around the anus and putting the penis in it the same way as it is placed in a woman's sexual part'.[11] Acts between women (as we will see) could be sodomitical too: Karma Lochrie has reminded us that sodomy was, in the words of Chaucer's Parson, a 'cursednesse doon men and wommen in diverse entente and in diverse manere'.[12] In fourteenth- and fifteenth-century Venice 'sodomy' referred usually to acts between men but also unnatural acts with women or animals: interfemoral sex between men was a common factor in fourteenth-century prosecutions; in the fifteenth century anal sex was more usually the bugbear but not infrequently concerned men's anal penetration of women.[13] Although the actual prosecutions did not reflect this breadth, French definitions of sodomy nearly always included women. Hence the entry in a late eighteenth-century French encyclopaedia of jurisprudence: 'Pederasty or sodomy is the crime of any man with man, of any woman with a woman, and even of a man with a woman, when, through inconceivable debauchery, they do not make use of the usual paths of reproduction.'[14] In early modern New Haven, it included some forms of masturbation and vaginal penetration of a prepubescent girl.[15]

Altogether, it is not entirely sex that defines the sin; rather, the premodern Sodomite is so deeply an enemy of God that his or her sins may include same-sex acts that contravene, in the words of thirteenth-century theologian Albertus Magnus, 'grace, reason and nature'.[16] '[S]odomy is seen as what disrupts established law, systems of classification, religious, ethnic, and gender boundaries.'[17] If 'sodomy' is primarily 'opposition to God', we can better understand its frequent medieval parallels with 'heresy'. From the mid-eleventh century, heresy accusations were often accompanied by allegations of same-sex acts; perhaps most famously, *bougre* ('Bulgar', 'bugger') may have originated as a nickname for Bogomils or Cathars, sects thought to have originated in Bulgaria. Helmut Puff shows that in fifteenth- and sixteenth-century Germany, *ketzern* ('to commit heresy') and *ketzerie* ('heresy') were often used in legal records to refer to same-sex acts.[18] Sodomy stood as shorthand for general crimes against the state, society and God – behaviour beyond the pale – and could be used to signify corruption, disorder or threatened societal disintegration.[19] The seventeenth-century theologian Benedicti placed sodomy on a continuum of damnation: 'Such shameless people fall from this miserable sin into others more terrible, such as apostasy, atheism, heresy, and finally, having reached the height of impiety, die damned.'[20]

Despite the term's enduring flexibility, from the twelfth century 'sodomy' was increasingly associated with sex acts between men. Why? John Boswell satisfied few (not even himself) with his suggestion that the posited shift from Christian 'tolerance' to 'intolerance' towards 'gay men' was due to increasing urbanization.[21] More recently Mathew Kuefler has suggested that twelfth-century male lovers were perceived to threaten maintenance of family lineages, while bonds between men of military classes threatened loyalties to large and ambitious political entities of 'church and state'.[22] Men's friendships, previously celebrated, were ever in danger of coming under the suspicion of 'sodomy'. Courtly love was offered up as an alternative to love between men, and the *unnaturalness* of male–male sex was increasingly harped upon. Bernard of Clairvaux was one who declared this 'plague' 'unknown to cattle, or dogs, or horses' and despised men who polluted each other with what they should give the inferior sex. Sodomy violated 'not only human nature but also especially masculine nature', most forcefully expressed in Alain of Lille's *Plaint of Nature*: 'the sex of the active gender trembles thus to degenerate shamefully into the passive gender', that is, the feminine.[23] Medieval homophobia, in Kuefler's account, was founded partly on misogyny.

William Burgwinkle's argument that sodomy was 'crucial . . . to the institution of a new model of heroic and highly monitored masculinity in the twelfth century', that is, knighthood, is compatible with Kuefler's hypothesis.[24] Yet he goes further, suggesting that by calling attention to erotic possibilities beyond theological and legal frameworks that attempt to confine it, 'sodomy' carried paradoxical, subversive potential. It made visible what some wished to destroy and (Burgwinkle suggests) enabled self-recognition among some men as a result. Moreover, the twelfth-century renaissance of classical learning and literature provided the educated with a host of homoerotic models to draw upon (Zeus, Ganymede, Aeneas, Julius Caesar). For example, Arnaud de Verniolles, tried for heresy and sodomy in 1323, confessed that he borrowed a 'book by Ovid' from Guillaume Roux, and on two or three later occasions the two men committed sodomitic acts together.[25] Thus recent scholarship makes apparent that the explosion of discourse on and increasingly male homoerotic connotations of 'sodomy' are best seen as a corollary of the rise of centralized, homosocial, political institutions including secular and papal monarchies, centralized legal systems, civic governments and inquisitions, but may also have helped to foster the sexual acts and inclinations those institutions wished to suppress.

Once implanted in medieval discourse, 'sodomy' as male–male sex found special favour as a term of accusation. 'Sodomy' is always 'a judgement' (Jordan); 'a discursive weapon' (Zeikowitz); a 'politics' (Brundage and Puff); a 'libel', 'slander' or 'defamation' (Puff); an item of 'hate speech' (Jordan); and when applied to an entire social or religious grouping it becomes a 'delusion' (Percy and Johanssen).[26] Sodomy defamation was variously applied to Gregorian reformers campaigning against clerical marriage in the eleventh century but also to Emperor Henry IV (1054–1106, famous for his role in the 'Investiture Controversy') by pro-papal writers. Emperor Frederick II (1220–50) was similarly defamed by the biographer of his opponent Pope Innocent IV, but not long afterwards Philip the Fair made such allegations against Pope Boniface VIII (1294–1303). Philip's trial of the whole order of the Knights Templar (1307–11) circled around sodomy.[27] A number of allegations are well known to historians of medieval England. In the late eleventh century criticism was aimed at the courts of William Rufus and his brother Robert Curthose, while in the twelfth century rumours swirled around Henry I and Richard I, and in the fourteenth century allegations of excessive intimacy with male favourites were used against Edward II and Richard II.[28]

Some modern political scholars have attempted to address empirical questions of whether such individuals or groups were actually 'homosexual', but aside from being anachronistic this is not our point. The terms 'sodomy' and 'sodomite' had tremendous charge in medieval propaganda and were thus deployed as effective weapons. Foreign peoples, too, especially Italians (according to English, French and German sources), the French (according to the English), Muslims and (by the early sixteenth century) 'Indians' of the New World were also subject to virulent accusations. In contrast, before around 1500, Chinese, Indians, southeast Asians and in most cases Mongolian people were not depicted as sodomites, although by the mid-sixteenth century, with increasing European trade and missionary activity in those regions, the Chinese often were.[29] The venerable tradition of denouncing heretics for unnatural vices took on a new lease of life with the German Reformation, when Martin Luther and others used invective against Catholics, and Italians and especially all involved with the Papacy in Rome were attacked in print.[30]

At the popular rather than political level, accusations of sodomitic acts are almost unheard of until the late thirteenth century, when Bologna, parts of Portugal and other regions embracing Roman civic law prescribed death by fire for convicted sodomites.[31] The earliest record of capital punishment for male sodomy in the Holy Roman Empire comes from 1277; the earliest case of female sodomy yet found is from Bologna in 1295.[32] Many regions imposed the death penalty rarely, if at all. The kingdom of England had no secular 'buggery' act until 1533, and we saw in the previous chapter that Church courts almost never punished such behaviour. Persecution intensified in some places in the fifteenth and sixteenth centuries, but still at a relatively infrequent level. In sixteenth-century Zurich and Lucerne there were respectively eight and seven executions for sodomy across a 100-year period (burnings and decapitations), with some further milder penalties such as banishment and 'exhortations' also imposed.[33] William Monter counts seventy-five sodomy trials in Geneva from 1400 to 1800 (of which one, in 1568, concerned a woman); of those whose fates are known, one was beheaded, four hanged, twelve drowned and fourteen burned and most of the remainder were banished.[34] Bruges, Venice and Florence, on the other hand, all recorded unusually high levels of prosecutions. The ninety executions in Burgundian Bruges, 1385–1515, represent 15 per cent of all executions in that city over the period. Ruggiero counts 514 cases in Venice from 1326 to 1500, nearly 500 of which came from the fifteenth century.[35] As Marc Boone has argued in regard to Bruges, the severe measures taken reflect these cities' political ambitions and self-perception as pre-eminent states within Christendom: 'the repression of sodomy had become a matter of highest political importance'. Sodomites were an 'internal enemy' that had to be beaten. 'If the authority of the [Burgundian] prince and his role as guarantor of the divine order was to be secured in any city, it had to be in Bruges.'[36] Venetian authorities were genuinely concerned their city could suffer the fate of Sodom and Gomorrah, especially pronounced given the devastating waves of plague in the fourteenth century.[37] Florence prosecuted more alleged sodomites than any other late medieval city, with around 17,000 allegations against individuals and almost 3,000 convictions over the period 1432 to 1502, but this exceptional rate of trials can be accounted for by the Office of the Night's decision to punish first offences not with castration or burning as earlier Florentine authorities had required, but with fines (which could be very large) and optional public humiliation. The Office also took mitigating factors such as youth and the passive role into account.[38]

The history of 'sodomy' as a tool of political control is unavoidable, but should not deflect from our abiding concern with histories of sex and desire between men. The nature of surviving sources, with few descriptions in court records from before the fifteenth century, means that most of our remaining examples come from the late medieval or early modern periods. Viewed sexually, sodomy was excessive rather than perverted sex, part of a propensity to loss of control rather than a specific tendency: Bernardino of Siena said in the 1420s that all 'unbridled and crazy young men' were prone to sodomy because of their acute lust.[39] When explaining the workings of the devil on those of a sanguine constitution, a medical text of 1576 referred to 'riot, wantonnesse, drunkenes, wastfulnes, prodigality, filthy and detestable loves, horrible lustes, incest, and buggerie'.[40] It could also be a pragmatic as well as erotic choice. Arnaud de Verniolles

testified to inquisitors in 1323 that he had taken up sex with boys
because of fear of catching leprosy from prostitutes. At the same time,
his attraction to males seems unquestionable. He believed 'his nature
inclined him to commit sodomy', but appears to mean this was as
natural to him as inclination to fornication with women. He told
many of his young male partners that sodomy was no more sinful
than simple fornication.[41] Like the other pre-homosexual categories,
then, the history of sodomy is as much a part of the prehistory of
heterosexuality.

The possibilities of male-to-male sex ranged across classes. In early
modern elite culture, adult male libertines were men who enjoyed
the bodies of both male and female.[42] Edward de Vere, Earl of Oxford,
was accused in the 1580s of habitually buggering his boy servants.[43]
The allegation that he said that 'when wemen were vnswete, fine
(yonge) boyes were in season' is interesting less for its veracity than
the recognition that sex with boys and women was on a continuum.[44]
The conviction and execution of the Earl of Castlehaven in the
seventeenth century belongs to the history of libertinism rather than
to that of homosexuality. The Earl was alleged to have enjoyed
sex between the thighs of his male servants and to have watched the
rape of his wife, as well as keeping a female prostitute and either
viewing or engaging in group sex. But Castlehaven was accused of
having 'given himself over to lust' rather than to homosexuality.[45]
Restoration England was notorious for its sexual excess; 'buggery is
now almost grown as common among our gallants as in Italy, and that
the very pages of the town begin to complain of their masters for it',
was the often-cited complaint recorded by Samuel Pepys in the
1660s.[46] The famous verse of John Wilmot, Earl of Rochester, was a
product of this milieu: 'There's a sweet soft *Page*, of mine, / Does
the trick worth *Forty Wenches*.' 'And the best Kiss was the deciding
Lot / Whether the *Boy* us'd you, or I the *Boy*.' '*Woman* or *Boy* ... /
Where e're it pierc'd, a *Cunt* it found or made.'[47] The behaviour of
the rake or libertine was characterized by its excess rather than by
its attraction to men. Indeed George Haggerty and others have
observed that Rochester's verse is neither homosexual nor homoerotic; it merely represents 'the libertine ability to "make a cunt"
wherever he chooses'.[48]

The figure of the libertine may have lingered longer than historians
recognize. 'In England the vices in fashion are whoring & drinking,
in Turkey, Sodomy & smoking. We prefer a girl and a bottle, they a
pipe and a pathic. – They are a sensible people.' Thus wrote Byron in
1810.[49] The celebrated Byron is best seen as an early modern rather
than modern figure. His passion for beautiful choirboys and pages
as well as (numerous) beautiful women, and both male and female

servants, makes perfect sense in terms of the sexual configurations that we have been discussing.[50] Notions of heterosexual, homosexual and bisexual are just not appropriate.

At a more popular level, male-to-male sex could surface in the unremarkable circumstances of daily work and recreation.[51] In early fourteenth-century Pamiers Arnaud de Verniolles solicited youths in gardens, a cemetery, the friars' refectory and open fields and had sex with them (forced or consensual) in fields or his own house. Arnold's own first same-sex experience was aged ten or eleven while living away from home for schooling and was with a fellow student with whom he shared a bed.[52] Helmut Puff has observed the everyday nature of sodomy cases in sixteenth-century Switzerland. Inns, hostels, shared beds, fellow workers or master and servant drinking and working together: such were the sites, occasions and relationships recurring in erotic encounters between Swiss males.[53] Cristian Berco has written of a similar breadth of sexual opportunity in early modern Spain: 'The veritable bacchanalia of semi-public and public sex that took place in early modern cities and villages delineates a sexual geography that rendered the public sphere an unofficial erotic theatre.'[54] The shared bed (a practice everywhere in Europe) also looms large in eighteenth-century English accusations of sodomy because that is where the alleged act commonly occurred.[55] One case arose out of sleeping arrangements at a printer's where those involved slept and worked together. The accuser claimed that his bedfellow had been interfering with him for four years: 'he over-persuaded me to let him bugger me'.[56] Such cases involved master and apprentice sleeping together, fellow workers sharing a bed, or the nightly arrangements of lodgers. Another indictment began when a watchmaker's apprentice was forced to share a bed with a Portuguese sailor who was lodging in the same room. He normally paired with a fellow apprentice, but they fought and he had to move in with the older man. (It transpired that there was another man in the bed too, and five more sleeping in the next room.)[57]

In an Italian Renaissance tale involving a beautiful young priest dressed as a woman and a lustful friar, the latter, when he discovered the deceit of the former, was no less ardent in his affections: 'Very well! I like you no less as a man than as a woman.'[58] The sex that we are discussing here spanned what we would term heterosexual and homosexual behaviour; though presumably this spanning varied according to the sexual availability of women in the respective regional cultures – women were less publicly accessible in Italy and Spain than they were in England and Switzerland. There are cases in the English court records of men who came between the legs of other males, telling them that they gave as much pleasure as 'a woman'.[59]

A naval court martial in 1761 heard that when a man who was buggering a boy was asked 'what he had got there, he said cunt'.[60] It
would be an exaggeration to claim that males competed with female
prostitutes for the attention of other men in early modern London,
for anonymous sex was predominantly between men and women.[61]
Nevertheless, they did turn to one another as well as to those women
described as whores. The descriptions of sexual aggression towards
males (often boys) in eighteenth-century London, grabbing, lunging
and exposure, is remarkably similar to the interactions with women
revealed in the early modern court records.[62]

Male–male sex was frequently described in terms of courtship and
pursuit. Boys and young men were approached in the street, asked
to go for a drink or food, bought little gifts, kissed and asked to spend
the night; or they were plied with drink, kissed and groped in ale-
houses or down laneways. '[H]e put his Hand into my Breeches, and
forced my Hand into his . . . he struggled with me till I was quite
tir'd.'[63] '[H]e said he'd f[uc]k me that night', a seventeen-year-old
reported of his assailant in 1749; 'then, said he, what countryman are
you? I told him Hertfordshire; he took me in his arms and kiss'd me
five or six times: then said he, I'll take you down in a coach, and make
you drunk as a owl all the way you go.'[64] The aptly named Henry Wolf
met a brandy merchant's servant out on an errand for his master,
invited him for a drink, bought him a nosegay and penny custard and,
much as a courting couple might, accompanied him to places of
popular entertainment. He then took him to a privy and fellated
him.[65] In early modern Spain, the strategies that men used with one
another, 'cajoling words, gifts, money, overt advances, and sometimes
violence mimicked the relationships established between men and
women'.[66] In a case in seventeenth-century Paris an elderly man
pursued a young notary's clerk, visiting him at work, taking him to
taverns and for walks, promising visits to a prostitute, and fondling
and kissing him – all quite publicly, though the alleged attempted
sodomy occurred in a private room in an inn.[67] It is interesting that
in premodern Florence the sites for opposite-sex and same-sex intercourse were identical. Michael Rocke's summary of erotic relations
in that Renaissance Italian city is doubtless applicable to other European regions: 'homoerotic relations were not necessarily an exclusive
alternative to sex with women, but one of several possible and probably overlapping options'.[68]

This is not to ignore those men whose preferences were more
exclusively male. Such tendencies had a long lineage.[69] In the twelfth-
century *Roman d'Eneas* Lavine's mother warns that Eneas is interested only in boys, because of his nature. 'He won't eat hens, but really
loves the flesh of a cock . . . you wouldn't find him hanging round the

hole in the gate; but he really goes for the crack of a young man.' If all men were like him, she warns direly, no woman would conceive and the human race would cease to exist.[70] In Marie de France's *Lanval* (late twelfth century), Guinevere turns on a knight who has spurned her advances with the accusation that he has no inclination (*talent*) for women but prefers to sport with young men.[71] There had been men in medieval Florence who, even in old age, retained a sexual preference for young males: Boccaccio's *Decameron* contains a character 'as fond of [women] as a dog of cudgels'.[72] Such men could be married but there was a predisposition to 'more dedicated' sodomy among a small group of men who remained unmarried.[73] Bernardino of Siena warned: 'if they don't marry they become sodomites. Make this a general rule: when you see a grown man in good health who doesn't have a wife, you can take this as an evil sign about him, especially if he hasn't chosen for spiritual reasons to live in chastity.'[74] The Dominican friar Matteo Bandello wrote a story in 1554 about a married Roman poet who was said to be 'a thousand more times eager for boys than goats are for salt'. When questioned by his confessor about 'the sin against nature', the man denied any wrongdoing: 'To amuse myself with boys is more natural to me than eating and drinking to a man, and you asked me if I sinned against nature! Just go, go away – you don't know what a good tidbit is.'[75]

A married New England man, prosecuted for sodomy in the 1670s, had been making sexual advances to men for some thirty years. He was a man of influence in the community who seemed only to approach social inferiors, often his own servants, who may have tolerated his behaviour much in the way that female servants put up with the sexual advances of their masters as part of the hierarchical nature of their relationship. But clearly examples such as his show that there were men who were attracted to their own sex, and who were recognized as such by others.[76]

Recent studies of early modern Frankfurt and Geneva have revealed similar individuals who were known 'buggers' long before any actions were taken against them.[77] The same was true of seventeenth-century France.[78] By the time he was indicted a seventeenth-century French priest had acquired a decade-long reputation for approaching soldiers and other young men and inviting them to sleep with him; it was common talk – they called him the 'cock jerker', 'the dear chaplain who wants to do it from behind'.[79] An elderly man in Mexico City who appeared before the Spanish High Court in 1656 said that he had been committing the crime against nature for his whole life: '"one should eat" men just like one "ate a frog": that is, "from the waist downward"'.[80] A Mallorcan water-carrier was reputed to have said of sodomy, 'these actions were more enjoyable with men than with women', while another early modern Spaniard, named Pizarro, was popularly known as (the feminine) 'la Pizarra' because of his penchant for being penetrated and his associated effeminacy.[81] Trials in the Dutch Republic in the eighteenth century revealed a handful of men who for long periods of time had shown no interest in women, confining their pleasure to men.[82] However, these instances, while important, indicate what Richard Godbeer has called 'erotic predilection' rather than sexual identity.[83]

Tim Hitchcock has observed that it is intriguing that people did not seem reluctant to engage in this sort of activity in public in parks or alleyways or while others were sleeping around them.[84] It implies an acceptance (rather than tolerance) of such behaviour, and certainly shows a gap between public morality and a draconian law that, at its extreme, punished sodomy with death. It is entirely possible that people had notions of sodomites as those beyond the pale yet did not necessarily connect this image with the behaviour that went on around them.[85] With the publicity of court cases, they may then have become more condemnatory. It is difficult to determine such attitudes. The preacher who delivered 'such a sermon against sodomy, and lifted up his eyes', when, 'about half an hour before, he had been acting such a vile action', may have maintained a separation in his mind between his own behaviour and the sins that invoked his wrath or may merely have been a hypocrite.[86] There is a question over how far we can trust the rationalization of the man who reassured another that 'he need not be troubled, or wonder at what he had done to him, for it was what was very common, and he had often practised it with many others; at the same time desiring the Deponent to act the same with him'.[87] If the man who said 'I think there's no Crime in making what use I please of my own Body' really believed what he said, why did he call witnesses to testify to his long marriage and the fact that he 'loved the Company of Women better than that of his own Sex'? And did he still believe it was not a crime after he had been fined, pilloried and imprisoned?[88]

Helmut Puff has distinguished two cultural attitudes to early modern sodomy: the age- or power-structured system (especially associated with Mediterranean contexts), where it mattered who was on top, and the Christian tradition (more generally noted north of the Alps), which did not distinguish between penetrator and penetrated in its condemnation of the practice.[89] The former is most clearly associated with ancient Greek and Roman pederasty. Indeed, the classicist Halperin confines his discussion of what he terms pederasty or 'active' sodomy to penetration of a subordinate male by a social and/or age superior, with its associated hierarchies of penetrator/penetrated, superior/inferior, masculine/feminine and active/passive.[90] Another archetypal case (closer to the remit of this chapter) is the age-graded, male–male sex of medieval Florence, where, despite the penalties and the activities of informants, a majority of Florentine males were involved in sodomitical activities and homoerotic activity was part of masculine work and neighbourhood interaction. (Not surprisingly, *'florenced'* became the European term for sodomized.[91]) Some 80 per cent of active partners prosecuted for sodomy were aged nineteen or over, and 90 per cent of passive partners were eighteen or younger.[92] The cultural assumption was that the older partner was the penetrator and the younger the penetrated, even if the age difference was minimal. The language of the streets referred to the active, those who sodomized, fucked, embraced, buggered, serviced, used, did, and the passive, those to whom such things were done. The penetrator was manly in his actions; the penetrated was sexually subordinate and woman-like. Later, when they got older (it was expected that a young man would shed his boy status between the ages of eighteen to twenty), the penetrated could become the penetrator with younger boys or men. Most would get married when they reached their thirties.[93] The older male who let himself be penetrated was subject to the greatest stigma and punishment; a twenty-six-year-old wool-washer who had confessed that he had been sodomized many times was convicted 'because he could be called a man, not a boy'.[94]

Cristian Berco has likewise demonstrated the role of sodomy in the culture of early modern Spanish masculinity. Here too large numbers of the passive/effeminized partners were younger men: 'the desire of mature men for male adolescents was considered normal, even if this normalcy often spilled into what authorities termed the grievous sin of sodomy'.[95] Nearly 90 per cent of those accused of active sodomy in the Aragonese trials reputedly had sex with males younger than themselves. Seventy per cent of those labelled passive in such cases were under twenty years old.[96] Sodomy was a means of demonstrating a man's dominance, power and . . . well . . . masculinity. Although the offence carried the death penalty for adults, there were remarkably few trials: Berco counts less than one a year in the cities of Valencia and Barcelona in the sixteenth and seventeenth centuries. Male-to-male sexual contact was embedded in Spanish culture rather than being peripheral or subcultural.[97] It was, as Berco expresses it, part of the ethos of 'penetrative virility'.[98]

Randolph Trumbach has suggested that this world was part of a European-wide system favouring age-structured sexual relations between men and male adolescents, and that the shift away from the age-structured system to the homosexual–heterosexual division occurred in the eighteenth century in north-western Europe but later in central and southern and eastern Europe.[99] It is a seductively neat hypothesis that explains much that we encounter in this chapter relating to master–servant interactions and sex with boys. Stephen Orgel has explained that, like women, attractive boys were accepted as male objects of sexual desire in early modern England: 'The love of men for boys is all but axiomatic in the period.'[100] Mary Bly's fascinating study of the homoerotic performances of the boy actors of the King's Revels or Whitefriar's company in London in 1607–8 is surely wrong when it confines their appeal to an erotic minority. Whatever the size of the audiences for these bawdy 'women' with male genitalia under their dresses, their 'libidinal economy' catered for the shared culture of a majority rather than any subcultural community.[101]

Some of the best examples of early modern homoeroticism involved the love or friendship of a younger male. Richard Barnfield's poem 'The Affectionate Shepheard' (1594) has lines such as: 'Of that faire Boy that had my heart intangled; / Cursing the Time, the Place, the sense, the sin; / I came, I saw, I viewd, I slipped in. / If it be sin to love a sweet-fac'd Boy.' The poem refers to the boy's amber locks, his lovely cheeks, the pearl and flowers in his hair. The boy's name is Ganymede, a common name for a young man used for sex by an older male.[102] A sixteenth-century English translation of a Greek novel of the second century CE omitted its more graphic extolments of sex with boys, but still contained descriptions of their beauty, scent and sweet kisses.[103]

B. R. Burg has demonstrated that the pattern of prosecutions for sodomy in the British Navy in the eighteenth century invariably involved the penetration of a boy by an older seaman. 'The largest number of naval courts martial for sodomy and sexual irregularity convened from the mid eighteenth century to the eve of the Victorian era involved warrant and petty officers accused of violating shipboard boys.'[104] These seaboard sexual configurations stretched across nations and time, as is clear from the intriguing nineteenth-century diaries of the American marine Philip Van Buskirk, which record the numerous cases of sodomy and mutual masturbation on the various ships he served on in the 1850s and 1860s. Van Buskirk thought that there was 'no school of vice comparable to the Navy'. 'Certainly ninety per cent of the white boys in the Navy ... are ... blasphemers and sodomites.' '[N]o boy can ever remain a year on board of an American man-of-war without being led or forced to commit this crime (which, by the way, is not regarded as a crime in a man-of-war).'[105] With a rather warped sense of crusading zeal, Van Buskirk recorded numerous instances of mutual masturbation on the ships that he served on, what the sailors called 'going chaw for chaw'. He noted semi-formalized on-board relationships between older boys and younger boys, or men and boys, based on superior/inferior relations (the junior partners were called 'chickens'). The marine claimed that he had only ever met one boy who had not had sex with his shipmates.[106]

While age-structured sodomitical behaviour was certainly an important element in these sexual histories, there is no evidence that sodomy was part of the male life course in Anglo-America as it seems to have been in Florence and Spain, and it existed alongside many forms of interaction. As has been said of early modern Switzerland: 'Same-sex behavior unfolded in a variety of social settings: it was practiced among adolescents; it existed in the milieu of workers or laborers with negligible age or social distinctions; and it flourished in cross-class and intergenerational relationships of masters with their dependents.'[107]

There was also ambivalence, if not confusion, in the languages and representations of active and passive in these sexual arrangements. Puff found that the Swiss courts showed 'little concern over who was active and who was passive in sexual intercourse. Neither do the daily interactions portrayed in these proceedings convey popular conceptions that attach significance to the question of who penetrated whom.'[108] The English courts both reinforced and undermined active/passive dichotomies. Indictments habitually separated those sodomizing and those sodomized, implying an active/passive distinction. In one informative case, the raison d'être of insertion was maintained despite the active partner having been the man penetrated.[109] But such distinctions were threatened on a daily basis in cases of perceived consensual sodomy where both parties were prosecuted, the penetrator for committing or attempting, the penetrated for consenting. There is no suggestion that the name 'sodomite' was reserved for one of the partners.

Several critics have suggested that male friendship was an important site of premodern homoeroticism. It was accepted and indeed expected that men would have close male friendships – what Alan Bray terms the 'masculine friend' – and would express that bonding, closeness and friendship in ways that can seem sexual to the modern observer but were not necessarily so for men in the past.[110] David Clark demonstrates that poems contained in the tenth-century Anglo-Saxon 'Exeter Book' have been interpreted in heterosexist terms based on little but modern critical assumptions; they could equally be read as expressions of deep affectivity between men.[111] Godbeer has referred to premodern American men embracing 'a range of

Image 6. In this portrait the artist Raphael rests his arm affectionately on his companion's shoulder. His friend, perhaps a fellow painter, perhaps his fencing instructor, turns to gaze at Raphael and reaches towards the viewer with his right hand, thereby including them in the intimacy of the portrayed interaction. It is a beautiful image of mature male friendship (both men are bearded) but there is no indication that they are anything more than friends. Raphael (Raffaello Sanzio of Urbino), *Self Portrait with a Friend*. Sixteenth century. Oil on canvas, 99 × 83 cm. Louvre, Paris. Bridgeman Art Library.

possibilities for relating to other men that included intensely physical yet non-sexual relationships' and has indeed outlined a series of such interactions in eighteenth-century America.[112] Seventeenth-century discourses on friendship and gentlemanliness referred to friendship as 'marriages of the soul', or as a state 'where two hearts are so individually united, as neither from other can be well severed'.[113]

Friendship was a central ingredient of monasticism and elite male culture. Some medieval male friends took oaths of 'sworn brotherhood'. Examples exist in contemporary literature such as the widely read romance of *Amys and Amylion* and Chaucer's *Knight's Tale*, *Friar's Tale*, *Shipman's Tale* and *Pardoner's Tale*, but also in the lived experiences of men such as the English knights William Neville and John Clanvowe, who died within days of each other on campaign in Turkey, 1391, and whose relationship is commemorated in the iconography of their shared tomb.[114] Both eastern and Latin Christianity possessed rites that endowed the relationships with divine approval. Such rites have sometimes been mistaken as a form of marriage, but it is perhaps more interesting that premodern cultures publicly endorsed masculine friendships as a distinct kind of relationship representing ideals of commitment and mutual affectivity. Friendship was brotherhood felt deeply, indeed of more import than a man's marriage, and declared in a series of public gestures: the embrace, the shared meal, the shared bed, the passionate letter and, very occasionally, a joint burial or memorial.[115] Yet potential for slippage between approved and condemned categories was always present. As Robert Mills has put it, wherever masculine friendship was found, 'the spectre of Sodom' lurked nearby, ever available to polemicists or satirists on the lookout for means for defaming men who fell out of favour or came under suspicion. This is illustrated powerfully in the case of King Edward II and Piers Gaveston, whose relationship was likely a conventional form of sworn or ritual brotherhood but was later condemned as 'sodomy' by political opponents.[116]

Yet premodern western cultures allowed men to express open physical affection for one another and to use homoerotic language without necessary aspersions of sexual involvement. One of the best-known medieval exponents of friendship was the Cistercian Aelred of Rievaulx (1110–67). Inspired by Cicero's *De amicitia* and the Old Testament story of David and Jonathan, Aelred celebrated close bonds between men but took care to distinguish carnal earthly love from sublime spiritual love. There are several indications that Aelred had physical sexual experiences with other men or boys during his adolescence spent at the court of King David of Scotland, or at least desired them. He referred to his own youthful 'vices' in delighting in the company of other youths and the 'filthiness', 'rottenness' and 'slimy concupiscence of flesh' brought on by 'the gushing up of puberty'.[117] As Brian McGuire suggests, while modern readers might want to know whether Aelred had sex with his friends, his self-revulsion could equally have been brought on by homoerotic desire and habitual masturbation.[118] After taking monastic vows he subdued his urges with fasting, whipping and cold baths, finally transforming his attraction for men into an emotion compatible with the path to spiritual closeness to people and thence to God. Appreciation of male beauty was licit within this philosophy. Aelred said of a young monk and particular friend, Simon, that one could only be 'amazed at this tender and delicate youth, outstanding in his parenthood, beautiful in his appearance', and elsewhere celebrated the attractions of Jesus as a twelve-year-old.[119] An earlier celebrated monastic figure, Anselm of Bec (*c.* 1033–1109), a Benedictine who spent the last sixteen years of his life as Archbishop of Canterbury, offers a more complicated example. While an older body of scholarship debated whether his expressions of ardent feeling for contemporaries signified platonic idealization, 'gay' orientation, asexual homoeroticism or monastic communal affectivity, Sally Vaughn has recently pointed out that his letters to female friends and laymen also use 'emotionally intense and sometimes physical language' and that he similarly exalted parent–child love, mothers and the relationship of master and pupil.[120] The openly expressive nature of premodern writing, especially at particular moments such as the twelfth century, can lead the modern reader into premature judgements about the relationships described there.[121]

This is why it is so difficult for the modern observer to interpret the relationship between James I of England and one of his favourites, George Villiers, the Duke of Buckingham. Buckingham's letters address James as 'Dear Dad and Gossip' (that is, godparent), and close with the words 'Your majesty's most humble slave and dog'. James addresses his favourite as 'My only sweet and dear child'; and describes himself as 'Your dear dad and husband'. Buckingham compared his longing to be with his king to a man's desire 'to be in the arms of his Mistress'; 'my thoughts are only bent of having my dear Dad and master's legs soon in my arms; which sweet Jesus grant me'. In one of his letters James proposes

> that we make at this Christmas a new marriage ever to be kept here-after; for, God so love me, as I desire to live in this world for your sake, and that I had rather live banished in any part of the earth with you than live a sorrowful widow's life without you. And so God bless you, my sweet child and wife, and grant that ye may ever be a comfort to your dear dad and husband. James R.[122]

Bray has interpreted their correspondence as Buckingham's demonstration of his power in his easy familiarity and friendship with the monarch (the letters were not sealed and thus open to the court), and as evidence of a jocular masculinity rather than the coded sex that we might be tempted to read it as. The reference to a 'new marriage' meant the renewal of their bond of friendship with the receiving of Holy Communion at Christmas, a public avowal of friendship. The mixed metaphors of the language of friendship (two men referring to one another as husband, wife, gossip, dad) merely represent amity.[123]

While Bray's critical caution is impeccable, the separation between friendship and desire was an uneasy one – as he was fully aware. Halperin included male friendship in his taxonomy precisely because the discourse of friendship allowed the expression of love and passion between men, an important aspect of the history of homosexuality.[124] There was semantic overlap between the terms 'friend' and 'lover' in medieval and Renaissance literature.[125] The metaphor of marriage was employed to describe bonds that were indescribable in their intensity, even for those experiencing them. Palamon and Arcite in William Shakespeare and John Fletcher's *Two Noble Kinsmen* (1634) were

> . . . one another's wife, ever begetting
> New births of love; we are father, friends, acquaintance;
> We are in one another, families . . .[126]

Mario DiGangi has stressed the normality of homoeroticism in the early modern period, before such things were proscribed for 'normal' men: 'early modern gender ideology integrated orderly homoeroticism into friendship more seamlessly than modern ideological formations, which more crisply distinguish homoeroticism from friendship, sexual desire from social desire'.[127] Michel Eyquem Montaigne (1533–92) saw friendship between men as superior both to love between men and women and to marriage. Affection towards women was 'a rash and wavering fire', whereas male friendship was 'a general and universal heat . . . all pleasure and smoothness'. But if 'lustful love' crept into friendship, it too was tainted. As for marriage, 'it is a covenant which hath nothing free but the entrance, the continuance being forced and constrained, depending elsewhere than from our will, and a match ordinarily concluded to other ends, a thousand strange knots are therein commonly to be unknit, able to break the web, and trouble the whole course of a lively affection'. Whereas in friendship, he continued, 'there is no commerce or business depending on the same, but itself'. Women, he thought, were constitutionally incapable of attaining such equilibrium.[128]

Such early modern male bonds were so strong that George Haggerty prefers the term *love* for the 'emotional intensity and erotic attachment ... in many eighteenth-century relationships between men'.[129] Sir John Oglander said of James I that he 'loved young men, his favourites, better than women, loving them beyond the love of men to women. I never saw any fond husband make so much or so great dalliance over his beautiful spouse as I have seen King James over his favourites, especially the Duke of Buckingham'.[130]

Halperin distinguishes male friendship between equals from relationships of the pederastic type, based on inequality. It is an important qualitative distinction that is culturally informative about a premodern separation between love and sex and the feasibility of a passionate friendship between equals unsullied by the imputations of lust associated with class or age inequality.[131] It was a differentiation made by contemporaries.[132] Yet the distinctions constantly collapsed, so much so that it is the noncompliance rather than the adherence that characterizes this category of pre-homosexuality. By definition, the relationships of James I could never be equal. His interactions with Buckingham were those of a superior in age and status. Even so, their correspondence contains one of the best descriptions of the indefinable borders between love and friendship:

> And for so great a king to descend so low, as to his humblest slave and servant to communicate himself in a style of such good fellowship, with expressions of more care than servants have of masters, than physicians have of their patients (which hath largely appeared to me in sickness and in health), of more tenderness than fathers have of children, of more friendship than between equals, or more affection than between lovers in the best kind, man and wife; what can I return? Nothing but silence. For if I speak, I must be saucy, and say thus, or short of what is due: my purveyor, my good fellow, my physician, my maker, my friend, my father, my all. I heartily and humbly thank you for all you do, and all I have.

While Buckingham was aware of his own status – 'Judge what unequal language this is in itself, but especially considering the thing that must speak it, and the person to whom it must be spoken' – the 'thing' claimed that the king's friendship was beyond that 'between equals' and his affection exceeding that 'between lovers in the best kind, man and wife'.[133]

The distinction between natural male friendship and unnatural sodomitical inclination, what Bray termed 'the shadow in the garden', was not always so easily observed.[134] Moreover, any such distinction would have been puzzling to the craftsmen and tradesmen of Renaissance Florence, where sodomy was part of male sociability and strongly associated with brotherhood and friendship.[135] The dividing lines of homosociality, homoaffectivity and homoeroticism should not be drawn too crudely. The category of the masculine friend is helping to overturn older scholarly assumptions about what to include in histories of sex. Moreover, as Bray's work so deftly illustrates, friendship (unlike sodomy or effeminacy) was a form of male intimacy claimed and celebrated by premodern men themselves. Coding love, desire and sex between men as sinful, unnatural or unmanly were means by which regulatory regimes of Church and government seized and repressed love between men. Premodern modes of friendship, including the laughter that often accompanied its expression, provided means for its repossession. We have not often given male friendship its due in history because it 'did not signify', but it is 'beginning to signify again'.[136]

Like friendship, effeminacy was a possible – though not invariable – indicator of same-sex desire. Loss of masculinity was a danger faced by all men. Courtship was an anxious time, for love countered reason, causing loss of control, and turning men into women. Romeo said that his love and sexual attraction to Juliet made him 'effeminate'.[137] It was a cultural commonplace in Machiavelli's Italy that love made men weak, passive and woman-like – 'laid low like a woman'.[138] In the premodern world, men who spent a lot of time around women in order to gain sexual access were often described as effeminate.[139] Even in Anglo-Saxon England, a man who seemed excessively fond of women could be deemed 'effeminate', with no connotations of same-sex attraction.[140] Crusade chronicles of the twelfth and early thirteenth centuries often portrayed Greek men as effeminate (excitable, unreliable, weak in warfare) as well as beastly (brutal, lacking reason or intelligence) without casting explicit aspersions on their sexual habits.[141] Manhood was not something inherited and enjoyed forever. It had to be constructed, and was an attribute in continual danger of being lost. Whether we look at Shakespeare's plays or sixteenth-century Italian literature, they are full of characters whose masculinity is under threat.[142] Fops, an eighteenth-century object of derision, were perceived as unmasculine because they were men who concentrated far too much on their appearance. They spent inordinate amounts of time in front of the mirror, took too long in dressing, wore excessive perfume, paraded themselves, and wasted time in the company of women.[143] Clearly, the history of effeminacy belongs as much in the prehistory of heterosexuality as it does in that of pre-homosexuality.

And yet effeminacy was also associated with male-to-male sexual behaviour. The Franciscan theologian Benedicti wrote in 1610 of the sins of *mollesse* or mollitude: that is, softness or effeminacy. This sin included masturbation but primarily focused on '[t]hose males or females who let themselves be defiled by sodomites [and] give

Image 7. This detail from a Florentine artist's large fifteenth-century painting of a church entrance and interior combines both architectural and human detail. Our focus is on the male interactions as elegantly dressed young men engage each other through looking, touching, gazing and waiting. Fra Carnevale (Bartolomeo di Giovanni Corradini), *Presentation of the Virgin in the Temple. c.* 1467. Oil and tempera on panel, 146.4 × 96.5 cm. Museum of Fine Arts, Boston: Charles Potter Kling Fund 37.108.

consent to and take part in the sin against nature ... when someone is passive in the performance of this sin and fulfils the woman's function'.[144] Benedicti invoked a series of names and associations to signify *mollesse*: *molles* (biblical), *bardashes* (French), *kedeshim* (Hebrew) and *cinaedi* (Roman); as well as Jupiter's Ganymede, Nicomedes' Caesar and Béza's Audebert. The relationships discussed were all of an older male and a younger man or boy, but the essence of the sin was effeminacy or an inappropriate lack of male hardness.[145] The well-known diatribes against 'effeminates' issued by the twelfth-century chroniclers Orderic Vitalis and William of Malmesbury are a little harder to decode. Both denounced the Anglo-Norman courts as degenerate and soft, tainted by imported French fashions for long hair, curly-toed shoes and walking with hips thrust forward. Orderic blamed William Rufus's untimely death (1100) on the 'effeminates' of his circle who 'carried on their debaucheries without restraint' and on 'loathsome Ganymedes' who 'abused themselves with foul-sodomite things', and elsewhere castigated contemporary 'foul catamites' whose indulgence in the 'filth of sodomy' would see them condemned to hellfire.[146] As Robert Mills points out, though, we can't be sure what 'sodomy' connoted for these authors. A number of twelfth-century poems celebrating the attractions of girl-like boys are ambiguous in implication. Bishop Marbod of Rennes, Baudri of Bourgueil and Hilary the Englishman eulogized both girls and youths in terms that make feminine and masculine beauty almost identical. A boy's girlish looks were the key to his charms. Bishop Marbod writes:

> Over his ivory neck flowed hair
> Brighter than yellow gold, the kind I have always loved.
> His brow was white as snow, his luminous eyes black as pitch;
> His unfledged cheeks full of pleasing sweetness
> When they flushed bright white and red.[147]

Boyish effeminacy is here admired, where in contemporary chronicles it was reviled, but in both instances any connection with sexual desire remains unsure.

Some premodern men desired males who resembled girls, while others were seen as wanting to be like women sexually. Their desires and different dispositions were written on their bodies in the effeminacy of the movement of their limbs and general bodily deportment. The Romans called them *mollitia*; the Greeks called them *kinaidia*. Michael Camille has detected such characteristics in representations of the demeanour of the fourteenth-century Italian sodomites.[148] A fifteenth-century Castilian tract, known principally for its misogyny, wrote of heretic sodomites who 'are like women in their deeds and like little sluts in their disordered appetites, and they desire men with greater ardor than women do'.[149] And we know of at least one medieval medical/scientific treatise that recognizes that some men enjoy the passive role in male-to-male intercourse.[150] Some Renaissance texts, claimed somewhat exaggeratedly as a species of early modern sexology, posited that a man's sodomitical inclinations – as insertor, or receptor and fellator – were detectable in his physiognomy, including marks on his hands (chiromancy) or forehead (metoposcopy): that is, the hands of *cinaedi*, the facial mark of the sodomite, the twitching lips, flashing eyes and flushed faces of the fellator.[151] There are also allegations that sodomy made early modern Dutch men effeminate; that their disposition was reflected in their beardless faces, 'wriggling' movements, 'whorish' eyes and 'effeminate posture'.[152] The problem is, of course, that such accounts deal with rhetoric rather than subjectivities.

Discussions of premodern, English effeminacy have been dominated by descriptions of the eighteenth-century mollies – a name with a striking likeness to the words *molles* and *mollesse*. Halperin includes the mollies in his prehistory of homosexuality, where they are characterized as 'effeminate men'.[153] We need to consider the mollies because it has become something of a historiographical orthodoxy that they represent an important stage in the formation of homosexuality as identity. As Bray expressed it in his pioneering study, the mollies signified a 'momentous' shift from male-to-male sex as something that mankind in general was capable of to something associated with a particular group with its own sense of self. It was an identity or subculture that emphasized effeminacy in a way that modern homosexuality would reject, but was '*an* identity nevertheless'.[154] This was an early statement, drawing on Trumbach's claim that the mollies embodied the birth of modern homosexuality. But others have more or less followed the framework. Hitchcock writes: 'The molly houses became synonymous with homosexuality, and gradually over the course of the eighteenth and nineteenth centuries contributed to the broader transition, both in perception and reality, from the sodomite to the effeminate homosexual.'[155] All these historians (and sociologists) stress the effeminacy of both the 'perception and reality' of molly culture, referring to the wearing of dresses and the use of female names.[156]

We remain unconvinced by the historiographical prominence of the molly. One major difficulty is with the source material, for the image of the mollies derives disproportionately from a notorious work of satire rather than any direct experiential account, whereas even the printed versions of the court records place far less emphasis on molly culture.[157] It is true that as late as the 1740s, Londoners refer to mollies in cases of sodomy or attempted sodomy. Molly was used as a shorthand term for sodomite in the language of the lanes and streets. People discussed both mollies in general and whether a particular individual was 'a Molly and a Sodomite'.[158] When a man was apprehended at an inn for his activities with a scholar from

St James Chapel, the landlord asked one of those who arrested him
if the prisoner was 'a Molley' – though, until then, he had thought
little of the man entertaining the boy alone in an upstairs room.[159]
People might accuse one another openly: 'I never mollied you', one
man replied indignantly when called a molly.[160] However, they were
far more likely to use the language of sodomy, talking in terms
of 'sodomites', 'sodomitical practices' or, less elegantly, 'sodomite
dog'.[161] 'I have heard talk of sodomites, and I believe these are
some,' one woman exclaimed when she saw two men in action in
her public house in the 1740s.[162] When two men were found together
in Stepney Church porch at night in each other's arms, naked from
the waist down, the jury 'concluded they were no better than two of
those degenerated Miscreants from the Race of Men, called
Sodomites'.[163]

If the court reports are any indication, the workers of the craft and
trade milieu of the city, women as well as men, knew how to describe
a person who was more attracted to their own sex than its opposite.
We can see this at work in the testimonies surrounding an alleged
sodomite in the 1760s, a servant who was said to have consented to
sodomy with a footman. 'What do you mean by that, all the world
that knows me, knows I love a woman too well, to be a sodomite.'
Numerous acquaintances testified on the servant's behalf: 'he has
lived with me six years . . . during that time, I never discovered any
unnatural inclinations in him. . . . I have no sort of suspicion, he was
in any ways addicted to this vice'; 'he was always amongst the women,
when he had any time. . . . I never saw any circumstances, that shewed
him inclined to any unnatural vice.' 'I look upon him to have a natural
passion for women, and none for his own sex.' 'I have known him
seven years, I have been in company with him often, I thought him a
great admirer of women; I never apprehended him any way inclined
to any filthy vice with his own sex.' 'I never saw he had any tendency
towards his own sex; no, far from it.'[164] These sorts of sexual verifica-
tions occurred again and again in the court material. The non-sod-
omite sought out the company of women; the sodomite delighted in
unnatural passions with men.

It is tempting to read such denials as a shift from sodomy as loss
of control towards something approaching sexual preference: he 'said
he receiv'd more pleasure in lying with a Man, than with the finest
Woman in the World'.[165] But we need to be careful. The focus was on
acts. Such men indulged in vice rather than in a declaration of identity.
In mid-eighteenth-century allegations involving Fellows of Wadham
College, a butler who claimed to have been the subject of unwanted
sexual advances told the accused Warden that 'he wondered Gentlemen of his Fortune did not provide themselves with Women, or Wives,

and did not act in so vile and beastly a Manner'. The Warden 'made Answer, that he would not give a Farthing for the finest Woman in the World; and that he loved a Man as he did his Soul'. Such examples indicate a situation where some men (the Warden) associated desire for men with exclusivity in sexual attraction, whereas others (the butler) saw these tendencies merely as excess or misdirected lust.[166]

It is clear that the Londoners of these court reports saw the behaviour of the sodomite as woman-like. Indeed this seemed to be the way that contemporaries reasoned such desires. The logic must have been that anal sex involved a penetrator, who assumed the male role, and the penetrated, who, in effect, played the part of a woman. Hence the use of such terms as 'he-bitch' when abusing a sodomite.[167] Witnesses who saw a man sodomizing a boy in an alehouse said that they also saw him 'kiss him, call him his Dear, and use several other fond and foolish Expressions, common betwixt persons of different Sexes'.[168] In other cases there were testaments to men who 'acted ... as in Cohabiting with a Woman', or who were 'acting as man and woman'.[169] A woman called out, 'What do you mean ... by two men acting as man and woman?'[170]

One of the partners in a sexual encounter was sometimes described in what we would call feminine terms. 'He never behaved with any effeminacy, that shewed him to have a liking to his own sex', was another defence that, in its denial, assumes that 'effeminacy' was a factor in such cases.[171] There is reference to a 'smooth Face and a fresh Countenance'; and an eighteen-year-old servant and male prostitute is purported to have said, 'I suppose I am not handsome enough for you, but if you don't like me, I have got a pretty younger Brother.'[172] But, generally, masculine and feminine roles were not assigned in these encounters. There was no strict demarcation between male and female role-playing (the he-male, she-male binary); the descriptions of femaleness applied loosely to the combined behaviour of the couple concerned. As a pair, they behaved 'as man and woman', which is different to strictly assigned sex roles.

Furthermore, there was almost no suggestion that the bodies, deportment or dress of the offenders was feminine or effeminate. The sexual acts of the sodomites were womanly by definition – when they paired off, one of them did as women did sexually – but they were not *effeminates*. The roles of penetrator and penetrated could interchange, even at an alleged molly house where the patrons called one another 'Bitch' and referred to male sexual partners as a 'Husband'. The witness said that the fruit-seller 'Orange Deb', one Martin Mackintosh, 'came to me, put his Hands [in] my Breeches thrust his Tongue into my mouth swore that he'd go 40 Mile [to] enjoy me and beg'd of me to go backward, and let him – but I refusing he offer'd to sit bare in my Lap'.[173]

The defences offered by accused sodomites always focused on their lack of interest in men and desire for women or the fact that they had shared beds with other men without attempting sodomy or encouraging other lewd behaviour. There was rarely any debate about their female dress or feminine behaviour. The focus on cross-dressing, female names and effeminate interactions is strongest in the satirical literature and in a few cases centred on what may have been a male brothel. This is not to deny that there were male brothels, known meeting places for men who wanted sex with men, recognized signals of intent or interest, or that there were male-to-female trans-vestites in that culture. The prosecution of the infamous Margaret Clap claimed that about fifty men gathered in her brothel, 'making Love to one another as they call'd it. Sometimes they'd sit in one anothers Laps, use their Hands indecently Dance and make Curtsies and mimick the Language of Women – O Sir! – Pray Sir! – Dear Sir! Lord how can ye serve me so! . . . Then they'd go by Couples, into a Room on the same Floor to be marry'd as they call'd it.'[174] Nor are we refusing to accept that the cultural trope of viewing male same-sex behaviour as woman-like may have encouraged a subjectivity that embraced such feminization. Our purpose is merely to set such activ-ity in a far wider context. Those described as favouring men were sodomites rather than mollies and the focus was on their acts (inter-preted as involving sex role reversal on the part of at least one of the participants) rather than their identities. Their environment was the same as that where men worked and socialized and sought out sexual contact with women. The venue for these encounters was more likely to be the neighbourhood pub, alley or the shared bed or room rather than the molly house. Significantly, the molly had no role to play in the British Navy's sodomy prosecutions during the eighteenth century; the signifiers 'effeminate' and 'womanish' were never used, if the records of courts martial are any indication of onboard sexual banter.[175]

Pre-homosexual practices and discourses comprised same-sex sexual behaviour but not homosexuality. When the young, future scientist Robert Boyle was in Florence in the 1640s and approached by two friars, he described it as the 'Preposterous Courtship of 2 of those Fryers, whose Lust makes no Distinction of Sexes, but that which it's Preference of their own creates'. Though their designs on him indi-cated a 'preference' – which, in itself is significant – it was a result of the 'Goatish Heates' of 'these 'gown'd Sodomites'. It reflected their lust rather than their sexual identity; Boyle was not, strictly speaking, subjected to the 'homosexual advances' that his modern editor claims.[176] People were not accused in the premodern courts of being homosexual; nor was homosexuality a cause of defamation or sexual slander.[177] Men were punished for buggery and sodomy, but these infractions were generally considered the excesses of mankind in general rather than the practices of a specific group. Berco writes of early modern Spain: 'Not merely an act relegated to a few deviants, sodomy formed an integral part of the male sexual mindset, a potential erotic encounter present at the core of male sociability.'[178] Hitchcock has argued that for most Englishmen who engaged in sodomy in the premodern period there was no sense that they were a separate group in society: 'They did not belong to a subculture, nor did they have a distinct self-identity. They would have seen sex with another man simply as an extension of the forms of sexual behaviour in courting and marriage.'[179] Guido Ruggerio's study of Niccolò Machiavelli certainly shows the famous sixteenth-century Italian's tolerance of same-sex behaviour (though his own tastes were in women).[180]

An important aspect of modern homosexuality is that those involved in such sexual activity see themselves, and are seen by others, as a separate group in society, defined by their same-sex sexuality. The only people who approximate this in the premodern period are the men of the disputed sodomitical subcultures, the eighteenth-century sodomites and mollies. In the early decades of that century, Parisian sodomites or pederasts (as the French called them) met in the Luxembourg, Palais-Royal or Tuilereries gardens, the Champs-Elysées, on the Pont-Neuf or the quai des Orfèvres, or under the Saint-Louis arcades.[181] They frequented particular inns and taverns, or loitered along the banks of the Seine and in parks, engaging in conversation: 'I see you here every evening. If you want to come with me under the yew trees ... I will f[uck] you.'[182] '[H]e asked me if I had a room where we could go jerk off our c[ocks] or butt-fuck each other.'[183] One man showed another his penis, saying, 'I'm sure you prefer that to a pinch of tobacco.'[184] By the 1780s pederasts – even working men – were said to adopt extravagant clothing as a marker of their sexual tastes, declaring themselves to one another. Police reports referred to those 'dressed like a pederast'.[185] There is evidence for sodomite meeting places in the cities of the early modern Netherlands – toilets in Rotterdam, the city hall in Amsterdam, a wooded area in The Hague, and inns and male brothels in most of the major towns. We know about the secret signals that men of that persuasion were reputed to have made to one another. Adhering to the subcultural thesis, Theo van der Meer claims a 'sodomite subculture' for the cities of the eighteenth-century Netherlands.[186]

However, our arguments for London could be applied to Amsterdam or Paris. The homosexual meeting places in Paris were the normal haunts for Parisian leisure, courtship and the prostitution of women. Priests figure in published accounts, and the authorities were preoccupied with combating the corruption of boys, but the majority of those arrested in the first half of the eighteenth century were both married and unmarried men employed in the crafts and trades or in service.[187] The documents from the archives of the Bastille do include men who claimed that they had nothing whatsoever to do with women. One thirty-eight-year-old, unmarried servant said that 'he was up for anything, that he put it in and that he had it put in him, that he didn't like women, that he had done nothing but fool around with men since his youth, that this pleasure was in his blood'.[188] Yet the French sodomites and their partners mostly reflected the general male occupational and household structure. Certainly, those with a liking for male flesh had no trouble indulging their predilections; they knew where to go. However, this is not the same as a subculture, and historians are premature in ascribing a 'homosexual subculture' to eighteenth-century Europe.[189] We should be wary of attributing too much coherence to these early modern practices and desires. They are best seen as part of the wider sex of the streets.

4

Between Women

The contours of female-to-female intimacy, while intersecting with
the themes of intimacies between men, have their own trajectories.
On the face of it, there is a topic consensus for such histories.
The chapter structure of the early modern section of Rebecca Jennings's *A Lesbian History of Britain* (2007) follows one template: the
early modern renaissance of representations of female same-sex
desire, female husbands and friendships.[1] Though such headings
can disguise a developing, uneven and contested historiography, they
are useful nonetheless. The word 'lesbian' in Jennings's title is more
contentious, for the act of naming – 'A lesbian history' – imposes
modern meanings and interpretations, when the very purpose of the
writing and research underpinning this historical synthesis may have
been to work against such assumptions and the lesbian of the 'lesbian'
history does not appear until chapter 7. 'Lesbian' (unlike 'homosexual' or 'heterosexual') does appear in premodern texts but only very
rarely, and with shades of meaning different from modern notions of
stable sexual orientation.[2] Writing of 'looking for lesbians in the past'
or employing the terms 'lesbian-like' and 'lesbianisms', whatever
authorial intent, risks restricting interpretation before it begins.[3] A
fascinating study of the marriage of two women in London in 1680
has raised the possibility of lesbian desire, but also shows the unwill-
ingness of contemporaries to describe it as such.[4] We have already
referred to Elizabeth Wahl's use of the term 'female intimacy' to
avoid some of these conceptual quandaries, her reasoning being
that '[s]ince neither the term "romantic friendship" nor "lesbian"
entirely suffices to describe intimate relations between women prior
to the nineteenth century, critics will need to continue to develop new

conceptual models and a more nuanced vocabulary to define the sexual, social, and psychological dimensions of premodern culture.'[5] Some of the more significant rethinking of sexual categories and mapping of historical diversity involves female-to-female intimacy before lesbianism.[6]

It was once possible for historians to write of the discursive silence about medieval and early modern female homoeroticism.[7] But the work of Valerie Traub has shown the ubiquity rather than the scarcity of such imagery and text, an early modern '*renaissance* of representations of female homoerotic desire', for the Renaissance rediscovery of classical texts uncovered a range of erotic possibilities with, as we will see, erotically charged, female same-sex intimacy articulated in medical writings, poetry, drama, travel literature, early modern pornography and art.[8]

While the claims for 'silence' on 'lesbianism' in medieval history are also no longer sustainable, evidence from the period remains more fragmentary. Even while renouncing older scholarly allegations of premodern lesbianism's absence, many treatments of the topic are marked by an (understandable) anxiety. The history of premodern female–female love and desire is only a few decades old and great energy has had to be expended on arguing for its validity.[9] Shortage of sources, especially before the mid-sixteenth century, is only the beginning of the problem. Feminist queries around meanings of modern lesbian identity compel historians of female intimacy to reconsider where to draw the lines around their subject. Do they insist on evidence of 'genital sexuality' or embrace more diverse expressions of physical contact and response? Do passionate friendships, which might or might not involve erotic contact or even desire, properly belong in a history of sex? Should our study include expressions of intense affectivity even when the nature of that affect is wide open to interpretation? If we have been enjoined to read the silences (the 'blanks'), on what evidentiary bases do we stake such readings?[10] Is ignorance of premodern lesbianism innocent or willed: how do we know whether we are 'failing to know' or 'refusing to know'?[11] Should we take our cue from the many scholars who renounce any cultural model which conceives of women in relation to men, jettisoning 'lesbian' in favour of 'woman-identified woman', or alternatively reframing lesbianism as the 'lesbian continuum' encompassing 'witches, *femmes seules* [*sic*], marriage resisters, spinsters, autonomous widows, and/or lesbians'?[12] Or should we begin by reminding ourselves that heterosexuality, far from being compulsory, did not exist? All of this can pose problems for a sexual historian or open up opportunities, depending on how one looks at it. When one reads that the thirteenth-century Provençal beguine and ascetic Douceline de Digne whipped one of her younger spiritual 'daughters' until she bled for the offence of watching some men working, one may see 'the homo-social and powerfully homoaffective aspects' of such a relationship and indeed infer other 'more complicated' meanings.[13] Alternatively, one could see Douceline as confined and defined by the spiritual, social and sexual limits of her Christian patriarchal inscription.

As a way through the methodological challenges posed by a diverse historiography, we like the path suggested by Traub. Rather than becoming unduly distracted by the task of identifying 'origins' of modern lesbianism or individual exemplars of its history, she keeps her gaze fixed on historical texts and visual artefacts and asks of them a few 'guiding questions': 'How was same-gender female desire rendered intelligible? What tropes, what images, figured such desire?' To the problem of what counts as 'desire' and more specifically 'erotic desire', Traub settles on 'intense emotional investment and compelling erotic attraction', expressed variously by premoderns as 'love, passion, appetite, lust' and manifesting variously as 'caresses, kisses, bodily penetration, and passionate verbal addresses expressing longing, loss, devotion, frustration, pleasure, and pain'.[14] Her approach enables a vision of female–female love and desire that is broad enough to take account of historical and individual diversity without drifting too far from the erotic. Yet in addressing medieval evidence, in particular, it may still be desirable to investigate a range of relationships between women beyond those which contemporaries 'rendered intelligible' as same-gender female desire, in order not to foreclose on potentially fruitful examples. Because of the notable shift by which female–female desire came to be much more frequently a subject of discourse after the mid-sixteenth century we divide our discussion chronologically.

The earliest known case of 'female sodomy' comes from Bologna in 1295.[15] Bertolina, known by the nickname Guercia, was accused in a civic court of being a 'public and well known sodomite [*sodomita*]' possessing a silk *mancipium* (here, a dildo, also referred to as a *virilia*) with two silk testicles, and of 'conducting herself lustfully with women with this mancipium as men do with women'. The act, according to the conventional language, is called 'unutterable and horrible, in opprobrium of God and the world and against human nature'.[16] A witness testified that Guercia had told him she had 'been interested in' a certain widow for two years. He replied that this was unlucky (*malafortunata*) for her, and asked how she could be interested in women. 'She said, "It is because I *tifuo* them with these *virilia* of silk that I have."' She showed him several silk *virilia* of different shapes and sizes kept in her purse. Carol Lansing, who discovered this document, wonders whether *tifuo* (which does not match any known Latin word) is a scribal error for *futuo* ('I fuck'), thus implying penetration. Guercia, who could not be found to appear in court, was banned from the commune and fined the enormous sum of 500 Bolognese pounds. She had good reason to keep a low profile. Although hers is the only known case of female sodomy from the Bolognese court, some cases of male sodomy exist from the period and the men were sentenced to death by burning.[17]

The Bolognese court explicitly used the language of sodomy to condemn Guercia. The act she committed was not perceived as materially different from penetrative sex between men. Regions which adopted Roman civil law in the later medieval period were influenced by the *lex foedissimam* of 287 CE, which originally referred in a general way to women who 'surrender their honour to the lusts of others' but which medieval Roman law commentators interpreted as defilement by men *or* by other women. It might be significant for Guercia's case that Bologna was the prime mover in the revival of Roman law, during the eleventh century. Around 1400 the Bolognese Roman law scholar Bartholomaeus of Saliceto argued that defilement of women by women should be punished by death.[18] So far a total of thirteen cases against alleged female sodomites in western Europe have been found down to 1500 (all except Guercia's from the fifteenth century), and a number of others occurred in the sixteenth and seventeenth centuries.[19] The geography of female sodomy conviction, covering Italy, France, the Low Countries, Germany, Switzerland and Spain, seems partly the result of Roman legal influence. England's notable absence from this list, and the apparent nonchalance of English courts towards women's same-sex activity, could correspondingly be explained by its preference for an independent common law over Roman civil law. Yet even where courts had recourse to a code and language to condemn female sodomy they rarely bothered to use it. Michael Rocke finds 'not a single case of sexual relations between women' among the thousands of Florentine sodomy cases from the 1320s to 1542, Guido Ruggiero claims that 'lesbianism . . . was not prosecuted' in fifteenth-century Venice, and Mary Elizabeth Perry finds little evidence of official concern with sex between women in early modern Seville.[20]

At first sight, the 1477 trial of Katherina Hetzeldorfer in Speyer has some similarities to Guercia's condemnation 180 years earlier.[21] Like Guercia, Katherina was said to have used a dildo in her sexual relations (involving at least three women), though hers was fashioned from leather stuffed with cotton and stiffened with a wooden stick. Prior to making her instrument she had progressed from using one, then two, then three fingers. As with Guercia, penetration is a focus. Both were harshly punished, though Katherina's execution by drowning was much more severe. Yet we should not overlook the differences. Although Helmut Puff claims the coinage 'female sodomy' to describe her crime, that terminology is absent in Katherina's trial records.[22] Roman law did not prevail in the Holy Roman Empire before the *Constitutio Criminalis Carolina* of 1532. Indeed the exact nature of the crime for which she was killed is never stated.[23] A dramatic difference between the cases concerns gender. Guercia's femininity is not in doubt. Indeed, added to her charge of sodomy are others of using love magic and fortune telling – crimes that Lansing notes as 'fairly common against women considered prostitutes'.[24] Guercia's chief crime is one of sexual abomination, not male impersonation, even though her use of the *mancipium* is explained as being like what men do with women. Katherina, on the other hand, appears to belong to the tradition of women passing as men in order (among other things) to facilitate their sexual encounters with women (see below). Although her clothing is not mentioned, several witnesses cite elements of her performative masculinity. She urinates through her 'penis' (which Else, wife of Wendel Muter, claims was a 'huge thing, as big as half an arm'); she stood, whored and grabbed a woman 'just like a man'; 'with hugging and kissing she behaved exactly like a man with a woman'. She was sexually dominant. Else Muter claimed Katherina tried to 'seduce her and to have her manly will with her'; Schrenkenspönn explained how Katherina three times 'committed an act of knavery with her'. Some of the language is of sexual violation. Else 'could hardly ward her off'; Katherina is said to have 'deflowered' the 'sister' who was her long-term partner. These women, who risked severe punishment alongside Katherina, insisted they had mistaken her for a man. As Puff points out, this was an essential 'defense strategy', but he also wonders whether her gender transgression was Katherina's real crime.[25]

The case of Jehanne and Laurence, apparently prosecuted for their sexual relationship in early fifteenth-century France, offers a further variant.[26] Laurence was sixteen and worked alongside Jehanne in fields and vineyards. Both were married. They had a number of sexual encounters, for which Laurence at least (and possibly Jehanne also) was imprisoned. Laurence appealed for royal clemency on the grounds that she was the passive partner and Jehanne (in Cadden's words) the 'manlike aggressor' in the relationship. According to Laurence's appeal for pardon, it was Jehanne who asked Laurence to be her 'sweetheart' (*mie*), to which Laurence agreed, thinking 'nothing evil in it', and Jehanne who 'climbed on her as a man does on a woman, and ... began to move her hips and do as a man does to a woman'. When Laurence rejected Jehanne's advances one night the latter attacked her with a knife. It was perhaps a combination of Laurence's claims for taking a feminine role, her self-representation as a penitent who desired pardon, and Jehanne's violence towards her which led to Laurence's pardon. Jehanne's fate is not recorded.

Sexual relationships between women were thus regularly comprehended – rendered intelligible – through various manifestations of male impersonation. The female sodomite and manly woman are persistent premodern types. As Jacqueline Murray has argued, 'Sexual activity without a penis was difficult to imagine.'[27] Use of an artificial phallus was the most serious offence, as an outrageous offence against nature, but masculine performances from cross-dressing, to courtship of women, to sexual aggression all provided lenses for making female–female sex visible. It is difficult, probably impossible, to identify whether such masculine performances represent real behaviour or the legal rhetoric of courts. The defence of feminine passivity seems to have been an effective means of avoiding the worst consequences.

Long before female sodomy became a matter for late medieval courts, Hincmar of Reims's ninth-century condemnation of royal divorce raised alarm about women's use of 'instruments' on one another. While sex between women was only rarely mentioned in early medieval penitentials, the Penitential of Theodore (668–90) ordered three years' penance for a woman who 'practices vice with a woman'. This is the same as penance for female masturbation and is considerably less than most of the penalities for male same-sex acts.[28] Other penitentials specified punishments for women who used dildos on themselves or others.[29] Female–female desire was rarely visible in medical texts, although in 1285 William of Saliceto, an eminent scholar of the Bologna medical school, wrote about *ragadiae* or fleshy growths protruding from the vulva with which women could penetrate other women.[30] Because the clitoris was unknown to the West between the sixth and mid-sixteenth centuries, the notion of the 'tribade' as a woman with an outsized clitoris (see below) had to wait for that organ's 'rediscovery'.[31] It is therefore difficult to be sure what is meant in the 1270 Orleans customary *Li Livre de Jostice et de Plet*, the only medieval secular law code to distinguish female from male sodomy, which orders that women offenders should lose their members (*perdre membre*) for their first two convictions for sodomy and be burned for a third. The penalty was clearly meant to parallel male sodomites' loss of testicles and penis for first and second convictions respectively, with burning on the third conviction.[32] The French estates poem *Le Livre des Manières* by Etienne de Fougères (d. 1178) takes another tack, ridiculing women's phallic lack when they 'bang coffin against coffin / without a poker to stir up their fire / . . . [who] join shield to shield without a lance / . . . [and] don't bother with a pestle in their mortar'. Saher Amer has persuasively argued that

Etienne drew on tenth- and eleventh-century Arabic homoerotic literature, as his imagery mirrors in key respects that found in the Arab
sources.[33]

Phallocentrism and stereotypes of performative masculinity do not
show up in theologians' discussions of sex between women. Peter
Damian did not include acts between women (or indeed between
women and men) in his *Book of Gomorrah* (1049), though in his tract
on miracles (*c.* 1063–72) the Virgin Mary intercedes to release from
Purgatory a Roman woman who when 'in tender age' had given in
to 'indecent lust and committed shameful acts' with her female contemporaries.[34] It is important that the woman was suffering the temporary torments of Purgatory rather than eternal hellfire of male
sodomites. In subsequent centuries Peter Abelard, Albertus Magnus
and Thomas Aquinas made female–female sex a more severe sin by
counting it among the vices against nature. Abelard said female genitals had been made for the use of men, not other women, while
Albertus and his pupil Aquinas equated female and male same-sex
acts as the worst forms of vice against nature.[35] These later medieval
churchmen took as their cue Paul's condemnation of women who
'exchanged natural relations for unnatural' (Romans 1:26), the sole
Scriptural reference to sex between women. Thus by the thirteenth
century female–female sex counted among the most serious branches
of lechery and a mortal sin, but it is unclear whether this had the
practical consequences which Roman legal proscriptions entailed.

The well-known example of the Tuscan abbess Benedetta Carlini,
labelled in modern scholarship as 'a lesbian nun', is worth reconsid-
eration in light of these observations.[36] Benedetta's relationship with
a younger nun, Sister Bartolomea Crivelli, came to light in the course
of ecclesiastical enquiries into Benedetta's claims to visionary and
stigmatic experiences. When first questioned in 1619, Bartolomea told
of how she often got into bed with Benedetta, placed her hand on
her heart or embraced her to calm and steady her in her battles with
the devil, and felt happiness and no fear.[37] When the enquiry was
reconvened by papal nuncios four years later, Bartolomea told a very
different story:

> For two continuous years, two or three times a week, in the evening,
> after disrobing and going to bed waiting for her companion [Bartolo-
> mea], who serves her, to disrobe also, she would force her into the bed
> and kissing her as if she were a man she would stir on top of her so
> much that both of them corrupted themselves because she held her by
> force sometimes for one, sometimes for two, sometimes for three hours.[38]

Bartolomea testified further that Benedetta kissed her breasts and wanted 'always to be thus on her', would take Bartolomea's hand and insert her finger into her genitals or 'by force' would do the same to Bartolomea. 'And when the latter would flee, she would do the same with her own hands.'[39] No artificial phallus was involved, but by placing emphasis on Benedetta's masculine forcefulness in instigating sex, on her assumption of the man-on-top position, and the use of fingers for penetration, Bartolomea frames the sexual encounters in conventional gendered terms. She, like Laurence, Else Muter and others mentioned above, is cast in a safely passive feminine role. A modern reader might read these as rape scenes, but there is no mention of *raptus*. As mentioned in chapter 2 above, premodern languages of sex cast males in a dominant sexual role which paid little attention to consent. However, a new rhetorical element appears. Bartolomea takes care to emphasize that she thought she was not sinning because not Benedetta but the 'angel, Splenditello, did these things, appearing as a boy of eight or nine years', or that through Benedetta Jesus was instructing her to be his bride.[40] The language of visions and mystical union further quarantined Bartolomea's actions and reduced her culpability. They served not so much to make female same-sex love intelligible as to divert interpretation, reframing the acts and the relationship in spiritual terms. This rhetorical tactic (if that is all it was) may have saved Bartolomea: Benedetta spent the remaining thirty-five years of her life in a monastic prison, while Bartolomea seems to have resumed a relatively normal convent life.[41]

The female homosociality of convent life must have produced all manner of ardent affective relations between women. In 423 Augustine of Hippo had warned the nuns of the convent headed by his sister, 'the love which you bear one another ought not be carnal, but spiritual'.[42] In later medieval England Aelred of Rievaulx and the author of the *Ancrene Wisse* issued similar warnings to nuns, while the 1395 'Twelve Conclusions of the Lollards' chastised nuns for their hypocrisy in taking vows of continence yet 'having sex with themselves'. Each of these is ambiguous about whether same-sex acts or masturbation is the problem, yet a Latin text of the Twelve Conclusions specified 'intimacy between women in carnal acts against nature'.[43]

But the unfolding story of medieval female homoeroticism becomes steadily richer, stranger and more interesting as we move beyond discourses of proscription and punishment. Many scholars have suggested that relative lack of attention paid to female–female desire and sex could have allowed for relationships to flourish unhindered.[44] What emerges is a picture of female–female intimacy 'made intelligible' not so much to medieval authorities but rather to modern readers seeking evidence on relationships between women in the premodern past.

An unnamed nun, probably from a Bavarian nunnery in the twelfth century, wrote 'To G., her singular rose', expressing distress at her beloved's absence. The language goes beyond that of passionate friendship: 'When I recall the kisses you gave me, / and how with tender words you caressed my little breasts, / I want to die.'[45] In another poem in the same manuscript a nun writes to another in terms that echo but also exceed Anselm's lament for his absent male friend: 'Why do you want your only one to die, who as you know, loves you with soul and body, who sighs for you at every hour, at every moment, like a hungry little bird.'[46] Also in Bavaria, in 1315, Margaret and Katherine, two 'beautiful well-disposed aristocratic maidens who were almost thirteen years old', jointly decided to dedicate their lives to Christ. These 'dear playmates, dearest friends', were allotted adjoining cells and had a door cut into the wall between them. Far from being subject to suspicion, the other nuns delighted in the girls and their friendship. Around the age of thirty they decided to flagellate each other with iron rods in celebration of their bridegroom, Christ. They suffered profuse bleeding then fell into a trance that lasted several days, and were finally found garlanded with roses. Rather than cause consternation, their act enhanced their spiritual aura and the prioress had the garlands placed in the convent's reliquary storeroom. They lived a further forty years before dying within days of one another.[47] Other Germans, the Benedictine Gertrude of Helta (d. 1265) and Dominican Margaretha Ebner (d. 1351), detailed a number of close affective friendships experienced in their nunneries.[48] During an inquisition by John of Schwenkfeld, a novice of a Silesian order of Beguines alleged that the sisters fondled each other and kissed with tongues during services and mass.[49]

Intense friendships were a common feature of thirteenth-century Italian women saints also. Elizabeth Petroff says 'almost every saint's life tells of a profound relationship with a woman friend': Benevuta had her sister Maria, with whom she shared her bedroom, her secular friend 'the devout widow Jacobina', and in the convent which she visited almost daily there was her 'beloved Margarita'.[50]

Ulrike Wiethaus claims Hildegard of Bingen's relationship with the younger nun Richardis of Stade equals 'in tragic passion and depth the letters between Héloïse and Abelard'.[51] Let us look at Hildegard and Richardis in more detail. Richardis of Stade (b. *c.* 1123) was around twenty-five years younger than Hildegard (b. 1098) and joined her small convent probably in childhood. Hildegard spoke of the 'deep love' she bore for Richardis and compared it to Paul's for Timothy.[52] When Richardis was appointed abbess of a convent near Bremen in 1151, Hildegard raised an outcry, citing simony (the von Stade family were looking to expand their influence in northern Germany) and invoking her prophetic persona in condemnation, but her emotional attachment to Richardis was clearly the sticking point. Susan Schibanoff suggests that Pope Eugenius III in his rebuking letter to Hildegard employs the moral diction of the confessional (*paralipsis*) to refer to events: 'that matter you wished to consult with us about'; 'that sister (the nun you delivered up to him)'. This allusive style, says Schibanoff, with its refusal directly to name the point of contention, echoes the advice given to confessors to avoid naming or describing the worst forms of sexual vice – 'the unmentionable vice', 'the unspeakable sin', 'the silent sin' – lest they unwittingly teach penitents new habits.[53] Hildegard's statement that Richardis 'bound herself [*coniunxerat*]' to her 'in loving friendship in every way' while she was writing *Scivias* employs, in Schibanoff's view, a 'telling metaphor' of physical connection.[54] She adds, Hildegard's condemnation in the *Scivias* of any woman who 'plays a male role in coupling with another woman' and of the female partner in such an act as 'devilish' and a 'most vile' sin may allude specifically to gender transgression and the use of dildos and is not necessarily incompatible with approval of strong love for another woman. Moreover, Hildegard's account of female sexual response avoids the phallocentric concepts of arousal and pleasure usually found in medieval medical literature. Her 'gynocentric' account of feminine *delectatio* likens women's pleasure to the sun, 'which gently, lightly, and continuously perfuses the earth with its heat'.[55] Bruce Holsinger, in his innovative study of Hildegard's music, draws upon these descriptions of female sexual response ('winds of pleasure', 'airey breezes' arising within the body's marrow and flowing to the womb) to support his argument that her hymn *Ave generosa* is 'an expression of intense, loving, and erotic devotion to the Virgin Mary' and that other compositions celebrate the beauty and fertility of the female body.[56]

However, Hildegard's feelings for Richardis could be explained as a particularly intense example of spiritual maternity. Her reference to Paul's relationship to Timothy evokes the relationship of master and disciple, spiritual father to his 'son in the faith'.[57] Wiethaus, despite her reference to Heloise and Abelard, also leans towards a spiritual mother–daughter reading, reminding us of Hildegard's own loss of her mother when sent as an oblate to Disibodenberg at age eight and her closeness to her early spiritual mentor, Jutta.[58] Hildegard's final, farewell letter to Richardis expresses a ferocious love not incompatible with maternal feeling, even if it is a spiritual or sublimated rather than biological maternity. 'Now, again I say: Woe is me, mother, woe is me, daughter, "Why have you forsaken me?" like an orphan? I so loved the nobility of your character, your wisdom, your chastity, your spirit, and indeed every aspect of your life that many people have said to me, "What are you doing? Now, let all who have grief like mine mourn with me. . . ."'[59] Whether or not this is homoerotic, as an expression of affectivity between women it is one of the most power-ful survivals of the medieval era.

The affective and ecstatic nature of medieval mysticism has prompted further queer readings. Karma Lochrie redirects scholarly debates over the sexual content of female mystics' ecstasies with the question, 'What does it signify when a female mystic desires and adores the feminized body of Christ?' Some portrayals of Christ's wound (*vulnus*) in books of hours seem obviously vulvic.[60] (It was not only 'female mystics' who meditated upon this imagery, however; some of the books' owners were laywomen, while male authors, including James of Milan, seem to have been conscious of the vulva/*vulnus* analogy. What, then, does it signify when a *male* mystic desires and adores the feminized body of Christ?) The thirteenth-century Brabatian mystic Hadewijch, who adapted the poetic traditions of courtly love and the minnesingers, produced highly original religious poetry in which she expresses ecstatic love for a sometimes feminine, sometimes masculine, God, and as speaker moves between gendered positions from feminine (a 'poor woman') to masculine (the courtly knight devoted to his lady, 'Minne').[61] Her passion for *Minne* has been read as homoerotic and a subversion of religious discourse that enabled her to 'speak her truth without speaking it'.[62] Others have read her letter to two younger pupils in which she enquires after another young woman, 'Sara', her best-beloved pupil, as suggestive of an intense woman-identified relationship.[63]

Apart from the handful of court cases already cited, intense intimacy between laywomen has proved harder to identify. One often-cited instance derives from an early thirteenth-century *canso* attributed to the woman troubadour Bieiris de Romans, in which the (apparently) female speaker expresses admiration for a woman, 'Maria', and expresses oblique longing for unnamed satisfaction.[64] Angelica Rieger's 1989 query as to 'whether the author was lesbian' looks rather blunt, and indeed Rieger's conclusions about female homosociality and affectivity are congruent with the more compre-hensive views of love and desire between women that have become the focus of recent scholarship. Elsewhere in medieval literature, romances such as *Yde and Olyve* and *Silence* featured cross-dressing women and mistaken gender identities, and offered readers the enter-tainments of gender play and desire between women.[65] Medieval authors made female love and desire for other women legible by creating female sodomites, phallic women and including sex between women among the unnatural vices. Modern scholars have, in contrast, made intimate relations between women visible by placing them in a genealogy of lesbianism – even if the outlines of that category are softened by concepts of woman-identification, lesbian continuum, lesbian-like, homoerotic and homoaffective. Both groups have prob-ably reduced the spectrum of feminine erotics and affectivities by thus confining them in rhetoric.

In the end, we are reluctant to attach clear labels to many of the relationships mentioned here. Female–female intimacy in medieval culture encompassed homoerotic desire, sex between women, ardent friendships, spiritual mother–daughter bonds, spiritual sisterhood and complicated triangulations involving Christ, the angels, the Virgin Mary, vulvic imagery and feminized 'Love'. Rather than reducing this richness to a 'history of medieval lesbianism' we prefer to remain open to interpretative possibilities. It is the great diversity of human erotic responses, and the likelihood that we will only ever stumble towards comprehension of many of them, that we find most interest-ing in the history of sex.

With the 'renaissance of lesbianism' identifiable at least from the later decades of the sixteenth century, female–female desire continued to be characterized by many of its medieval tropes, especially performa-tive masculinity, but also gained new forms (the female husband, the hermaphrodite, the tribade, the friend, the Sapphist) and new expres-sions (mythological art, pornography). As with male effeminacy, female masculinity did not necessarily imply same-sex desire. An early modern English ballad told the story of a woman who cut her hair, changed her name from Elise to William, and disguised herself as a male servant. She became the King's chamberlain and then ended up marrying him when her true identity was discovered: 'He took sweet William for his Wife / The like before was never seen / A Serving-man to be a Queen.'[66] Warrior women, transvestites who donned male clothing to seek adventure at war and sea, and who were the subject of a whole genre of ballad literature, invariably found true love, returned to their female state, and settled down to marry someone of the opposite sex.[67] The chapbook heroine Long Meg wore men's clothing and fought with 'manly courage', but she married, pledging obedience to her husband.[68] Other women passed as male workers so that they could earn a living as a labouring man; here, the motive was economic.[69]

However, there are also women who pretended to be men in order to live with, or even marry, women. Amy Poulter, although already married (to a man), became James Howard in order to court and marry the soprano and lutenist Arabella Hunt in 1680.[70] Fraser Easton distinguishes the tolerated women warriors from the less culturally acceptable 'female husband', the latter treated with ridicule or reproach because such women were assuming not merely the clothing of a man but his 'sexual body'.[71] *Comical News from Blooms-bury* told of a woman who took on the identity of a man and who courted and married a gentlewoman, living with her for a month, and 'using a strange Instrument for generation':

> But what he did with it, or whether 'twas put
> I'll leave you good Folks to consider:
> The innocent Bride no difference knew,
> and seem'd to be greatly delighted;
> But Lasses I'll warrant there's none among you
> that would be so cleverly cheated.[72]

Henry Fielding's *The Female Husband or the Surprising History of Mrs Mary, alias Mr. George Hamilton* (1746) and John Cleland's *Historical and Physical Dissertation on the Case of Catherine Vizzani* (1751) left little doubt about the sexual aspects of the role of the female husband, both pamphlets hinting at artificial means of phallic pleasure (the thing that made Mary Hamilton 'the best man in Ireland' and Vizzani's leather contrivance) as well as at preferences for female–female sexual contact ('irregular passion', 'unnatural affections', 'unnatural desires').[73] Both cases demonstrated, without actually naming as a category, love between women: Hamilton, wrote Fielding, enjoying the gender play, 'declared, she was really as much in love, as it was possible for a man ever to be with one of her own sex'.[74] As with male homoerotics, the acts were seen as vice rather than identity, a propensity in every woman: 'if once our carnal appetites are let loose, without those secure and proper guides, there is no excess and disorder which they are not liable to commit, even while they pursue their natural satisfaction; and, which may seem still more strange, there is nothing monstrous and unnatural, which they are not capable of inventing'.[75] Vizzani's adventures were instances of 'a libidinous Disposition' and 'Perversion in the Imagination'.[76]

While the various court records are a source for male sodomy, they are less revealing of female same-sex activity. Few female sodomites were prosecuted in Europe and none in England.[77] The cross-dressing female husbands were prosecuted as vagrants (that catch-all legal category) if they were prosecuted at all.[78] The offences of those few whom one eighteenth-century Dutch judge termed 'tribades' are unclear, and at least one of the more revealing descriptions arose out of a murder charge, but their dossiers are nonetheless informative regarding female same-sex attractions.[79] Witnesses described seeing two women engaged in oral sex as well as having 'lain with their lower bodies nude and kissed and caressed one another, like a man is used to do to a woman'.[80] One of the accused was reputed to have said to another woman, 'You do have something in your being that attracts both male and female. If I just see you I shoot.'[81]

One of the ways in which female–female sexual acts were imagined in the Renaissance was in terms of the hermaphrodite, a being with both male and female bodily characteristics. In the case of the married women in England in 1680, midwives examined the groom because of his suspected 'double gender (being usually called an hermaphrodite)' but found her to be 'a perfect woman in all her parts'.[82] The notion must have had cultural resilience. In 1824, when Anne Lister (more of whom later) recalled attempting to make sense of her sexual attraction to women, one of the possibilities that she had examined and then discounted was hermaphroditism: 'No exterior formation accounted for it.'[83]

The tribade was another figure of imagined female same-sex erotics. Traub has associated the tribade with enlarged clitoral penetration. The translated Arabic writings and rediscovered medical texts of ancient Greece describing African women (an 'other') with enlarged clitorises, combined with the sixteenth-century European rediscovery of the clitoris (as a small penis), raised the spectre of female penetrative sex.[84] The anonymous author of the semi-pornographic *Tractatus de Hermaphroditis* (1718) discussed the penis-like characteristics of the clitoris, claiming lengths of two or three inches and the pleasures derived from that organ:

> Women well furnish'd in these Parts may divert themselves with their Companions, to whom for the most part they can give as much Pleasure as men do, but cannot receive in any proportion the Pleasure themselves, for want of Ejaculation. . . . I am inform'd that Diversions of this nature are frequently practis'd by robust and lustful Females, who cannot with any prospect of safety for their Reputations, venture upon the Embraces of a Man, though they are never so strongly enclin'd.[85]

The clitoris, as Traub puts it, became 'the disturbing emblem of female erotic transgression'.[86] And 'accompanying, influencing, haunting every anatomical discussion of the clitoris and its pleasures was the monstrous figure of the tribade'.[87] But we should not exaggerate the association. Tribadism literally referred to the practice of rubbing, thereby invoking female–female sexual interaction through bodily contact. The tribade was not necessarily phallic in her attributes. However, she was certainly what Harriette Andreadis has called a signifier for women who desired or had sex with other women.[88]

Then there was the figure of Sappho, the Greek poet from Lesbos, whose name was given to female same-sex acts and desires, including sapphic (a late nineteenth- and early twentieth-century term) and, eventually, lesbian. Sixteenth- and seventeenth-century commentators and editors of Ovid's comments about Sappho's love of women – 'What did Lesbian Sappho teach the girls if not love' – were more forthcoming in Latin than they were in English texts, but even the latter managed to convey a sense of her tribadism, her same-sex proclivities.[89] She had concubines and 'used' her friends 'libidinously'; she 'was with other women a tribade, this is abusing them by rubbing'. She emerges also in discussions of the clitoris in early modern human anatomies as a practitioner of clitoral tribadism: a confricatrice or rubster.[90] Joan DeJean has argued that in the French texts Sappho was rarely permitted to be sapphic, but that one of the moments of her same-sex attribution was in the sixteenth and seventeenth centuries. (Another would be in the late nineteenth and early twentieth centuries.)[91]

Clearly art, drawing on classical imagery, was an important site for same-sex eroticism. Lush paintings depict semi-clothed or naked women kissing. The fact that one of the 'women' was a male in disguise or a male god assuming female form did not mar the surface representation of open female erotic contact. Titian's *Diana and Actaeon* (1559), where the viewer should focus not on the presence of the man (the hunter Actaeon) but on the scene that he has interrupted, was just one of a series of images representing female–female erotic interaction. The same artist's *Diana and Callisto* (c. 1560), with Jupiter disguised as Diana seducing Callisto, Gerrit van Honthorst's *Jupiter in the Guise of Diana Seducing Callisto* (c. 1590–1656), Hendrick Bloemaert's *Diana and Callisto* (1635–40), Peter Paul Rubens's *Jupiter and Callisto* (1613) and Jacob van Loo's *Diana and Her Nymphs* (1654) were all powerful visual depictions of female intimacy. In van Loo's *Amarillis Crowning Mirtillo* (1645–50), the shepherd Mirtillo disguised himself as a woman to approach the nymph Amarillis and joined in a kissing-game that she was playing with her female companions. Visually, however, it looks like two women kissing. Although the female kissing is absent from Adriaen van Nieulandt the Younger's painting of the same name, it is central to many other representations of this story, and, as Traub has pointed out, Amarillis had once 'believed this fabulous kisser to be a woman'. Eighteenth-century versions of this classical female homoeroticism continued this same-sex imagining: Jacob de Wit's *Diana Seducing Callisto* (1727), François Boucher's *Jupiter and Callisto* (1744) and his *Jupiter in the Guise of Diana and the Nymph Callisto* (1757).[92] Patricia Simons's study of Italian Renaissance portrayals of Diana bathing with her nymphs suggests that such imagery of female intimacy and male repudiation could have had homoerotic connotations for viewers even in the late fourteenth and certainly early decades of the fifteenth century. Her essay, which offers the kind of historically nuanced account of female–female desire later developed by Traub, hints that elements of the 'renaissance of lesbianism' can be traced somewhat earlier than Traub's English-focused chronology suggests.[93]

Early modern pornography is another important source for imagining female-to-female sexual acts and demonstrations of desire.[94] *Tractatus de Hermaphroditis* (1718) alternated between serious discussion of hermaphroditism and salacious and tenuously linked musings and descriptions of the assumed propensity of women to sexual experimentation with those of their own sex.[95] We are introduced to an archetypal pornographic tale in which a male servant observes two female friends who 'mutually employ'd their Hands with each other, in the same Manner, and with the same force of Inclination, as a juvenile Gallant would make his Approaches to what he most admires'.[96] In another story two female companions fashion an 'artificial *Penis* of the largest Dimensions', attached with ribbons,

Image 8. This painting, by a seventeenth-century Flemish artist who worked in Amsterdam, is one of a series of images representing female–female, erotic interaction. Note the powerful visual depictions of female nudity and intimacy, the touching and easy familiarity. Historians use such imagery as visual evidence for same-sex imagining. Jacob van Loo, *Diana and Her Nymphs*. 1654. Oil on canvas, 99.5 × 135.5 cm. Statens Museum für Kunst (National Galley of Denmark).

'to use their utmost Artifices for the Relief of each other' and 'another Instrument ... us'd ... with an Injection of Moisture, which, with the rubbing, occasion'd such a tickling, as to force a discharge of matter and facilitate the Pleasure'.[97] The story ends with a male admirer, cross-dressed as a female servant, substituting the inevitable real thing for the artificial penis and marrying the woman concerned. The finale has the woman, 'experiencing a material difference between Art and Nature', singing

> The Shadow I'll no longer try,
> Or use the pleasing Toy;
> A sprightly Youth I can't defy,
> The Substance I'll enjoy.

Yet her journey involved considerable same-sex gratification.[98]

'Lord! You have set me all on a Flame. Ah! This fooling is lascivious. Retreat, I beseech you. Ah! How you clasp me. I am perfectly devoured!' were the exclamations of one nun to another in *Venus in the Cloister* (1725).[99] Women pleasure one another, indeed bring their partner to orgasm, through manual stimulation, kissing and rubbing.[100] 'If you continue to caress me, after this manner, you will soon reduce me to ashes; for I find myself now all on Fire.'[101] In the Latin text *Satyra Sotadica de Arcanis Amoris et Veneris* (c. 1665), Nicholas Chorier has two female cousins engaged in what James Grantham Turner terms sustained discursive and corporeal pleasure, 'mouth to mouth, breast to breast, womb to womb'. 'I am in love with you the way you are in love with your fiancé.'[102] Pierre de Bourdeilles, the Seigneur de Brantôme, asked in a text written in the sixteenth century but published in the seventeenth whether two married women 'in love one with the other' committed adultery and made cuckolds of their husbands if, in bed together, they did 'what is called *donna con donna*, imitating in fact that learned poetess Sappho, of Lesbos'.[103] He quoted Martial's phrase about uniting 'twin cunts', and wrote of acts involving rubbing rather than penetration. Brantôme's tribades were fricatrices or fricarelles, meaning to rub 'or to rub each other'.[104]

> 'Tis said how that Sappho the Lesbian was a very high mistress in this art, or even, so they say, the inventress of the thing, and that in after times the Lesbian dames have copied her therein, and continued the practice to the present day. So Lucian saith: Such is the character of the Lesbian women, which will not suffer men at all, but do go with other women like actual men.[105]

That is, his Lesbians meant women from Lesbos rather than lesbians as we might understand the word.[106] While this libertine text saw such acts as 'practice for the real thing with men', it still represented scenarios of sex between women, the possibility that some women sought out such contact, became infatuated with and loved other women, and wanted such partners even when they had constant access to men because these practices (quoting Lucian) could be 'much more pleasant than with a man'.[107] His fricarelles, it should be noted, courtesans, women of the court, gentlewomen and ordinary married women, also had sex with men. 'How many of these women of Lesbos have I seen who, for all their fricarelles and rubbings together do not forsake recourse to men!'[108] The Marie Antoinette of French Revolution pornography, who excited women with 'the royal finger', enjoyed sexual relations with both men and women.[109]

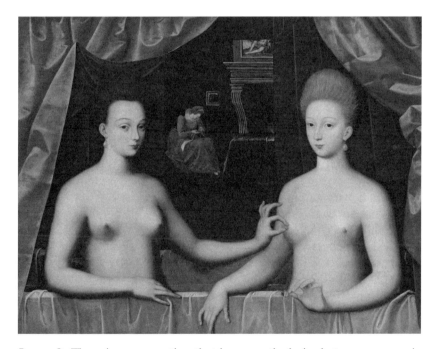

Image 9. There is no suggestion that homoerotic desire between women is literally depicted in this image. Rather it is thought to show the Duchess drawing attention to the beauty of her sister Gabrielle (who was the mistress of Henry IV of France, r. 1572–1610), in particular her fashionably small breasts. However, it is a highly playful image that may well have amused contemporary viewers with its allusion to fashionable sexual play between high-status women. *Gabrielle d'Estrees and Her Sister, the Duchess of Villars*, Late sixteenth century. Oil on panel. Bridgeman Art Library.

Female friendship did not enjoy the same open cultural endorsement as male friendship.[110] The historian is immediately confronted with the disparity between the richness of textual sources on the discourse of male friendship and the paucity, indeed the same recurring name (that of the seventeenth-century English poet Katherine Phillips), in accounts of the literature of female friendship.[111] Andreadis contrasts the over seventy-page essay on male friendship in Richard Brathwait's *The English Gentleman* (1630) with that author's silence about female friendships in his companion volume, *The English Gentlewoman* (1630).[112] Worse, male writers slighted the female capacity for friendship: 'it is too weak, too slight, too trivial!'[113] Yet it has been argued that women drew on classical discourses of male friendship to construct a language of female amity, what the French called *tendre amitié* (tender friendship), expressed in poetry, in letters and doubtless in verbal interaction.[114] The historian Nicole Eustace has contrasted the prevalence and intensity of loving correspondence between eighteenth-century American female friends with the relative paucity and silence of similar letters from young women to their male suitors.[115]

As already hinted, there were the same tensions as in male friendships with the possibility that such closeness could become sexualized. Like the medieval penitentials, early modern convent constitutions and instructions ruled against 'particular friendships'. Hence the Carmelites: 'we strongly encourage peace and love among all our nuns ... particular friendships are not permitted but rather everyone should love each other equally and if there is some specific affection it should be stopped immediately'.[116] *La Esposa de Christo Instruida con la Vida de Santa Lutgarda, Virgin Monja de San Bernardo* warned of the slide from the spiritual to the carnal: 'the love that begins spiritual and for superior motives can become twisted and end up foolish and useless carnal love'.[117] As Sherry Velasco has written, 'some of the most compelling accounts of women who loved other women can be found in documents associated with all-female communities'.[118]

Although an early nineteenth-century figure, the Yorkshire gentlewoman Anne Lister belongs more to the early modern environment of the long eighteenth century. While her edited journals are most often quoted for their sexual scenarios (as we will see), they also contain much of interest on a lived rather than publicly proclaimed female friendship. 'I felt that my happiness depended on having some female companion whom I could love & depend upon' was an early entry.[119] Lister's diaries show that two women could think themselves married to one another (as 'husband' and 'wife'), although one had gone through the actual ceremony with a man, her legal husband, and that their ties overrode opposite-sex bonds. 'Mary, there is a nameless tie in that soft intercourse which blends us into one & makes me feel that you are mine. There is no feeling like it. There is no pledge which gives such sweet possession.'[120]

The tensions within female friendship were similar to those between men. Friends might proclaim that 'heroic love is an antidote to the poison of vulgar love' and offer their 'tender friendship, which has greater worth than the love of more than half the world'.[121] But there were accompanying suspicions that such friendships could include something more than friendship, hints 'Of some dark Deeds at night' and 'stuff not fit to be mentioned of passions between women'.[122]

An early contribution to the literature of passionate female friendship is a Scottish poem, known merely as 'Poem XLIX' (1586), in which a female speaker invokes a number of famous classical pairs (Perithous and Theseus, Achilles and Patroclus, David and Jonathan) and adds a female couple (Ruth and Naomi). In partial echo of the discourse on female husbands mentioned earlier, the speaker exclaims that she wishes to be transformed into a man so that she can wed her beloved and end their torment. Jane Farnsworth argues that the poem's allusions, metaphors and vocabulary imply a wish for sexual consummation, not only chaste friendship.[123] When Anne Lister recorded her sleeplessness – 'Dozing, hot & disturbed ... a violent longing for a female companion came over me ... It was absolute pain to me' – she was not thinking of mere companionship.[124]

That friendship for women could involve something more is apparent in Lister's suspicions in 1822 that the relationship between two famous female friends was not merely platonic: 'I cannot help thinking that surely it was not platonic. Heaven forgive me, but I look within myself & doubt. I feel the infirmity of our nature & hesitate to pronounce such attachments uncemented by something more tender still than friendship.'[125] When she later attested to the warmth of her own friendships but denied that they went any further, we know – indeed she tells us – that she was lying.[126]

What is so compellingly fascinating about Lister's journals is that they record conversations about homoeroticism, distinguishing between mere physicality and sexual acts excused by 'mutual affection', theoretical and practical knowledge, and nature and artifice, and include Anne's later speculations on how many such women there are, yet where the thing discussed is never precisely named though the subject clearly understood as 'something more' or going 'beyond the utmost verge of friendship'.[127] That the language existed is clear from the same discussant's references to female–female relationships that involved bodies as well as souls. Lister wrote privately: 'In my mind thought of her using a phallus to her friend.'[128] In France in 1824 Lister conversed with another woman about the accusations that Marie Antoinette was 'too fond of women'.[129] They discussed the difference between 'Saffic regard', which Lister associated with the use of a dildo and did not sanction, and her own 'connection with the ladies'. Although Anne and her companion, the widow Mrs Barlow, were guarded in their disclosures of their respective sexual knowingness, while simultaneously reading one another's responses for deception, and repeatedly referred to this thing called 'it', they knew what they were both talking about. 'She begins to stand closer to me,' Lister wrote of Barlow the day before. 'I might easily press queer to queer [genitalia to genitalia]. Our liking each other is now mutually understood and acknowledged.'[130] We will see shortly that Lister had no difficulty recording what she once termed her 'erotics', the bodily responses of her lovers, including Barlow, and what one woman can do, or will not do, with another.[131]

Lister had ample opportunity for same-sex seduction. Her diaries list her successes: the love letters, 'grubbling', breast and open-mouthed kissing, feeling of genitalia, the repeated mutual orgasms, the serial seductions of sisters, the love-struck widow, the maidenhead taking, the exchanged lockets of pubic hair, the continuous flirtations.[132] She tried to make sense of what we (though not she) would call her sexuality, based on her reading of such behaviour in the classics, her interaction with similar women, and an awareness of her own same-sex desires.[133] As she wrote: 'I love, & only love, the fairer sex & thus beloved by them in turn, my heart revolts from any other love than theirs.'[134]

Annamarie Jagose has warned against imposing modern lesbian identities on such texts.[135] Anne saw herself – and was seen as – masculine, man-like. Women flirted with her as they might with someone of the opposite sex. As Jagose notes, these were not relations between those of the same gender. Lister had affairs with young women who later married, a widow with a child, and a long-term lover, Marianna Lawton, who was married to a man but to whom, as we have seen, Lister nevertheless considered herself 'married'. When we focus on these women, as much a part of this history as Lister, it is clear that they, as Jagose has expressed it, 'do not understand themselves, any more than she understands them, as sharing with Lister a sexual preference, let alone anything like a sexuality'.[136] It is significant that in her declaration of attraction to 'the fairer sex', she does not describe them as *her* sex.[137] She describes her desires in terms of gender rather than sex: 'All this ordering & work & exercise seemed to excite my manly feelings. I saw a pretty girl go up the lane & desire rather came over me.'[138]

There is a different possibility, however, not incompatible with Lister's masculinity: Lister was a sapphist. Susan Lanser uses the terms 'sapphic' and 'sapphist' to describe bodies and persons in the eighteenth century that were 'visibly female but metonymically masculine'.[139] These women, whose same-sex desiring was proclaimed by some visible indicator of masculinity (clothing or demeanour), replaced the tribade in what Lanser terms a mid-eighteenth-century shift from the focus on anatomy ('genital deviance').[140] Lister's masculinity, Lanser argues, 'suggests at least one shape, and one etiology, for modern sapphic identity'.[141] But surely this explanation is too reductive. The word 'sapphist', it should be stressed, is the literary critic's rather than that of the archive; its anachronistic use (for the term was not employed in this manner at that time), with implied identity-formation in references to 'sexual identities', is close to lesbianism under a different name.[142] Lister, we recall, used the term 'Saffic regard' in contrast to what she understood as her erotic constitution. And what of the place of Lister's various lovers in this sapphist framework: the woman who was wife to both man and woman, the young women courted before they married (men), the homoerotically accessible widow? Though her examples are from pornography and literature rather than from Lister's journals, Lanser's answer – with further anachronism – is that such women, 'feminine bodies who are preferentially heterosexual but happily homoerotic', are what would later be termed situational homosexuals: 'women for whom homoeroticism is a temporary excursion inspired either by the absence or the ill behavior of men'.[143] However, this privileges 'the woman who loves women as a primary or exclusive choice'.[144] Such history would exclude the desires of many of the women represented in the pages above.

A woman in Richard Brome's play *The Antipodes* (1640), married for three years without the consummation of her marriage, mused about what such consummating might entail: 'What a man does in child-getting.'[145] Her dramatic licence occasioned thoughts about female–female sexual interaction:

> A wanton maid once lay with me, and kiss'd
> And clipp'd and clapp'd me strangely, and then wish'd
> That I had been a man to have got her with child.[146]

It was a remembered part of her history, mentioned as of no great moment, and was also contemplated (along with adultery) as a remedy for her husband's marital neglect. Hence her reply to a female acquaintance's question 'Does not your husband use to lie with you?'

> Yes, he does use to lie with me, but he does not
> Lie with me to use me as he shoud, I fear;
> Nor do I know how to teach him. Will you tell me?
> I'll lie with you and practice, if you please.
> Pray take me for a night or two, or take
> My husband and instruct him but one night.[147]

A Spanish fictional character in a 1647 novella by María de Zayas, a male cross-dressed as a female in order to gain access to a young woman, argues for the legitimacy of same-sex desire: 'since the soul is the same in male and female, it matters not whether I'm a man or a woman. Souls aren't male or female and true love dwells in the soul, not in the body'.[148]

We have seen that female same-sex activity went beyond such literary representations. That some real premodern women desired other women, and acted upon such needs, is not in doubt. Sherry Velasco provides an extensive list of terms and descriptions for early modern Spanish women engaged in such acts: *Sahacat* (tribade), *bujarronas* ('female sodomites'), *bujarronas de las monjas* ('sodomite nuns'), *somética* ('sodomite'), *cañitas* ('little canes'), *marimacho* ('butch'), *medio hombre y mujer* ('half-man, half-woman'), *incuba* and *succuba*, *subigatrices* ('dominators or those who bounce up and down'), 'not the marrying type', *bellaca baldresera* ('dildo-wielding scoundrel'), *amistades particulares* ('special friendships'), 'fruitless love', 'love without reward', 'like man and woman' and 'making themselves into roosters'.[149] In early seventeenth-century Castile, two women confessed to having 'carnal relations like a man and woman', one on top of the other, 'emitting her semen into the vagina' of the other 'while kissing, hugging, and saying loving words like a man and woman': '"my love", "my life", "do you want to fuck?"'[150] Velasco also relates the case of Ana Aler and Mariana López, one a widow and the other a laundress, in trouble with the Inquisition in Aragon in 1656. A witness testified that 'Mariana lay down on the bed and Ana was between her legs and they were moving around, kissing each other and saying shameful things like when a man and woman are together carnally.'[151] However, whether such women were lesbians – what Velasco calls 'criminal lesbians' – is another matter.

The stories of women who showed exclusive sexual interest in women are indeed part of the premodern history of female same-sex desire. One Castilian servant said to her companion that 'when women sleep with each other it is enjoyable and with no risk of pregnancy ... and that after sexual relations with Maria de la Paz from Madrid three or four times, she couldn't imagine having sex with men because they repulsed her'.[152] Brantôme, despite his tendency to view acts *donna con donna* as a charming prelude to penetrative sex with men, mentions women who 'of their nature hate to marry and fly the conversation of all men they ever can'.[153] Queen Christina of Sweden (abdicated 1654) seems to have avoided all sexual contact with males in preference to relationships with women.[154]

The incredibly detailed trial records of Catharina Linck, executed for sodomy with another woman (her wife) in the German town of Halberstadt in 1721, stated that '[o]ften when a woman touched her, even slightly, she became so full of passion that she did not know what to do', that she had had sexual or intimate relations with prostitutes, maidens and widows and 'had never been intimate with a man', and that before she was beheaded she declared that 'even if she were done away with, others like her would remain'.[155] Yet this last example serves also to reaffirm warnings against premature lesbian identification. According to the trial documents, since adolescence Linck had mostly dressed and lived as a man, including several years as a soldier, wore a leather penis and testicles made of a pig's bladder, pissed standing up, was violent towards her wife, and tried to force her to perform fellatio. The court which tried her displayed no concept of 'lesbian orientation' but instead questioned whether she were a hermaphrodite, examined the size of her clitoris, compared her case with the example of Eastern or African women, and queried whether the use of an instrument constituted true sodomy. Through such rhetorical means they made Linck's desires for women intelligible to themselves. We need to keep such historically specific interpretations in view as we develop techniques for understanding the varied textual traces of premodern women's passions for other women. One of Velasco's Castilian 'lesbian partners' was still sexually involved with men.[156]

Martha Vicinus agrees with Terry Castle that historians need to stop treating the lesbian as a ghostly 'apparitional' figure, lurking in darkness at the margins of history, but rather should put her at the centre: if 'sexual behaviour is polymorphous, changeable, and impossible to define absolutely', then there is no justification for placing lesbian desire in a marginal position to a posited heterosexuality.[157] We agree up to a point, but argue that this will only be achieved for the premodern period by renunciation of both category *and word* 'lesbian', along with 'gay', 'homosexual' and (most urgently of all) 'heterosexual'. Indeed forcing abandonment of the last of these (which Vicinus, along with many historians of lesbianism, retains) will be the conceptual manoeuvre that finally enables a satisfactory account of sexual histories.[158]

5

Before Pornography

Robert Darnton has written that pornography is good to think with.[1]
We say pornography, but, like so many of the terms we encounter in
the history of sex, historians have argued that it did not exist as a
separate category before the modern period. As Bradford Mudge has
explained,

> Before 1750 . . . pornography simply did not exist as a recognizable
> generic category; on the contrary, it was discursively entangled among
> other closely related genres and subgenres. Sensational romances,
> scandal novels, bawdy poems and stories, whore dialogues and rogue
> biographies, pseudo-medical manuals, political exposes, and anti-
> ecclesiastical tracts all made use of 'pornographic' strategies and tech-
> niques. But without a clearly defined discursive terrain of its own,
> without clear-cut generic boundaries and stable readerly and authorial
> expectations, those strategies and techniques were hard to distinguish
> from other kinds of obscene writing. In short, pornography as we know
> it emerged over the course of the eighteenth century, not in any kind
> of smooth evolutionary progression but instead by fits and starts and
> according to a logic peculiarly its own.[2]

These assertions make sense only if we have a clear idea of what
'pornography as we know it' might be. Lynn Hunt offers a concise
definition: pornography is 'the explicit depiction of sexual organs and
sexual practices with the aim of arousing sexual feelings', and notes
that it was 'almost always an adjunct to something else until the
middle or end of the eighteenth century'.[3] Ian Frederick Moulton
suggests that 'pornography is writing aimed primarily at sexually
arousing its reader; its structure is one of infinite enumeration (or

positions, of partners) within a field that is always and only sexual'.[4] The novelist Angela Carter, more pithily, called it 'propaganda for fucking'.[5] Moreover, modern 'pornography', unlike premodern sexually explicit expressions, is a commodity unto itself. One may purchase an item of 'pornography', having a good idea (because of the expectations imposed by modern notions of textual and visual genres) of what one will probably get. No such generic expectations apply to the diverse range of sexually explicit materials on show to medieval and early modern audiences. The word only became common in the mid-nineteenth century, although it is attested in one ancient source – a Greek work of the second century CE – where it is used in a literal sense to refer to a painter of (or one who wrote about) prostitutes.[6] When 'pornographer' re-emerged in English *c.* 1850 (following French coinages) it was first applied to the painters of erotic frescos recently discovered at Pompeii and soon after by medical writers describing works on the moral and health dangers of prostitutes, only slowly taking on its range of current meanings.[7] Like 'lesbian', 'pornography' is an ancient word but its premodern meanings were not at all identical with modern ones.

Scholars have argued about how to date the development of modern discourses of pornography. Lynn Hunt locates it in the early sixteenth century with the work of Italian humanists Giulio Romano and Pietro Aretino. But some medievalists have attempted to identify sexually explicit material from before *c.* 1500 as pornographic; Lisa Bitel has written of the fascination with powerful women in early medieval Irish literature (*c.* 700–1100) as a 'veritable pornography' of sex and violence.[8] P. J. P. Goldberg has suggested that sexually explicit details in Church court records of marital disputes contain elements of pornography and voyeurism, while the detailed accounts of varieties of lechery in pastoral manuals and vices and virtues literature may have produced a 'vicarious frisson' for their (supposedly) celibate clerical readers.[9] In response, one might argue that while we cannot entirely discount any erotic *effects* felt by medieval readers of legal and moral texts, arousal was not the works' primary *purpose*. Secular entertainments may, however, have incorporated pornographic elements. James A. Brundage finds plenty of warnings to clerics in canon-legal texts to avoid songs, dances, plays and stories lest they be aroused to lust by what they heard, indicating that medieval audiences could be fully alert to their pornographic potential.[10] We can also glimpse the now familiar concern that sexually explicit material might influence audiences' erotic choices. Bernadino of Siena warned his Perugian listeners in 1425 not to read lewd books, including the

Image 10. The eroticism of this large painting by the engraver of Pietro Aretino's famous sexual postures resides in the draped bodies, open mouths and eyes, and the close, mutual gazing, but also, as with Image 1, in the action of the woman as she gently lifts the sheet from her partner's groin. The work anticipates the erotics of eighteenth-century pornographic imagery, with the onlooker reminding the viewers of the painting that they too are voyeurs. Romano, Giulio (Giulio Pippi) (?), *Love Scene*. Oil on canvas (transferred from panel), 163 × 337 cm. Italy. 1524/1525. Photograph © The State Hermitage Museum. Photo by Vladimir Terebenin, Leonard Kheifets, Yuri Molodkovets.

Corbaccio and the *Decameron* (mid-fourteenth-century works by Boccaccio), because of the vices they taught – the former especially condemned for making 'millions of men' into sodomites.[11]

There is no doubt that medieval visual and literary arts encompassed ribald material that now seems decidedly explicit but has often stumped critics in attempts at interpretation. Until recently many preferred to ignore or play down the extent of obvious nudity, crude language and sexual references in medieval culture. Could the problem be the modern invention of pornography as a readily identifiable genre? If it is assumed that naked sex organs, depictions of sex acts and words and euphemisms for sex are intended to cause arousal, then such images can be taken as pornographic. On the other hand, we have no reason to suppose that pilgrim badges featuring vulvas on horseback, church carvings of arses or French comic tales of fucking and farting were necessarily sexually arousing. Their bodily explicitness is unmistakable; what is harder to determine is the reaction of contemporary observers. Our contention is that it is not especially helpful to view medieval material as part of a historical continuum of pornography and that the more recent development of pornography as an autonomous discourse has hindered scholarly interpretations. While acknowledging that some items may have had arousal value for contemporary viewers, they are better understood as products of a culture that appreciated the socially satirical, moralistic and misogynistic potential of explicit art and literature as well as or more than their arousal factor.

Archaeologists and metal detectives have uncovered thousands of pilgrims' badges from sites in the Netherlands, France and Britain, including significant quantities of apparently obscene objects (we take 'obscene' to mean 'offensively or grossly indecent', *OED*). These cheap, mass-produced lead-tin trinkets dating from the thirteenth to mid-sixteenth centuries take the form of figures including a vulva on horseback brandishing bow and arrow, ambulant or flying belled-phalluses, a vulva and phallus on the brink of penetration, female pudenda on stilts, vulva pilgrims with staff and rosary, hyper-phallic beasts and wild men, and phallic roastings attended by female cooks.[12] No one can say for sure what these artefacts meant to their medieval wearers. Some have hazarded that they were meant to ward off 'the evil eye', others that they commemorated visits to brothels.[13] Jos Koldeweij suggests they were meant to mock pilgrims and religious processions and, he implies, would have suited Chaucer's Wife of Bath.[14] More recently Karma Lochrie has proposed we do best to regard the badges as multi-layered parodies that targeted both the conventional pieties of more traditional pilgrims' badges and the sexual activities of their wearers.[15] Ann Marie Rasmussen, placing them in the context of concerns voiced in contemporary German literature, wonders whether they stood for anxieties about unsettling groups of travellers (such as mercenary knights and acrobatic troupes) which were at once part of and external to the prevailing social order.[16] Nicola McDonald prefers not to close down on interpretation. Referring to the mounted vulva badge, she finds it

> defies modern interpretation. It cannot simply have been used to ward off evil; it seems purposefully ludic, yet we do not know the gender, age or social identity of its wearers, whether it was festally specific or quotidian [that is, designed for use on a particular feast day or for more daily use], whether it served to titillate or shock, excite or repulse; indeed, we do not really know whether it was obscene at all.[17]

The 'autonomous sexual organs' of the obscene badges have many parallels in bawdy medieval literature, especially the French fabliaux, some illuminated manuscripts of the *Roman de la Rose* and (most notoriously) the 1487 diatribe against witches, the *Malleus Maleficarum*.[18] Classicists are probably familiar with the phallic statues, relief sculptures and hanging 'tintinabulli' (bronze penises hung with small bells) which seem to have been ubiquitous in the classical Mediterranean.[19] What may not be so well known is that sex organ imagery also decorated the persons, houses and churches of later medieval north-western Europe. Phallic carvings have been found on the corbels of some French medieval churches, while some early modern farmhouses in Normandy and Wales had phallic emblems carved on fireplaces.[20] Michael Camille has noticed an abundance of bottom carvings in medieval French buildings, lay and ecclesiastical, especially in the thirteenth-century cathedral of St Stephen at Bourges. Bourges, he says, 'is a cathedral that is filled with bottoms', though art historians have not always been keen to acknowledge them.[21] The city was notorious to contemporaries as a den of sodomy, so that to say of a man that he was 'from Bourges' was to allege a passive homosexual role to him, though anus imagery on cathedrals also seems to have functioned as an architectural joke (for example, the anus at the 'fondement' [fundament or foundations] of the edifice.) Rather than read these as 'obscene', Camille contends, we do better to accept that explicit images of body parts and illicit sex were commensurate with rather than in opposition to sacred and moral messages. Bottoms and anuses were likely much more often on public view in the premodern than the modern world – medieval civic ordinances, for example, regularly complained about inhabitants shitting in the street or from open windows onto streets below – and it was not inconceivable that witty uses could be found for them in sacred symbolism. Anal imagery may have been meant to make viewers laugh, but with a deeper message attached.

Camille's is one of several recent pieces that employ the term 'obscene' for explicit medieval imagery even while querying whether it is appropriate or helpful to our interpretation.[22] *Sheela-na-gigs*, which decorated the walls, roofs, windows or doorways of several rural churches in Ireland and England (with handfuls of others in Wales, Scotland, France, Germany and Denmark), have prompted similar questions.[23] These sculptures, generally a stylized female form with gaping legs and prominent vulva, date from the twelfth to seventeenth centuries and by the late medieval period were also found on exterior walls of some Irish castles and tower houses, bridges, town walls and other public settings.[24] They are often bald with large staring eyes and commonly feature jug ears, lined faces, gritted teeth, shrunken breasts and emaciated torsos. Some reach down to pull open their vulvas. The usually rough standards of their carving suggest production by local amateurs rather than professional stonemasons, with a few exceptions. The antiquity of the term *Sheela-na-gig* is open to debate: it may be modern, attested in some nineteenth- and early-twentieth-century sources as equivalent to 'hag', which has come to

Image 11. This bottom carving is found below the 'misericord' or narrow shelf which provided relief to a member of the clergy required to stand for long periods during church services. Misericords were frequently carved with playful or scurrilous images apparently at odds with their sacred setting. Misericord of man with open legs in the air. Fourteenth century. St Mary's Church, Swine-in-Holderness, Yorkshire. *www.misericords.co.uk/ about_us.html.*

be widely applied to the lewd woman carvings, or it may have centuries-old connotations of feminine wantonness and giddy behaviour. Some posited Irish etymologies (*Sighle na gCioch* – 'the old hag of the breasts' – or *Sile-ina-Giob* – 'sheela [old woman] on her hunkers [haunches]') are highly dubious.[25] Modern scholars have offered diverse interpretative suggestions of their meaning and function. Sheelas have been viewed as guards against the evil eye, relics of Norse or Celtic fertility cults, representations of the Earth Mother or Mother-goddess, an incitement to marital sex, or even as *Ecclesia* (the institutional Church) giving birth.[26] One reading that emphasizes the paradoxical rather than mimetic qualities of medieval art suggests that the sheela could celebrate female virginity.[27] One more insistent scholarly view argues that far from being pagan these were Christian sculptures with the moral purpose of warning sinners to leave off lustful thoughts. Jørgen Andersen argues the sheelas derived from Romanesque 'exhibitionist' sculpture from eleventh- and twelfth-century French churches and Anthony Weir and James Jermin concur, placing sheelas alongside the 'coital couples, simple frontal nudes, anus-showers, acrobatic penis-swallowers, testicle-showers, [and] megaphallic men' widely found in Spanish and French church art. Through their very ugliness, they offered visual support for ecclesiastical castigation of lascivious sin.[28]

One point on which most recent scholars agree is that the sheelas are far from pornographic or even erotic.[29] In Barbara Freitag's words, the baldness, grimaces, awkward gestures, sagging vulvas or splayed legs could hardly 'be interpreted as either erotic or an invitation to lovemaking. In fact, they are not even remotely indicative of sex or sexual pleasure.'[30] She believes the posture is much more resonant of childbirth, and their dual imagery of fertility and grotesque emaciation served as an image of the interconnectedness of birth and death. The placement of these essentially pagan remnants on churches was, she suggests, congruent with medieval Christian habits of incorporating pre-Christian elements of imagery and ritual into Church practices.[31]

The images have the power to shock modern viewers – projection of the startling twelfth-century sheela from Kilpeck Church in Herefordshire, to take a good example, is bound to draw gasps from an unsuspecting audience – but perhaps in the medieval British Isles they were not obscene at all. The same could be said of the often highly explicit carvings itemised by Weir and Jermin, such as the image of a squatting, frontally exposed woman approached by a leering man with a giant erection which graces stonework at Whittlesford Church near Cambridge.[32] The *purpose* of such imagery cannot have been meant to arouse, given clerical casting of all sexual desire as at best venial and often mortally sinful (see ch. 1 above). Yet much as Weir and Jermin insist on the morally didactic nature of explicit sculpture, no one can be sure of the range of viewers' responses. Who can say that the parishioners of Whittlesford never sniggered or nudged one another as they passed that image of blatant lust or amused themselves through the longueurs of the liturgy with erotic daydreams? Later generations, especially after the mid-seventeenth century, often saw filth where medieval viewers were meant to read a moral message. An image of sodomites was cut off the north portal of Reims cathedral in the eighteenth century; the destruction of *Sheela-na-gigs* at the orders of bishops and provincial authorities began after about 1630.[33] According to Camille, defacement of sexually explicit images in medieval manuscripts may have begun in the fifteenth century when a more prudish mood is noticeable in new copies of old texts and the works of Christine de Pisan and Jean Gerson.[34] Perhaps censorship emerged earlier in learned than in popular culture. Regardless of the timing, it seems that medieval ethics and aesthetics tolerated sexually explicit scenes that some early modern and modern tastes would deem offensive.

It is intriguing how frequently medieval scholars, such as contributors to Jan Ziolkowski's collection on *Obscenity*, resort to the word 'taboo' despite their caution around use of the title word itself.[35] 'Taboo' is even less securely applicable to medieval culture than 'obscenity'. At least the latter existed in medieval Latin, though not in contemporary vernaculars; taboo was borrowed from Pacific languages (*tabu* in Melanesian and Micronesian, *tapu* in Polynesian languages with some other variants) and was introduced through Captain Cook's 1777 description of his experiences in Tonga.[36] Mary Caputi's oft-quoted suggestion that 'obscenity incorporates transgression and taboo' should be more carefully scrutinized before application to premodern contexts.[37] Medieval visual and literary culture suggests that the visually outrageous is not always taboo; indeed, it raises the possibility that in that era no subject was entirely off-limits. Not wishing to neutralize the impact of bottom carvings, lewd badges or *Sheelas* – for surely shock-value was central to any artistic power they possessed – we suggest that medieval culture could incorporate a kind of *useful* obscenity. Where more recent viewers have blanched at or destroyed explicit material, unable to cope with its bawdy challenge, medieval observers found moral, social and entertainment value therein.

Scenes of the torture and deaths of the 'virgin martyr' saints have been viewed as potentially pornographic by several scholars.[38] The martyrs – who included the Saints Margaret, Katherine, Agnes, Lucy, Christina and Cecilia, to name a few – are generally beautiful Christian maidens in their teens who attract the attention of pagan potentates and find themselves threatened with torture and death for refusing sexual advances. Stripped naked to the view of all bystanders, the virgins suffer violent assaults. In the *Golden Legend*, Margaret 'was hung upon a rack and was beaten with rods and then lacerated with iron rakes, so cruelly that her bones were laid bare and the blood poured from her body as from a pure spring'. Agatha was stretched on a rack and tortured, and when she avowed that 'These pains are my delight' her angry persecutor ordered her breast to be twisted and finally cut off.[39] Such moments of violence were regularly depicted in medieval art, such as in the magnificent *Belles Heures* made for Jean, Duc de Berry, but women are also known to have commissioned and owned texts of the lives.[40] Several scholars have objected that these scenes, far from paralleling bondage and torture elements in modern hard-core porn, should not be viewed sexually at all but rather as celebrations of the courage and determination of the Christian virgin.[41] However, the idea of 'parasexuality', developed by Peter Bailey for his study of nineteenth-century barmaids, allows one to grant erotic connotations to the legends without jumping to the conclusion that they were designed for male titillation. 'Para' has a dual meaning – 'almost' or 'beside' (as in paramedic), and 'against' or 'protection from' (as in parachute) – thus 'parasexuality' (in Bailey's account) is 'a secondary or modified form of sexuality', 'everything but' actual sex, and 'protection from or prevention from sexuality ... an inoculation in which a little sexuality is encouraged as an antidote to its more subversive properties'.[42] Viewing virgin martyrs as 'parasexual' allows us to acknowledge their 'obvious but safely anchored sexuality' and suggest that its deployment helped to make the ideals of virginity and premarital chastity more alluring for girls and women.[43]

Some of the most sexually explicit content is in late medieval Welsh poetry, which includes celebrations of penises and explicit sex in the form of riddles or multi-layered metaphors. Most authors, who wrote for oral performance in the halls of gentry patrons, were male, and their productions sometimes misogynistic ('A most bloody crotch, nasty lair of seven hundred fucks'), but the fifteenth-century amateur female poet Gwerful Mechain countered with poems that emphasized female ability to withstand and indeed outlast the efforts of any 'sturdy cock', and eulogized the vulva: 'You are a body of boundless strength, a faultless court of fat's plumage ... a girl's thick grove, circle of precious greeting, lovely bush, God save it.'[44] Yet erotic content was ubiquitous in medieval literature. One of the most popular poems of the Middle Ages was the lengthy, allegorical *Roman de la Rose*, which takes in numerous philosophical and moral themes along the way but culminates with a highly wrought scene of literal 'defloration', when the Lover 'plucks the rose'. In the early fifteenth century Christine de Pisan railed against the explicit language and anti-feminism of the poem, while Jean Gerson, Chancellor of the University of Paris, reviled its celebration of sexual pleasure, but with around 250 manuscripts surviving (comparable to *The Book of John Mandeville*, around 100 more than Marco Polo's *Description of the World*, around 170 more than the eighty surviving copies or fragments of Chaucer's *Canterbury Tales*) it appears that many readers did not agree. Boccaccio's *Decameron* was also widely read in its day and includes numerous bawdy stories, including several of lustful priests, monks and nuns.[45] Around 200 *pastourelles* – poetic pieces usually telling of a nobleman's seduction of a peasant girl, sometimes involving rape – survive in various European vernaculars.[46]

One can hardly get away with discussing medieval obscenity and erotic literature without mention of the fabliaux. Most of the poems, of which around 150 survive, are in Old French: short comic verses that deploy erotic themes and imagery for satirical and moral ends. As Norris Lacy has argued, the diversity among fabliaux is such that they resist generalization, but sex features as an almost universal feature of their narratives.[47] A popular example was *The Miller and the Two Clerks*, variously rendered in Jean Bodel's 'Gombert et les dues clers' (Gombert and the Two Clerks), Boccaccio's *The Decameron* (ninth day, sixth tale) and Chaucer's *The Canterbury Tales* ('The Reeve's Tale'), respectively. In a classic farce of mistaken identity, two young men (Cambridge students in Chaucer's version) lodge for a night with a married couple and their children (a young unmarried woman and a baby boy) all in one tiny bedroom. Under cover of darkness one visitor manages to have sex with the daughter while the other tricks the wife into bed with him by moving the baby's cradle to the side of his bed. The first young man returns to what he thinks is the bed he shares with the other guest to boast of 'fucking' the host's daughter, only to discover his bedfellow is the cuckolded host. Different versions of the story take up contrasting social messages. In Boccaccio's rendition the tale ends on an almost proto-feminist note as the wife cunningly manages to persuade her husband that he was so drunk he was mistaken to think any bed-hopping had occurred, and the daughter convinces her mother that the first man had been dreaming to think that he had slept with her. In Chaucer, however, the tale turns into a satire against the vulgarity and pretensions of the miller-host, his wife (the illegitimate daughter of a priest) and their ugly daughter.[48] Chaucer's 'Miller's Tale' also involves student and clerkly lust for a host's sexy wife (Alison), features raunchy adulterous couplings, and climaxes with arse-kissing, farting and bottom-burning.[49] Apart from Chaucer's renditions few fabliaux were written in Middle English, but in France they seem to have enjoyed great popularity among both aristocratic and middling-rank audiences.[50]

Many fabliaux display cynicism about human motives and in particular contain the theme of the 'cupidity and deceitfulness' of women: one finds women are 'fickle, shrewish, hypocritical, and ruled by an insatiable desire for sex', although, given the variety within the genre, some are to the contrary neutral or admiring in presenting women's cunning in deception or achieving sexual satisfaction.[51] Stupid husbands are the butt of many stories also, but this is not misandric humour; rather the point is that men should take their proper positions of authority over women.[52] The humour is often scatological and socially satirical as well as bawdy. They are notoriously 'conservative, even reactionary, compositions, using humour to preserve and enforce a status quo considered to be natural or even divinely instituted'.[53] R. Howard Bloch finds the fabliaux highly conventional in their presentation of erotic possibilities: 'The stock characters – the frivolous wives and lecherous priests, the innocent maidens and roguish seducers – are remarkably lacking in perverse imagination. In the fabliaux there is almost no suggestion of homosexuality [*sic*], sodomy, sadism, masochism, oral sex, incest, or transvestism.'[54] The fears that Bernadino of Siena expressed about the *Decameron* and *Corbaccio* – that they would lead their listeners to sodomitic vice – do not apply. Perhaps this helps account for the apparent popularity of the genre and appeal to respectable courtly and mercantile audiences.

The question of whether fabliaux ever served a pornographic purpose is more open to question. They are not 'pornography' as we know it, but Norris Lacy perhaps overdoes caution in stating that 'exciting prurient interest in the reader . . . is foreign to the purpose of the fabliaux'.[55] Sex acts are often dealt with in a few abrupt words ('he stretched her out in a bed, such that he fucked her three times'; a priest mounts and dismounts a woman 'in less time than it takes to sing a prayer'), though perhaps audiences could be roused even by such brief coital glimpses, mirroring a fabliau knight who 'almost swoons' with excitement while watching his squire screwing a lustful widow.[56] Many fabliaux, and the related genre of farce, employ straightforwardly coarse language (*foutre, cul, vit, coilles, con* [fuck, arse, prick, balls, cunt]), though it is arguable whether these terms were as offensive to contemporaries as their modern equivalents.[57] However, others prefer an extravagantly inventive range of metaphors. The sex act is variously 'a ferret's hunting for a rabbit in its lair, a squirrel's searching for nuts, . . . feeding or watering a horse, and . . . feeding a piglet'. Metaphors based on eating are also popular: to have sex is 'to have the final course, to have some bacon or a roast, to nurse, to be skewered or turned on the spit'. Then there are all manner of agricultural images: 'to seed a garden, to grind (grain), to plow a field, to reap, to crush grapes, to exercise pasture rights, to draw in the shafts', and other figures (for example 'to polish the ring', 'measure the length', 'get plugged', 'get greased' and to 'sharpen up with a stone'). Several metaphors emphasize male dominance or military allusions: 'to give justice, to dub, to take the maidenhood, to give the King's blows', to tear 'her banner to shreds'. Terms for sex organs are perhaps less inventive, including 'tool', 'thing', 'member', 'lance' and 'staff' for penis, though also 'squirrel', 'relic' and 'parsnip'; testicles are 'pendants', 'gear', 'bells', 'eggs', and so on; a vulva is a 'tool', 'hole', 'belly', 'gate', 'wound', 'fountain', but also 'glutton' or 'pig'.[58] The often playful language of the fabliaux is not usually coy or euphemistic; rather it testifies to the composer's skill and is central to the works' entertainment value.[59] If in early modern pornography sex became good to think with, in medieval literature sex was good to write with. Fabliaux and farce may contain pornographic elements, but they are nonetheless not *pornography* as we know it. Word play, social satire, anti-feminism, anti-clericalism and (in Charles Muscatine's view) an ethos of hedonistic materialism distance the genre from anything more familiar from modern cultures.

In concluding his influential work *Image on the Edge*, Camille suggests that the presence of scurrilous images such as hybrid creatures, monsters, scatological themes and sexual imagery in the margins of psalters, books of hours and other upright medieval texts was enabled, not repressed, by a dominant moral order. 'Representation has to be policed more thoroughly in the modern world, I would argue, precisely because the truths being articulated are no longer so fixed and stable as they once appeared to be. . . . Gothic marginal art flourished from the late twelfth to the late fourteenth century by virtue of the absolute hegemony of the system it wished to subvert.'[60] While it is hard to be sure of any subversive intentions of artists responsible for sexually explicit images in art and literature, Camille's point about the relative openness of medieval culture is valuable. It was not tolerant, open-minded or liberal in its responses to sexual expressions in the way we might expect of modern Western cultures, but in the absence of an autonomous discourse of pornography and under the sway of a Catholic Christian hegemony it was able to confront explicit sex and desire in a way that has, paradoxically, become more difficult in the modern era.

What we might call sex narratives also appear in a range of early modern sources – we have drawn on such texts throughout this book. Sexual scenarios were enacted in performance in popular entertainment, traces of which can be found in the early modern ballad.[61] 'The Wanton Widows Pleasant Mistake' was a song about a widow who slept with a carved model of her dead husband Simon until a suitor managed to substitute himself for the carving:

> She thought she toucht somthing that did not feel wooden
> For something she felt which was all soft and warm,
> Nay, at last something stir'd too; but thinking no harm
> She hug'd him still closer, resolv'd to be try'd,
> What had alter'd the wooden old Sim by her side.

The tale ends with the ravenous couple consuming vast quantities of food the following day, and burning the wooden Simon for fuel.[62] Or there was the song about the servant who carried her lover over her shoulders up to her room so that her employers would only hear one pair of footsteps: 'I first mean to try him, and if bad's his Gear, / I'd not have him, if he had ten Thousand a Year.'[63] Ballad after ballad told of single women craving married sex.

> My fancy it is set on fire,
> As Love-sick as another,
> I love to taste of Married joys,
> as well as did my Mother:
> you are the Engine that must quench
> the flames of my affection,
> If you will be my Husband dear,
> I'le follow your direction.[64]

They told of married women craving more sex. 'For he lyes by me like a cold stone in the Wall, / And will do a poor woman no kindness at all.'[65] '[G]ive me a Lord, if he can be had, / that will do it at Night and Noon.'[66]

We can imagine the dramatic potentials of the voyeuristic ballads in which the narrators recount watching lovers: 'I laid me down and I listen'd a while, / To hear if the Man could the Maiden beguile.'[67] Sometimes it was requited love, sometimes it was an unrequited passion that ended in tragedy, but the eye-witness fiction was a common technique to engage the reader or hearer.[68] A few authors recounted their own supposed experiences so that the audience became imagined spectators of predatory sexual behaviour.[69] 'Faint Heart Never Won Fair Lady', a particularly nasty ballad in Samuel Pepys's collection, described courtship that amounted to rape:

> Tickle her Knees, and something that's high'r,
> kissing and feeling go hand in hand;
> No Flesh and Blood but what will take fire,
> tho' she may seem at first to withstand ...
>
> When the Outworks they fairly are won,
> enter the Fort, it now is your own;
> Plunder and Storm it from Sun to Sun,
> Revel and Sport until weary grown:
> Fie Sir, why Sir, I'll sooner dye Sir,
> now are exchang'd for another Tone ...[70]

It is likely that the printed ballads are sanitized versions of oral renderings. Francis Place remembered ballads from the 1780s, including one about a man whose wife's sexual demands reduced him to a skeleton. Place recalled the rousing finale: 'For which I'm sure she'll go to Hell / For she makes me fuck her in churchtime.'[71] The performative elements have disappeared forever as far as the early modern material is concerned – the inflections of tone, the facial expressions, bodily gestures and rapport with the audience central to every oral rendition. 'Sandman Joe' had lines such as:

Why blast you, Sall, I loves you!
And for to prove what I have said,
This night I'll soundly fuck you.

Place recalled that the female performers who sang the song on Saturday nights outside an alehouse off London's Strand thrust their bodies backwards and forwards to mimic intercourse, and feigned sexual ecstasy: 'This used to produce great shouts of applause at the end.'[72]

Laura Gowing's work on litigation in early modern London suggests that popular culture contained a series of narratives of sex and marriage, romance, conflict and fantasy, found not only in the repertoire of chapbook, ballad and folk tale, but in the stories told by those who appeared in court. She writes of 'a stock of stories in both oral and printed form whose contexts, events, and results could be rifled for the tales told in everyday life, in the moments of dispute, and at court'.[73]

So there were interesting narrative loops between the various spheres of popular culture. The court records certainly contain sexual scripts more explicit than many literary sources, as we have seen elsewhere in this book. The Somerset innkeeper Mary Coomb was alleged in 1657 to have lain on the Axbridge road, calling 'all good fellows to come & occupie wth her', 'spreading of her leggs abroad, saying come play wth my Cunt and make my husband a cuckwalld'. She put her hand down the codpiece of a wheelwright's apprentice. She told the wheelwright, John Barber, that his wife was 'fucking with William Fry'. On one occasion, when Barber went to her house, 'shee shut ye door and would force me to be naught with her spreading of her legs & shewing her comoditie saying come rouge look thee here wt thou shalt play withall'. She said 'come & thrust thy pricke in my Cunt and there shalbe an end to all bussiness'.[74] These secular court records speak the sexually explicit in ways reminiscent of Goldberg's medieval Church courts, and to a similarly circumscribed audience. Presumably the recorded languages of such depositions reflected the sexual expression of city street and village lane. And the stories and scenarios may well have become part of popular sexual folklore. Whether they evidence 'vicarious frisson' or non-remarkable sexual banter is another issue.

The sixteenth and seventeenth centuries certainly witnessed the production of sexually explicit literature: for example, the sixteenth-century writing of the Italian Pietro Aretino, including the illustrations of his famous sexual postures/positions.[75] But the significant thing about this early erotica, if we can begin to employ that term, was that it was imbricated in other discourses. Ian Moulton has explained that Aretino's work was highly satirical and political.[76] Sarah Toulalan refers to seventeenth-century 'pornography' as similar but 'substantially different' from its modern variant: 'some texts can be seen as more "pornographic" than others, but *no* text, whatever its nature or origin, was entirely "pornographic" in the modern sense that it focused exclusively on repeated explicit descriptions of the sexual body and acts of sexual intercourse in a variety of sexual scenarios'.[77]

One of the imbricated discourses was reproduction: medical advice for the married has been described as 'concealed pornography'.[78] The young John Cannon was provoked to 'lustful thoughts' by *Aristotle's Master-piece* in the 1690s or 1700s, and masturbated after reading Nicholas Culpeper's *The Book of Midwifery*. It has earned him a place in Thomas Laqueur's famous history of masturbation.[79]

Or what we would term pornography was used to attack the crown, the Church or aspects of society; political pornography was employed during crises in seventeenth-century England, France and Sweden.[80] James Grantham Turner refers to the discursive merger between political comment and sexual arousal in literature in seventeenth-century England.[81] The sometimes sexually explicit prints produced in London in the long eighteenth century in their thousands represented the imagery of sex in the service of social satire: gentlemen lining up to have sex with Lady Worsley, for example, or the serial, sexual indiscretions of the Prince of Wales.[82] In France, much of this literature was so hostile to the Church that it seemed to be more about religion than sex. As Lynn Hunt has expressed it, 'between 1500 and 1800, pornography was most often a vehicle for using the shock of sex to criticize religious and political authorities'.[83]

Indeed pornography was used in the service of the Enlightenment. Darnton has described an eighteenth-century French work, *Thérèse Philosophe* (1748), where a Jesuit priest flogs a young woman while giving her a radical philosophy lesson:

> Strange as it may seem to a modern reader, the sex and the philosophy go hand in hand throughout the novel. The characters masturbate and copulate, then discuss ontology and morality, while restoring their forces for the next round of pleasure. This narrative strategy made perfect sense in 1748, because it showed how carnal knowledge could open the way to enlightenment. . . .[84]

Thérèse was a philosophical materialist: 'there is a need which the immutable laws of nature put in us; it is also in the hands of nature that we hold the remedy for alleviating that need'.[85] Such literature rarely existed purely for sexual titillation. Pornography as an end in itself is another recent construct.[86]

A distinction between the premodern erotic and the modern pornographic is certainly good to think the history of sex with but at the risk of obscuring the intricacies of both cultures. The contrasts and categorizations should not be overdrawn. Turner has shown that the libertine literature of early modern Italy, France and England, much of it expressed in the freedom of Latin before it was translated into the vernacular, came very close to representing sex for the sake of sex. Arousal was expected. However, sex, especially the sexual education of women, led to intellectual as well as bodily freedom, 'a bold new fusion of desire and reason'. The aim was to arouse passion to challenge convention – 'to form an erotic-didactic counter-discipline'.[87]

This pornography before pornography certainly provides an entry into the complexities and flexibilities of the sexual regime that we have been exploring. In a fascinating study Marta Vicente has unpacked an incident in eighteenth-century Madrid where an obscure Mexican priest and a more famous Mexican theologian, José Mariano Beristain, were detained by the Inquisition for reading the forbidden French book *Histoire de Dom Bougre* (1741). It was alleged that Beristain had read the text aloud – as he translated, using a 1784 edition – not only to his companion as he sat beside his bed late at night but also to actresses or prostitutes who visited the men in their room during the daytime. One of the witnesses was a button-maker who lodged in an adjoining room but hid (as in the very text they were reading) in a nearby closet to observe and listen to the nightly readings. Vicente has observed the multiple readings and hearings of this central text of Enlightenment pornography before pornography: the Censor who prepared himself with prayers and the rosary before embarking on the forbidden words; the landlady who only had access to the book's illustrations of varied fornications; the button-maker who heard the Spanish translation from the secrecy of the closet; the theologian who read the original French before translating and (if the reports were true) mimicking some of the described acts. 'They heard a prominent priest uttering sentences such as "there is no other God than sensual pleasure" and "If women would do justice to the penis they would call it God".'[88]

Or take the mingling of desires in John Cleland's *Fanny Hill or Memoirs of a Woman of Pleasure* (1748–9). When Fanny is introduced to sex it is with a woman, Phoebe, whom she shares a bed with, and although this woman (who introduced her to 'pleasure') was hired by a bawd to prepare her prostitutes, there is a hint that the woman has same-sex tastes. Cleland refers to

> the gratification of one of those arbitrary tastes for which there is no accounting. Not that she hated men or did not even prefer them to her own sex; but when she met with such occasions as this was, a satiety of enjoyments in the common road, perhaps to a secret bias, inclined her to make the most of pleasure wherever she could find it, without distinction of sexes.[89]

Phoebe is a kind of female rake, but the description hints at those who prefer the same sex. It also provides an example of female–female sex as titillation for the male reader and for female–female sexual desire as a preparation for male–female sex. Switching gender adds to the sexual confusion. The novel was written by a man yet takes the fictional form of a letter from one woman to another. The reader, of course, could be either male or female. This ventriloquism has unsettling effects.[90] When Fanny narrates descriptions of the male sexual organ and the impact that this has on her, it is actually a male (the author) who is describing the desire: 'Her sturdy stallion had now unbuttoned, and produced naked, stiff, and erect, that wonderful machine, which I had never seen before, and which, for the interest my own seat of pleasure began to take furiously in it, I stared at with all the eyes I had.'[91] When the text refers to 'a maypole of so enormous a standard . . . such a breadth of animated ivory, perfectly well turned and fashioned, the proud stiffness of which distended its skin', is the loving fascination with a lover's penis of 'smooth polish and velvet softness' Fanny's or Cleland's or the female or male reader's?[92]

Moreover, there is gender ambiguity in the described bodies of the young men, although their monstrous organ – 'that terrible spitfire machine' – resolves any questions of their masculinity.[93] Fanny's first love, a young rake, is beautiful in a way that a woman is beautiful.

> Figure to yourself, Madam, a fair stripling, between eighteen and nineteen, with his head reclined on one of the sides of the chair, his hair in disordered curls, irregularly shading a face, on which all the roseate bloom of youth and all the manly graces conspired to fix my eyes and heart. Even the languor and paleness of his face, in which the momentary triumph of the lily over the rose was owing to the excesses of the night, gave an inexpressible sweetness to the finest features imaginable: his eyes closed in sleep, displayed the meeting edges of their lids beautifully bordered with long eyelashes, over which no pencil could have described two more regular arches than those that graced his forehead, which was high, perfectly white and smooth; then a pair of vermillion lips, pouting and swelling to the touch, as if a bee had freshly stung them.[94]

These are descriptions of bodies that could be female if not for the references to a manliness that, to us, seems scarcely masculine: 'Oh! could I paint his figure as I see it now still present to my transported imagination! A whole length of an all-perfect manly beauty in full view. Think of a face without a fault, glowing with all the opening bloom and vernal freshness of an age in which beauty is of either sex.'[95]

Sex is invoked in this explicit novel but never named. The descriptions of Fanny's sexual awakening do not mention the word.[96] Other terms convey the experienced passion: 'licentious courses', 'a lambent fire', 'enflamed', 'her lascivious touches had lighted up a new fire that wantoned through all my veins', 'tears of pleasure gushed from my eyes and somewhat assuaged the fire that raged all over me'.[97] And yet desire is no less powerful for the absence of that word 'sex':

> I began to enter into the true unallayed relish of that pleasure of pleasures, when the warm gush darts through all the ravished inwards. What floods of bliss! what melting transports! what agonies of delight! too fierce, too mighty for nature to sustain: well has she therefore, no doubt, provided the relief of a delicious momentary dissolution, the approaches of which are intimated by a dear delirium, a sweet thrill, on the point of emitting those liquid sweets in which enjoyment itself is drowned, when one gives the languishing stretch-out, and dies at the discharge.[98]

Fanny's (women's) desire for men builds from an itch to a fire that has to be satiated. Annamarie Jagose has brilliantly dissected the descriptions of orgasm in this novel, where the female sexual passion associated with mutual orgasm at the moment of conception (the so-termed mingling of seed that is part of the one-sex model of the body) retains all its powers of erotic description but never actually displays the association with reproduction that historians have come to expect of premodern sex.[99] It is almost as though *Fanny Hill* represents a switching point in the history of pornography where sex associated with generation gives way to sex for the sake of sex; the languages and imagery of generative sexual pleasure are there in Fanny's narrative of pleasure but without reproductive consequences (apart from occasional subtextual references to bastardy).

But to think of some sexual moment of transformation would be to misunderstand the complexity of these premodern representations of bodily desire. The severance of pleasure from reproduction was an earlier phenomenon. For it is becoming increasingly clear that the valorization of female desire, originally associated with conception, rubbed off on libertine descriptions of female sexual engagements – with both men and women – *before* Fanny Hill. It is a feature of

the libertine and erotic literature of the seventeenth and early eighteenth centuries.[100] The female protagonists in *The School of Venus*
(1680) say that 'the Woman's pleasure is greater than the man's,
because she is not only pleased with her own fucking, but also hath
the satisfaction of perceiving her Gallant so extreamly delighted'. 'I
believe that we were created for fucking, and when we fuck, we
begin to live.'[101] Moulton sees early modern erotic writing's focus on
female sexual desire as one of its distinguishing characteristics, different to modern pornography's tendency to privilege male pleasure
and female passivity.[102]

The power of the penis, vaginal pleasure and the focus on male–
female and female–male sex should not deceive us into interpreting
Fanny Hill as a heterosexual text. Jagose is critical of those who
assume a heterosexuality that was in the process of its constitution.[103]
The bodies in this text are not modern bodies. Premodern, humoral
theories of bodily temperature explain much of what occurs. Fanny's
heat, long after she has been whipped, is a build-up of desire due to
the stimulation of her blood flow rather than a masochistic sexual
response; hence the delay in the arousal and quest for satisfaction.

We have seen that what we have termed pornography before pornography provides an entry into the sexual regime of the early
modern world. But pornography can also be invoked to demonstrate
the sexualization of *modern* culture. It was to be shaped by and
helped to shape heterosexuality, male homosexuality and lesbianism.
It, like postmodern sexual culture, fragmented into its multiple identities: significantly, Lisa Sigel's recent collection of scholarly articles on
modern European pornography finishes with transsexual pornography and its presence on the Internet.[104] The range of pornography
now is virtually limitless. Computer-generated imagery can replace
human bodies. Hard-core, cartoon imagery can show what film cannot
show and indicate female pleasure in a way impossible in filmed sex
acts. Most commentators would agree that we are now in a totally
different period in the history of pornography, what some historians
have called a 'pornographication' of mainstream culture.[105]

Linda Williams has described the current situation, the recent historical shift in pornography's visibility, as on/scenity. Obscenity, the
use of sexual images and scenarios that were previously obscene –
that is, literally off-stage – has been replaced by on/scenity, where they
are now on-stage in the public domain.[106] And Williams provides data
for the sheer volume of pornography in the early twenty-first century.[107]

But if we step back to the premodern period, on-scene could almost
be a description of its written, spoken and visual imagery – what Tim

Image 12. This drawing comes from the historical borderland between premodern and modern pornography. Apart from its phallocentrism, the image is interesting for its rendition of group and male–female oral sex as well as the promise of female-same-sex coupling, with one woman reaching up to kiss the other. Indeed, with its depiction of cunnilingus and the lure of woman–woman sex it may hint at the supplanting of the primacy of the male member rather than its celebration. Baron Jean-Baptiste Regnault, *A Phallic Rite*. Late eighteenth/early nineteenth century. Ink and sepia wash on paper. The Kinsey Institute for Research in Sex, Gender, and Reproduction.

Hitchcock has called a public culture of sex.[108] As we have discussed, sexually explicit themes, depictions and descriptions abound: in the court records of marital dispute, pastoral manuals, lewd books, comic tales, poems, medieval manuscripts, printed imagery and text; on pilgrim badges, in church and domestic carvings and satirical prints. The scripts of medieval examinations for impotence, where women, probably prostitutes, bared their bodies and handled the alleged impotent's genitals and incited him to sex in an effort to test his manhood, were, Goldberg muses, pornographic in a literal sense given that they wrote about prostitutes: 'each in turn fondled and held the yard and testicles, and displayed their breasts . . . and, embracing the same John around the neck, kissed him and spoke various jestful words . . . telling him that he should for shame show these women his manhood if he were a man'.[109]

This on-scenity, however, was not pornography as the modern world has come to know it. In the French impotence trials vaginas were prodded with fingers and wax phalluses to ascertain virginity, penises were fondled and measured to determine potential potency, and couples were monitored to see if sexual congress had occurred. These were public displays of sex in front of midwives, surgeons and physicians, written up in reports to be pondered over by those in judgment, and often combined with the equally intrusive verbal examinations of lawyers and judges. They were then sometimes relayed in print and gossip to a wider audience.[110]

Are they pornographic? Some of the female cases come close. Louis Servin, writing in 1587 and 1627 under the pseudonym of Anne Robert, was unambiguously prurient, despite his/her protestations of the shamefulness of the described spectacle:

> Would you have this spectacle depicted in words? Forgive me, gentle reader whose ears are chaste, if in describing a shameful matter my words do reek of I know not what unchaste and shameful thing. A maid is obliged to lie outstretched to her full length on her back, with her thighs spread to either side so that those parts of shame, that Nature has wished to conceal for the pleasure and contentment of men, are clearly visible. The midwives, matrons all, and the physicians, consider these with much earnest attention, handling and opening them. The presiding judge adopts a grave expression and does hold back his laughter. The matrons in attendance remember old fires, long since cooled. The physicians, according to their age, do recall their first flushes of vigour. The others, seeming busy, do gorge themselves on the vain and futile spectacle. The surgeon, holding an instrument that is fashioned expressly for the purpose, called *the mirror of the womb*, or with a male member made of wax or other matter, explores the entrance to the cavity of Venus, opening, dilating, extending and enlarging the parts.

The maid abed does feel her parts itch to such a degree that, even if she be a virgin when examined, she will not leave other than corrupted and spoiled. It would be shameful to speak further of this.[111]

This imputed arousal implicated the examined ('her parts itch') as well as her examiners, and the text's author likewise 'gorges' himself on the 'unchaste and shameful thing'. Presumably he anticipates that his readers will also participate in the self-righteous titillation. However, the male trials were more likely to provoke jocularity than carnality: 'just looking at you makes me wilt', retorted an early eighteenth-century Marquis to his male examiners who were questioning his virility.[112] 'What penis', argued the lawyer of an Amiens draper in the 1730s, 'however swollen it might be, . . . would not wilt on the very spot' when 'handled and examined' by one physician while another held a candle to observe? 'Did this oracle from Bourges flatter himself that he was of sufficiently comely appearance and had a sufficiently enlivening hand to stroke the imagination of a man of modesty?'[113] These heteroerotic and homoerotic encounters are of failed masculinity and femininity. Moreover, their raison d'être is cheated fertility. The propagation of the species, the virgin who remains a virgin, and the penis that fails to respond are not exactly modern pornographic tropes.

Arousal was expected in some early modern forms. But this excitation of the senses was to challenge convention rather than merely aid masturbation or serve as Carter's propaganda for fucking: such pornography, it seems, was an important servant of the Enlightenment. The sexually explicit, we have seen, was often entangled with other discourses: medical advice, social or political comment, anti-clericalism. But more importantly, much of the premodern on-scene may not have been sexually arousing, erotic – or even interpreted as obscene. Some might seek a term to describe materials that ranged from the incitement of arousal to explicit texts and images that were not necessarily erotic; others will be content to avoid gathering such scattered materials under a generic heading. In the meantime, 'before pornography' will have to do.

Epilogue: Sex at Sea?

When the western voyagers, missionaries, settlers and traders met the Oceanic peoples of the Pacific in the eighteenth and nineteenth centuries, it was as much an 'exploration and exchange' of sex as any of the other multiple motivations that lay behind the contact between European and indigene. It was, as in the title of Lee Wallace's book on the subject, a sexual encounter.[1] The Europeans, Greg Dening once observed, found themselves 'in a sea of sexuality'.[2] There is no denying that for most of these male voyagers the sex encounter was with women. Historians have enjoyed toying with such possibilities. Nails were exchanged for sex, so many so that at times the ships seemed in danger of demolition. When the *Dolphin* visited Tahiti in 1767, two-thirds of the men had to sleep on the deck because their hammock nails had gone on food and sex. 'Young girls only wanted a Long Nail each.' Four inches was not enough; 'some was so Extravagant as to demand a Seven or nine Inch Spick'.[3] As Roy Porter joked, sailors could get a screw for a nail.[4]

Journals of early voyages read like fantasies of carnal excess. Louis Antoine de Bougainville (1768) wrote of the Tahitians as a people who 'breathe only rest and sensual pleasures. Venus is the goddess they worship.'[5] 'The chief offered me one of his wives, young and fairly pretty, and the whole gathering sang the wedding anthem. What a country! What a people!'[6] 'It is the true Utopia.'[7] In 1773, 'Encouraged by the lucrative nature of this infamous commerce, the New Zealanders went through the whole vessel, offering their daughters and sisters promiscuously to every person's embraces, in exchange for our iron tools, which they knew could not be purchased at an easier rate.'[8] On Easter Island, local women had sex with the sailors

Image 13. An image that hints at some of the pleasures available in Tahiti. Note that the male body is on display more than the female. John Keyes Sherwin, *A Dance in Otaheite*. 1784. Engraving, 26.5 × 41 cm. National Library of Australia.

in the shade of the famous Easter Island statues.[9] One woman had repeated sex with sailors on board the *Resolution*. The diarist George Forster compared her to the classical figure Messalina, of whom Juvenal said, 'She went away, exhausted by the men but unsatisfied.'[10] In Tahiti, women and girls boarded the visiting ship: 'The decks were ... crouded with natives, among whom were several women who yielded without difficulty to the ardent sollicitations of our sailors.' When the same men returned to Tahiti in 1774, the women again came aboard: 'the excesses of the night were incredible'.[11]

The later voyages of the *Resolution* and *Discovery* continued in a similar vein. David Samwell, the surgeon of the *Discovery* on James Cook's third voyage, noted the attractions of the women of the Pacific Islands: 'We found no great Difficulty in getting the Girls on board, for the Charms of a Hatchet, a Shirt or a long nail they could no more withstand than we could theirs which were far from despicable.'[12] In Tonga in 1777 'we had constant Intercourse with the Women both on board the Ships and on Shore, & the price was a Shirt or a Hatchet for the Night. . . . They are of a very amorous Complexion & highly deserving of what they got.'[13] It is significant that Samwell's 'short

Specimen' of the Tongan language included the words for a woman's breast, 'make me a present' and venereal disease.[14] The references to sexual exchange with women are numerous on this voyage, and men deserted to be with female companions. The women of the Sandwich Islands (Hawaii) were considered 'to have no more Sense of Modesty than the Otaheite women, who cannot be said to have any'.[15]

It was a sex tour, eighteenth-century style, though this is not an interpretation favoured by Cook scholars. At Nootka Sound, because the sailors had used up all their axes and linen in the Pacific Islands, they had to trade pewter plates for sex.[16] In Unalaska,

> If we may be allowed to judge from the short acquaintance we had with these people we should conclude that the Chastity of the Women whether married or unmarried is an object of small Concern to the Men, for we did not perceive that the least Restraint was imposed upon any of them, for taking them promiscuously according to our fancies we never met with an unkind fair one if We had but a leaf of Tobacco in our Hands.[17]

Cook repeatedly attempted to limit sexual traffic in an effort to contain venereal disease; but the descriptions of opposite-sex promise continue.[18] In Hawaii, 'When any one of us sees a handsome Girl in a Canoe that he has a mind to, upon waving his Hand to her she immediately jumps overboard & swims to the Ship, where we receive her in our arms like another Venus just rising from the Waves.' 'We live now in the greatest Luxury, and as to the Choice & number of fine women there is hardly one among us that may not vie with the grand Turk himself.'[19] Even when the British were engaged in warfare with the Hawaiians, women were coming on board. And when the slain Captain Cook's body was returned in pieces to his ship, Hawaiian women were still visiting at night.[20]

A decade later, William Bligh was convinced that the sexual allure of indigenous women was a principal motivation for the mutineers of the *Bounty* in 1789:

> I can only conjecture that they have Idealy assured themselves of a more happy life among the Otaheitans than they could possibly have in England, which joined to some Female connections has most likely been the leading cause of the Whole business.
>
> The Women are handsome, mild in their Manners and conversation, possessed of great sensibility, and have sufficient delicacy to make them admired and beloved ... what a temptation it is to such Wretches when they find it in their power, however illegally it can be got at, to fix themselves in the midst of plenty in the finest Island in the World where they need not labour, and where the alurements of disipation are more than equal to any thing that can be conceived.[21]

It is difficult to unravel the issue of agency in these relationships. As Kathleen Wilson has expressed it, what for the voyagers was traffic in women was for the Polynesians traffic in European men in terms of supernatural access or material gain.[22] Certainly, this exchange was far from romantic. Male kin exploited the situation, as suggested in the description of Maori interactions above.[23] The traffic also included venereal disease. The surgeon Samwell recognized in 1777 that venereal disease had been left in Tonga during the previous voyage of the *Resolution* and *Discovery*, and saw its effects, including some people who had lost their noses.[24] Bligh also discovered that traces of the *Resolution*'s visit to Tahiti consisted of more than the name 'Lieut Watts' on an old calico shirt that presumably had been traded for sex.

> Among the Women who were now come on board to the Men, I found one who had been on board the Resolution in 1777. She was a shrewd Girl, & among other questions put to her, were, if the Venereal disease was still among them. I was instantly answered in the affirmative, and such a string of descriptive circumstances of the havock it had made came out, as shocked me to the greatest degree. Many fine Girls she said had died of it, and described the many forms this dreadful disease puts on as left me no room to doubt of the truth of the relation. . . .[25]

Such sexual interactions are depressingly predictable by the early nineteenth century. Like others before him, the Russian physician and naturalist G. H. von Langsdorff recorded the allure of the Marquesan women and their trade in sex with sailors. Their 'pantomimic gestures, by which we were sufficiently given to understand that they were making us the most liberal and unreserved offers of their charms', included those of very young girls of eight or nine years old. 'We were not, however, allowed a long time to make philosophical observations upon our new Venuses; for one after another they vanished, hand-in-hand with the sailors, to the interior of the ship, while the goddess of night threw her dark veil over the mysteries that were celebrated.'[26] The American Captain David Porter made similar observations during a voyage in 1812–14. The female inhabitants of Madison's Island (in the Marquesas) 'possess much cunning, much coquetry, and no fidelity'. 'Virtue among them, in the light which we view it, was unknown, and they attached no shame to a proceeding which they not only considered as natural.' It was a society where 'the girls, from twelve to eighteen years of age, rove at will', a sexual culture of 'unbounded pleasure', 'unrestrained by shame or fear of the consequences', whose young women lived in a state of 'the most pleasurable licentiousness'. Unsurprisingly, the visitors made the most of this paradise:

> With the common sailors and their girls, all was helter skelter, and promiscuous intercourse, every girl the wife of every man in the mess, and frequently of every man in the ship; each one from time to time took such as suited his fancy and convenience, and no one among them formed a connexion which was likely to produce tears at the moment of separation.[27]

The convict settlement of colonial Australia in the late eighteenth and early nineteenth centuries also had a sexual history, and again most of the interaction involved opposite-sex attraction. As Joy Damousi has shown, male officers and diarists were both attracted and repelled by the sexual nature of their female charges on the convict ships to Australia and in the populations under their command.[28] The dangerous allure of female convicts fascinated upper-class men. Lt Ralph Clark wrote of the depraved convict women, consorting with the sailors during the voyage of the *Friendship* in 1787–8, 'damed whores. . . . I never could have thought that there wair So many abandond wreches in England, the[y] are ten thousand time worse than the men.'[29] Clark's diary contrasts the absent wife at home – 'the most tender best and Beautifulest of her Sex', 'dear Heavenly woman the best of wives the most Sinceerest friend and the kindest of Mothers' – with the female depravity and temptation in the decks below.[30] He was equally appalled by the behaviour in the new settlement, condemning sexual interaction in the women's convict camp at Port Jackson in 1788: 'a good God what a Seen of Whordome is going on there. . . . I hope the Almighty will keep me free from them as he has heather to done.' 'I would call it by the Name of Sodem for ther is more Sin committed in it than in any other part of the world.'[31] But this did not stop Clark and other officers in the colony from having convict mistresses and illegitimate offspring from those relationships.[32]

So there were many examples of what we have come to call 'heterosexuality before heterosexuality' in these Oceanic encounters on the cusp of modernity. Shocked contemporaries disapproved of the voyagers' easy acceptance of the sexual excess that they encountered. John Hawkesworth's 1770s account of Cook's voyages was received in some quarters as tantamount to pornography.[33]

Nineteenth-century commentators (especially missionaries) were particularly so affected. An outraged reviewer in a nineteenth-century periodical refused to pollute his pages with the descriptions in Porter's *Journal of a Cruise Made to the Pacific Ocean* (1822). Porter replied by simply referring him to the voyages of Cook.[34] Sometimes the observers were so horrified by what they found that the act remains undescribed, outside linguistic formulation – other than in the attention drawn by this very denial. The missionary C. S. Stewart recounted his reaction to the dance and song of the *koika*, witnessed in the Washington Islands in the late 1820s:

> In almost every instance, language and allusions of the most objectionable character ... and many are abominable, almost beyond belief. ... Before the grossness of one half that was forced upon me had passed in view, I was compelled in the thoughts of my very soul to exclaim, 'Stop – it is enough!' but I had gone beyond the point of escape, and the whole truth, in its abominable details, was riveted upon me.
>
> There was less of licentiousness in the dance than I had expected; but in a hundred things else, there were such open outrages on all decency, that I hurried away in a horror of disgust, with a heart too much humbled for the race to which I belong, and too much depressed at the depravity and guilt of man, to think or feel upon any other subject. ... So completely was I prostrated, that, for the first time in my life, I believe ... I looked to heaven, and exclaimed, 'Oh! why, why was sin ever permitted to enter a world otherwise so fair!'[35]

William Ellis stumbled over his depiction of the practices and ceremonies of the Arioi society of Tahiti:

> And these were abominable, unutterable. ... The mysteries of iniquity, and acts of more than bestial degradation, to which they were at times addicted, must remain in the darkness in which even they felt it sometimes expedient to conceal them. I will not do violence to my own feelings, or offend those of my readers, by details of conduct, which the mind cannot contemplate without pollution and pain.[36]

All this righteous indignation indicates that there was a counter-romance amidst the fantasies of opposite-sex attraction. For these sexual explorers also went dizzy at the thought of a range of other encounters.[37] The Pacific was far more than a 'heterosexual paradise'.[38] Damousi has shown examples of woman-to-woman sexual contact in the female factories in colonial Australia: of one woman 'having connexion' with another with her hand; of women acting in 'the capacity of men' by 'artificial means' of a 'mechanically secured ... substitute ... male organ'; of a 'man-woman' and the women who 'bestowed their affections' on her, 'decorating themselves, cleaning themselves scrupulously and making themselves as attractive as they can'. As the reader will know, we would question whether this same-sex attraction is best described as 'lesbianism' (and the 'man-woman' as the prototype of the butch as Damousi suggests) or as what contemporaries called 'licentious and unnatural practices' and 'depraved habits'.[39] But the existence of female–female desire certainly accompanied the sort of opposite-sex activity outlined above.

While the most noticeable feature of the literature that we have been discussing is its relative silence on female same-sex desire, the thick descriptions of male desire for the bodies of women and girls are frequently accompanied by even thicker descriptions of masculine flesh. '[H]is features were so mild, comely, and at the same time majestic.' 'His whole body was remarkably strong and heavily built, so that one of his thighs nearly equalled in girth our stoutest sailor's waist. His ample garments, and his elegant white turban, set off his figure to the greatest advantage.'

> They were all without cloathing, having nothing but a small piece of cloth to cover the loins. They were tall, and extremely well limbed ... among the youths, who were not yet marked or tattowed, it was easy to discover beauties singularly striking, and often without a blemish, such as demanded the admiration of all beholders. Many of them might be placed near the famous models of antiquity, and would not suffer in the comparison.

These were George Forster's descriptions of Tahitian and Marquesan men in the 1770s.[40] However, there are many other such images. Samwell's account of Cook's third voyage describes both the Hawaiian *aikane* ('their business is to commit the Sin of Onan upon the old King') and the chiefs' assumption that the Europeans similarly kept young men on board for sexual purposes. One man – in a strange attempt to reverse the flow of sexual commerce – offered six hogs to the captain for 'a handsome young fellow': 'such is the strange depravity of these Indians'.[41]

Bligh's *Log of the Bounty* contains several descriptions of male bodies in Tahiti. When a group of travelling performers danced the Heivah before him in 1789, the girls' performance was short: they took off their dresses. However, the men embarked on elaborate manipulations and distortions of their genitalia, 'making at the same time wanton and lascivious motions'. The audience were highly amused, but Bligh 'desired them to desist'. This was an excess of masculinity: one man extended his penis with a ligature, 'swelled and distorted out into an erection'; another stretched his genitalia 'untill they were near a foot in length'.[42] These bodies performed femininity as well as masculinity. Bligh's ethnography contains a description of the Tahitian *mahu*. The *mahu* were 'particularly selected when Boys and kept with the Women solely for the carnesses [*sic*] of the men. ... those who are connected with him have their beastly pleasures gratified between his thighs, but are no further Sodomites as they all positively deny the Crime'. I referred earlier to dizziness, but

Bligh was actually rather matter-of-fact about his inspection of the body of one of these men:

> the Young Man took his Hahow or Mantle off.... He had the appearance of a Woman, his Yard & Testicles being so drawn in under him, having the Art from custom of keeping them in this position.... On examining his privacies I found them very small and the Testicles remarkably so, being not larger than a boys of 5 or 6 Years Old, and very soft as if in a State of decay or a total incapacity of being larger, so that in either case he appeared to me [as] effectually a Eunuch as if his stones were away. The Women treat him as one of their Sex, and he observed every restriction that they do, and is equally respected and esteemed.[43]

Then there are the bodies of the mutineers, also described in the log. Fletcher Christian was 'Strong Made. A Star tatowed on his left Breast, and tatowed on the backside.' Other mutineers were similarly profiled as tattooed on the backside or elsewhere: 'Very much tatowed on the backside and Several other places.'[44] Bligh's book contains a log of possibilities of male-to-male desire and chartings of the masculine (and unmasculine) body seemingly at odds with the focus on women outlined earlier.

The Pacific was a world of naked and inscribed male bodies; the gaze is drawn to thighs, loins, penises and backsides – including those of the European visitors. When Roy Porter discussed sexual interaction between European and Tahitian in the eighteenth century, he simply assumed heterosexuality. Yet we have seen that Oceanic sexual encounters were more complex than that. Ironically, one of the descriptions quoted by Porter describing Tahitian beauty, and comparing it to that of the Greeks, was actually describing the bodies of males not females.[45]

The nineteenth-century travel accounts that had recounted the beauty and sexual accessibility of Oceanic women *also* contained descriptions of male adoration. Although Captain David Porter thought Marquesan women beautiful, he considered their attractiveness as inferior to that of the men, who were 'as beautiful as those of any part of the world'.[46] Langsdorff's *Voyages and Travels* (1813) actually contains more visualization and dwelling upon male bodies than those of the women. His discourse upon the beauty of the people of the Marquesas starts with that of the men: 'such general beauty and regularity of form, that it greatly excited our astonishment. Many of them might very well have been placed by the side of the most celebrated chef-d'oeuvres of antiquity, and they would have lost nothing by the comparison.'[47] Langsdorff and his companions spent

Image 14. The male body is even more central to this image. Note the muscular backs and buttocks. Samuel Middiman, *An Offering Before Capt. Cook in the Sandwich Islands*. 1784. Hand-coloured engraving, 26 × 41 cm. National Library of Australia.

much time admiring and measuring male bodies. One man was found to be in direct proportion to 'the Apollo of Belvedere ... that masterpiece of the finest ages of Grecian Art, in which is combined every possible integer in the composition of manly beauty'.[48] They recorded the statistics of every body part but the genitals.[49] Initially, they touched too, breaching taboo: 'At our first arrival we were very desirous of stroking our hands over the heads of some of the handsomest men.'[50] In short, there is a male preoccupation with the form of its own sex. The engravings of partly clothed, heavily tattooed, male bodies in Lee Wallace's monograph on male homoeroticism in the Pacific come from Langsdorff.[51] Langsdorff's account also contains a description of same-sex sexual practice, though, as with the *mahu*, one of the parties is rendered feminine. On the island of Oonalashka, in the Aleutian Islands (between North America and Russia):

> Boys, if they happen to be very handsome, are often brought up entirely in the manner of girls, and instructed in all the arts women use to please men: their beards are carefully plucked out as soon as they begin to appear, and their chins tattooed like those of the women: they wear ornaments of glass beads upon their legs and arms, bind and cut their hair in the same manner as the women, and supply their places with

the men as concubines. This shocking, unnatural, and immoral practice, has obtained here even from the remotest times; nor have any measures hitherto been taken to repress and restrain it: such men are known under the name of Schopans.[52]

Langsdorff thought that 'male concubines' were even more common on the island of Kodiak.[53]

An edited collection on Pacific interactions has cleverly referred to Europeans 'at sea' in more ways than one when it came to the sexual and other mores with which they had to deal.[54] Serge Tcherkézoff has proposed that the offering of young women to eighteenth-century western visitors in both Samoa and Tahiti was a coerced ritual sacrificial offering rather than a proclamation of female sexual freedom. In Samoa, 'The Europeans were seen as "*Papalagi*", beings in some measure endowed with super-human powers. The young girls were presented to them, perhaps according to a mythical logic of theogamy, the strategy being to bring about the creation of sacred progeny.'[55] Building on Tcherkézoff, the historical anthropologist Anne Salmond has emphasized the depth of sexual misunderstanding in early Tahitian–European cultural contact. Of Bougainville's visit in 1768 she writes: 'the islanders frequently offered the French young girls to sleep with, no doubt seeking to acquire the *mana* and *ora* (life force) of these sacred strangers, enhancing the fertility and power of their lineages'.[56] Ritual displays of female power were sexualized either as sexual invitation or primitive innocence. Intended ridicule was misread. Invocation of the gods was seen as lasciviousness and cosmology interpreted as carnality.[57]

However, we contend that the gaps of understanding were not quite as wide as Tcherkézoff and Salmond suggest. At least one of the European participants in Tahitian public copulation was aware of its link to fertility: 'If wise people carry out these ceremonies in association with the planting of seeds,' the Prince of Nassau mused in his journal, 'why should the reproduction of the finest species of things ever created not also be a public festival?'[58] But the French certainly interpreted such things in terms of the precepts of the Enlightenment. 'Happy nation that does not yet know the odious names of shame and scandal.'[59] Charles-Félix-Pierre Fesche, another journal keeper on Bougainville's voyage, mused about moral relativism in his entry concerning public sex:

> however great the ardour that drives you, it is very difficult to overcome so quickly the ideas with which you have been brought up. The corruption of our morals has made us discover evil in an act where these people rightly find nothing but good. It is only someone who is doing

or thinks he is doing evil who fears the light. We hide in order to carry
out such a delicate action, they do it in public and often. Several French-
men less susceptible to delicacy, found it easier, that same day, to shrug
off these prejudices.[60]

Wallace has also suggested the novelty of the encountered sexual
worlds:

> Male homosexuality, such as we have come to understand it, was con-
> stituted in no small part through the European collision with Polynesian
> culture, whose systems and activities of sexual attraction and desire
> were so different, or different in such a way, as to throw the European
> observer into positions of reaction, denial, or injunction that helped to
> reify modern categories of sexual identity.

Critical of the manner in which the voyages to the Pacific read as
'confirmation of an unspoken heterosexual warrant', Wallace notes:
'One of the most far-reaching consequences of this blindness to the
hybridized structure of sexual contact and sexual colonization is its
failure to recognize the disruptive force of Polynesian sexuality within
European discourse.'[61]

While not disputing Wallace's picture of the homoerotic strands in
the supposed heterosexuality of the European encounter with the
Pacific and other geographical areas – for our account draws heavily
on her work – we are less persuaded by the novelty of the meeting.
We should think of a hybrid rather than homogeneous European
sexuality.[62] Wallace observes of Bligh, for instance, that the 'newly
discovered behaviors' that he found could not be placed within his
European framework; she refers to 'sexual possibilities between men
that cannot be recuperated to extant European models'.[62] Yet sex
between the thighs and even the ambiguous figure of the man-woman
were certainly not outside the ambit of European erotics. As we have
seen in the pages of this book, there was little that Bligh found that
did not have a European parallel (apart from the deeper cultural
differences discussed by Tcherkézoff and Salmond). It is fascinating
that one of the supposed manservants on Bougainville's voyage
turned out to be a woman in disguise, Jeanne Baret, accompanying
her lover, the naturalist Philibert Commerson (she is thus claimed as
the first woman to voyage around the world), and that the Tahitians
detected 'his' femininity and, it seems, saw him as a *mahu*.[64]

In fact, the uneven blend of heteroerotic and homoerotic that
characterized the sexual islands and continents that we have been
charting was not so out of alignment with desires and practices in
Europe and North America, what has been termed an Atlantic sexual
culture encompassing the contact points between Europe, the Ameri-

cas and the Caribbean.[65] The Spanish colonization of Latin America was a sexual colonization too.[66] This is not to deny that Europeans imposed their own meanings on the behaviour that they observed. Pete Sigal has unravelled the complexities of Spanish translations of the bodies and acts observed in sixteenth-century Mexico.[67] However – for the purposes of our argument – it matters less that the translations of Mexican practices and roles were displaced or imperfect and that the Spanish could never grasp the real meanings of *cuiloni*, *xochihua* and *patlachuia* than the fact that there was a sufficient range of Spanish bodies and erotics to displace them in: as the *puto* (faggot), *sométtico* (sodomite), transvestite, hermaphrodite and tribade. Ward Stavig detects similarities between the sexual practices of Spain and indigenous Peru, for example.[68] Ramón Gutiérrez has observed that berdache, the name given to the North and South American men forced to adopt the clothing and social and sexual roles of women, was based on the Arabic term *bradaj*, which meant male prostitute, 'something Europeans were quite familiar with in the fifteenth and sixteenth centuries'.[69] The confessional manuals used in the eighteenth-century Spanish missions of California likewise indicated a familiarity with the combinations of potential sinning: 'Have you sometimes thought about doing bad things for pleasure with a woman, with women, with a man, with men?'[70]

When Europeans interpreted the sexual cultures of others, they saw them much as they would in Europe. Bligh discussed the range of sexual practices that he encountered, interpreting them as the exaggerated tendencies of the whole culture rather than the behaviour of a specific group in society (we need to focus here not on the *mahu* but on the Tahitian men who had sex with them). Male-to-male sex was discussed in exactly the same context as male-to-female sex.

> It is strange that in so prolific a country as this, Men should be led into such sensual and beastly acts of gratification, but perhaps no place in the World are they so common or so extraordinary as in this Island. Even the mouths of Women are not exempt from the polution, and many other as uncommon ways have they of gratifying their beastly inclinations.[71]

Langsdorff considered the prevalence of what he called male concubines on the island of Kodiak to be a function of the dissolute mix between the local population and Europeans employed by the Russian–American company engaged in the fur trade, a result of the general collapse in moral restraint. Rather than a separate category of sexuality, the practice was part of a continuum of sexual excess, including incest and 'the most promiscuous intercourse between the sexes'. Indeed, male concubinage and male–female intercourse are paired within the same sentence in Langsdorff's account.[72]

Even the missionary William Yate, dismissed in 1837 by the Church Missionary Society for his sexual behaviour in New Zealand, described his desires in terms of the framework of marriage as he urged a young Maori male convert to mutual masturbation: 'He said to me, All Europeans act thus while they are single men. Then because they sleep with their wives this practise is left off. But as for me my wife is this, a hand.'[73] Yate, whose activities went far beyond mere admiration of the physical beauty of Maori males, allegedly had sexual relations with as many as a hundred of his young indigenous converts, exchanging tobacco for male sexual favours – mutual masturbation, oral sex and sex between the thighs – much as generations of voyagers had traded for access to female bodies. This is not to say that Yate was responsible for introducing novel sexual practices to an innocent population; there was a Maori term for male mutual masturbation, *titoitoi*, in its shortened form, and the depositions of the young men share none of the missionaries' speechlessness about indescribable acts.[74]

To make sense of these Oceanic cross-cultural encounters from Europe's perspective we need only take a further step back in time to the eighteenth-century voyagers' own recent history, where, as we saw of the sexual landscape of Europe *c.* 1100–1800, we find 'heterosexuality' that is inexplicable without including the homoerotic, and homoeroticism that does not correspond to modern homosexuality. But this is not a voyage that many historians have made.

Notes

INTRODUCTION: SEX BEFORE SEXUALITY

1   *The Belles Heures of Jean de France, Duc de Berry*, The Metropolitan Museum of Art, New York, The Cloisters Collection, Purchase, 1954, 54.1.1, fol. 191r. For a reproduction see T. B. Husband, *The Art of Illumination: The Limbourg Brothers and the Belles Heures of Jean de France, Duc de Berry* (New York, 2008), p. 231. The manuscript was made between *c.* 1405 and 1408/9.
2   J. de Voragine, *The Golden Legend: Readings on the Saints*, trans. W. G. Ryan, 2 vols (Princeton, 1993), vol. 1, p. 84.
3   M. Camille, '"For our devotion and pleasure": the sexual objects of Jean, duc de Berry', *Art History*, 24 (2001), 169–94.
4   'Saint Jerome is tempted by dancing girls', *Belles Heures* fol. 186r (Husband, *The Art of Illumination*, p. 223).
5   Camille provides several examples of the theme of the sexually assertive or controlling woman in medieval secular art in his richly illustrated volume, *The Medieval Art of Love: Objects and Subjects of Desire* (London, 1998).
6   St Catherine, *Belles Heures* fols 17r and v; Agatha, fol. 179r; and Cecilia, fol. 180r. (Husband, *The Art of Illumination*, pp. 99, 101, 213, 214.) Other virgin martyr scenes in the book (Margaret, Agnes and Ursula and the 11,000 virgins) are more erotically neutral. B. Buettner, 'Dressing and undressing bodies in late medieval images', in *Artistic Exchange: Papers of the XXVIII Internationaler Kongress für Kunstgeschichte* (Berlin, 1992), 382–92, discusses the sensual appeal of the martyrs of the *Belles Heures*, though see chapter 5 below for brief discussion of virgin martyrs as 'parasexual' rather than 'pornographic'.
7   Camille, *The Medieval Art of Love*, pp. 27–39.
8   Buettner, 'Dressing and undressing bodies in late medieval images', 386.

9   K. El-Rouayheb, *Before Homosexuality in the Arab-Islamic World, 1500–1800* (Chicago, 2005), esp. pp. 6, 12, 47–9, 54, 137, 153–4.

10 Some important proponents of the hierarchical model of Greek homosexualities include K. J. Dover, *Greek Homosexuality* (Cambridge, Mass., 1978); D. Halperin, numerous works including *One Hundred Years of Homosexuality and Other Essays in Greek Love* (New York, 1990), esp. pp. 29–38; and J. J. Winkler, *The Constraints of Desire: The Anthropology of Sex and Gender in Ancient Greece* (New York, 1990). J. Davidson argues fervently against the idea of Greek sex as a 'zero-sum game' of dominant penetrator and subordinate penetrated and contends that 'erotic' relationships between men encompassed both sexual and asexual relations: 'Dover, Foucault and Greek homosexuality: penetration and the truth of sex', *Past and Present*, 170 (2001), 3–51. His argument for wide variety among 'Greek homosexualities' is much expanded in *The Greeks and Greek Love* (London, 2007), esp. pp. 466–92.

11 Catherine Belsey's book *Shakespeare and the Loss of Eden: The Construction of Family Values in Early Modern Culture* (Houndmills, 2001) deals, chapter by chapter, with courtship, marriage and parenthood – showing that the tension-ridden, jealous, cruel, perilously passionate family she describes is far from the loving, caring institutional ideal of modern stereotypes.

12 J. E. Howard, 'Sex and social conflict: the erotics of *The Roaring Girl*', in S. Zimmerman (ed.), *Erotic Politics: Desire on the Renaissance Stage* (London, 1992), p. 173.

13 M. Shapiro, *Gender in Play on the Shakespearean Stage: Boy Heroines and Female Pages* (Ann Arbor, Mich.,1994), pp. 46–7.

14 Ibid., p. 62.

15 See P. Rackin, 'Shakespeare's crossdressing comedies', in R. Dutton and J. E. Howard (eds), *A Companion to Shakespeare's Works: Volume III: The Comedies* (Malden, MA, 2003), ch. 6; C. M. Billing, *Masculinity, Corporality and the English Stage 1580–1635* (Farnham, 2008), p. 60.

16 S. Orgel, *Impersonations: The Performance of Gender in Shakespeare's England* (Cambridge, 1996), pp. 27, 29.

17 A. Sinfield, 'Near misses: Ganymedes and page boys', in his *Shakespeare, Authority, Sexuality: Unfinished Business in Cultural Materialism* (London, 2006), ch. 7 (esp. p. 128).

18 G. Ruggiero, *Machiavelli in Love: Sex, Self, and Society in the Italian Renaissance* (Baltimore, 2007), p. 36.

19 D. A. Walen, 'Constructions of female homoerotics in early modern drama', *Theatre Journal*, 54 (2002), 411–30; J. Crawford, 'The homoerotics of Shakespeare's Elizabethan comedies', in Dutton and Howard (eds), *A Companion to Shakespeare's Works: Volume III: The Comedies*, ch. 7; D. A. Walen, *Constructions of Female Homoeroticism in Early Modern Drama* (New York, 2005).

20 P. Crawford and S. Mendelson, 'Sexual identities in early modern England: the marriage of two women in 1680', *Gender and History*, 7 (1995), 372.

21 M. Rocke, 'Gender and sexual culture in Renaissance Italy', in J. C. Brown and R. C. Davis (eds), *Gender and Society in Renaissance Italy* (London, 1998), p. 170.

22 W. Stephens, *Demon Lovers: Witchcraft, Sex, and the Crisis of Belief* (Chicago, 2002). Stephens argues that the extent of the debate reflects ideological uncertainty, but the important point is that such discussion exists. Sex with demons is also a recurrent theme in D. Elliott, *Fallen Bodies: Pollution, Sexuality and Demonology in the Middle Ages* (Philadelphia, 1999).

23 C. S. Mackay, *The Hammer of Witches: A Complete Translation of the Malleus Maleficarum* (Cambridge, 2009), pp. 129, 310–11, 313.

24 B. K. Mudge (ed.), *When Flesh Becomes Word: An Anthology of Early Eighteenth-Century Libertine Literature* (New York, 2004), p. 46; J. G. Turner, *Schooling Sex: Libertine Literature and Erotic Education in Italy, France, and England 1534–1685* (Oxford, 2003), pp. 151–2; and the ejaculating, eighteenth-century dildo illustrated in R. Aldrich (ed.), *Gay Life and Culture: A World History* (London, 2006), p. 131.

25 V. Traub, *The Renaissance of Lesbianism in Early Modern England* (Cambridge, 2002), p. 27.

26 J. Bristow, *Sexuality* (London, 1997), ch. 1.

27 A. I. Davidson, *The Emergence of Sexuality: Historical Epistemology and the Formation of Concepts* (Cambridge, Mass., 2001), p. xiii.

28 Ibid., p. 37.

29 R. Porter and L. Hall, *The Facts of Life: The Creation of Sexual Knowledge in Britain, 1650–1950* (London, 1995), p. 39 (Porter wrote this chapter).

30 N. Largier, *In Praise of the Whip: A Cultural History of Arousal*, trans. G. Harman (New York, 2007). See also S. Toulalan, *Imagining Sex: Pornography and Bodies in Seventeenth-Century England* (Oxford, 2007), ch. 3.

31 Mudge (ed.), *When Flesh Becomes Word*, p. 197.

32 L. Stone, 'Libertine sexuality in post-Restoration England: group sex and flagellation among the middling sort in Norwich in 1706–7', *Journal of the History of Sexuality*, 2 (1992), 518, 523.

33 A. I. Davidson, 'Sex and the emergence of sexuality', *Critical Inquiry*, 14 (1987), 16–48. Reprinted in Davidson, *The Emergence of Sexuality*, ch. 2.

34 J. H. Meibomius, *A Treatise on the Use of Flogging in Venereal Affairs* (London, 1718), pp. 9–10. The book is a composite of writings from 1639, 1669 and 1718.

35 Ibid., Preface.

36 Ibid., p. 51.

37 Ibid., pp. 17, 52.

38 M. Menon, *Unhistorical Shakespeare: Queer Theory in Shakespearean Literature and Film* (New York, 2008), esp. pp. 1–25: 'The argument: unhistoricism, or homohistory' (quotes from pp. 1, 3).

39 Ibid., p. 3.

40 B. Reay, *New York Hustlers: Masculinity and Sex in Modern America* (Manchester, 2010).

41   Menon, *Unhistorical Shakespeare*, p. 7.
42   Ibid., p. 5; M. Menon, *Wanton Words: Rhetoric and Sexuality in English Renaissance Drama* (Toronto, 2004), p. 6 (for quote).
43   M. Menon, 'Afterword', in V. Nardizzi, S. Guy-Bray and W. Stockton (eds), *Queer Renaissance Historiography: Backward Gaze* (Farnham, 2009), p. 234.
44   P. Cryle, *The Telling of the Act: Sexuality as Narrative in Eighteenth- and Nineteenth-Century France* (Newark, DE, 2001).
45   Ibid., p. 278.
46   Ibid., p. 363.
47   By discourses we mean ideologically charged modes of expression conveying authority based on such factors as shared vocabulary and generic conventions: for example 'legal discourse', 'religious discourse'.
48   A. Clark, *Desire: A History of European Sexuality* (New York, 2008), p. 3.
49   R. M. Karras, *Sexuality in Medieval Europe: Doing Unto Others* (New York, 2005), p. 5.
50   For example, K. M. Phillips and B. Reay (eds), *Sexualities in History: A Reader* (New York, 2002). Karras (*Sexuality*, p. 6) contends that a history of 'sexualities' is different from a history of 'sexuality' in that the former is an account of past sexual orientations or identities, but we did not employ the plural in this narrower fashion. If we had followed her rationale with the present book it would have been called *Sexuality before Sexualities*: the argument would be the same.
51   It is the title of Part 1 of P. Stearns, *Sexuality in World History* (London, 2009), p. 9.
52   J. Weeks, *Sexuality*, 3rd edn (London, 2010), p. 7.
53   D. M. Halperin, J. J. Winkler and F. I. Zeitlin (eds), *Before Sexuality: The Construction of Erotic Experience in the Ancient Greek World* (Princeton, 1990), esp. pp. 5–7. For some objections: A. Richlin, 'Not before homosexuality: the materiality of the *cinaedus* and the Roman law against love between men', *Journal of the History of Sexuality*, 3 (1993), 523–73; H. N. Parker, 'The teratogenic grid', in J. P. Hallett and M. B. Skinner (eds), *Roman Sexualities* (Princeton, 1997), esp. p. 59; J. Murray, 'Twice marginal and twice invisible: lesbians in the middle ages', in V. L. Bullough and J. A. Brundage (eds), *Handbook of Medieval Sexuality* (New York, 1996), pp. 191–3.
54   M. Foucault, *The History of Sexuality*, vol. 1, *The Will to Knowledge*, trans. R. Hurley (Harmondsworth, 1978), p. 43.
55   D. Halperin, 'Forgetting Foucault: acts, identities, and the history of sexuality', in Phillips and Reay (eds), *Sexualities in History*, pp. 42–68; Winkler, *The Constraints of Desire*, pp. 45–6; M. W. Gleason, *Making Men: Sophists and Self-Presentation in Ancient Rome* (Princeton, 1995); C. A. Williams, *Roman Homosexuality: Ideologies of Masculinity in Classical Antiquity* (New York, 1999), pp. 175–6 on the *cinaedus*.
56   For a trenchant analysis of the dead-ends of the 'essentialist/ constructionist' divide see E. Stein, 'Conclusion: the essentials of constructionism and the construction of essentialism', in E. Stein (ed.),

Forms of Desire: Sexual Orientation and the Social Constructionist Controversy (New York, 1990), ch. 12.

57 *Aristoteles [sic] Master-piece* (London, 1684), Title page: 'a word of Advice to both Sexes in the Act of Copulation'.

58 *OED*, s.v. 'sex' and 'sexual'.

59 Compare the Latin and English versions of H. Institoris and J. Sprenger, *Malleus Maleficarum, Vol. 1: The Latin Text and Introduction*, ed. and trans. C. S. Mackay (Cambridge, 2006), pp. 254 (26C), 307 (52C and 52D), 628 (217D); and *Vol. 2: The English Translation*, ed. and trans. Mackay, pp. 84 (26C), 138–9 (52C and 52D), 512 (217D).

60 Taken from quoted passages in T. Hitchcock, *English Sexualities, 1700– 1800* (New York, 1997), ch. 3.

61 Cryle, *The Telling of the Act*, pp. 270–1.

62 Weeks, *Sexuality*, p. 10.

63 'The disappearance of the homosexual: interview with Henning Bech', in S. Seidman, N. Fischer and C. Meeks (eds), *Handbook of the New Sexuality Studies* (London, 2006), p. 151.

64 V. Mottier, *Sexuality: A Very Short Introduction* (Oxford, 2008).

65 Stearns, *Sexuality in World History*.

CHAPTER 1 SIN

1 J. Weeks, *Sexuality*, 3rd edn (London, 2010), p. 32.

2 A short discussion of celibacy in the major religions is E. Abbott, *A History of Celibacy* (New York, 2000), ch. 4.

3 M. Foucault, *The History of Sexuality*, vol. 1, *The Will to Knowledge*, trans. R. Hurley (Harmondsworth, 1978), p. 59. He later develops connections between medieval confession and late nineteenth-century sexologists (pp. 63–70). Also relevant is M. Foucault, 'The battle for chastity', in P. Ariès and A. Béjin (eds), *Western Sexuality: Practice and Precept in Past and Present Times*, trans. A. Forster (Oxford, 1985), pp. 24–5.

4 M. Foucault, 'Sexuality and solitude (1980)', reprinted in J. R. Carrette (ed.), *Religion and Culture: Michel Foucault* (New York, 1999), p. 183. Compare with Brown's statement that early Christianity displayed 'a muted but tenacious tendency to treat sexuality as a privileged ideogram of all that was most irreducible in the human will': 'Bodies and minds: sexuality and renunciation in early Christianity', in K. M. Phillips and B. Reay (eds), *Sexualities in History: A Reader* (New York, 2002), p. 130. Karma Lochrie is among those who have pointed out inconsistencies in Foucault's scattered writings on sexuality, subjectivity and the Middle Ages: 'Desiring Foucault', *Journal of Medieval and Early Modern Studies*, 27 (1997), 3–16.

5 M. W. Bloomfield, *The Seven Deadly Sins* (Michigan, 1952), esp. pp. 43–104; R. Newhauser, 'Virtues and vices', in *Dictionary of the Middle Ages, Supplement 1*, ed. W. C. Jordon (New York, 2004), pp. 628–33;

R. Newhauser (ed.), *In the Garden of Evil: The Vices and Culture in the Middle Ages* (Toronto, 2005).

6   P. J. Payer, *The Bridling of Desire: Views of Sex in the Later Middle Ages* (Toronto, 1993), p. 9. The list follows St Thomas Aquinas, *Summa Theologiae* (Blackfriars, 1963–), vol. 43, 2a2ae. 154, I, p. 205, but there were many variants; see T. N. Tentler, *Sin and Confession on the Eve of the Reformation* (Princeton, 1977), pp. 140–4.

7   Quoted in J. T. Noonan, Jr, *Contraception: A History of Its Treatment by the Catholic Theologians and Canonists* (Cambridge, Mass., 1965), p. 261; see also F. Mormando, *The Preacher's Demons: Bernadino of Siena and the Social Underworld of Early Renaissance Italy* (Chicago, 1999), p. 119.

8   Noonan, *Contraception*, pp. 261–2; Mormando, *The Preacher's Demons*, p. 124.

9   Exodus 20: 2–17 and Deuteronomy 5: 6–21.

10   Leviticus 18.

11   Foucault, 'Sexuality and solitude (1980)', p. 184.

12   Finding Noonan's study too 'meticulous' in documenting change, Flandrin asserts 'only two stages seem to me to be essential from the point of view of doctrine: the formation of the traditional doctrine during the first centuries A.D. and its radical transformation in the twentieth century. Between these two periods lie seventeen or eighteen centuries of stability': J. L. Flandrin, *Sex in the Western World: The Development of Attitudes and Behaviour*, trans. S. Collins (Chur, Switzerland, 1991), p. 89. Payer says this 'is substantially correct' but that it gave rise to many theological questions: *The Bridling of Desire*, p. 4.

13   For example, A. Rouselle, *Porneia: On Desire and the Body in Antiquity*, trans. F. Pheasant (Oxford, 1988); P. Brown, *The Body and Society: Men, Women and Sexual Renunciation in Early Christianity* (London, 1990).

14   A. F. Segal, *Rebecca's Children: Judaism and Christianity in the Roman World* (Cambridge, Mass., 1986); E. Pagels, *The Origin of Satan* (Harmondsworth, 1997), pp. 3–34.

15   Pagels, *The Origin of Satan*, p. 8.

16   Matthew 19.12.

17   Matthew 5.27–8.

18   For example Mark 7.20–3, 10.2–12; Matthew 15.19–20, 19.3–9.

19   1 Corinthians 7.

20   Contrary to tradition, 1 and 2 Timothy and Titus were not written by Paul, and nor, probably, were Ephesians, Colossians and 2 Thessalonians: see E. Pagels, *Adam, Eve, and the Serpent* (Harmondsworth, 1988), pp. 23–5.

21   Segal, *Rebecca's Children*, pp. 48–51. It has been suggested that the 'Dead Sea Scrolls', discovered in caves at Qumram in 1947, represented the doctrines of one Essene sect, but recent scholarship has denied any connection: for example, N. Golb, *Who Wrote the Dead Sea Scrolls? The Search for the Secret of Qumran* (New York, 1995).

22   S. B. Pomeroy, *Goddesses, Whores, Wives, and Slaves: Women in Classical Antiquity* (New York, 1975), pp. 210–14; M. Beard, 'The sexual status of

vestal virgins', *Journal of Roman Studies*, 70 (1980), 12–27; E. Cantarella, *Pandora's Daughters: The Role and Status of Women in Greek and Roman Antiquity*, trans. M. B. Fant (Baltimore, 1987), pp. 154–5.

23 M. Foucault, *The History of Sexuality*, vol. 2, *The Use of Pleasure*, trans. R. Hurley (Harmondsworth, 1985), and vol. 3, *The Care of the Self*, trans. R. Hurley (Harmondsworth, 1986); P. Veyne, 'La Famille et l'amour sous le haut-empire romain', *Annales*, 33 (1978), 35–63; P. Veyne, 'The Roman Empire', in P. Veyne (ed.), *A History of Private Life* (Cambridge, Mass., 1987), vol. 1, pp. 202–5. Also Noonan, *Contraception*, pp. 46–8; M. Kuefler, *The Manly Eunuch: Masculinity, Gender Ambiguity and Christian Ideology in Late Antiquity* (Chicago, 2001), pp. 78–80, 82.

24 Segal, *Rebecca's Children*, p. 95; H. North, *Sophrosyne: Self-Knowledge and Restraint in Classical Antiquity* (Ithaca, NY, 1966).

25 Kathy Gaca emphasizes the changing nature of Stoic sexual ethics from the third century BCE to the early centuries of the Christian era and the divergence between those ethics and Christian thought, the latter deriving primarily from the Septuagint or Greek Bible: K. L. Gaca, *The Making of Fornication: Eros, Ethics, and Political Reform in Greek Philosophy and Early Christianity* (Berkeley, 2003).

26 S. Garton summarizes some key arguments in this debate: *Histories of Sexuality: Antiquity to Sexual Revolution* (New York, 2004), pp. 48–63. D. Boyarin and E. A. Castelli note inconsistency between the fragments for Foucault's fourth volume, where in some places he argues for a clear break between pre-Christian and Christian sexual ethics, and in others claims to the contrary that in the latter there was nothing new: 'Introduction: Foucault's *The History of Sexuality*: the fourth volume, or, a field left fallow for others to till', *Journal of the History of Sexuality*, 10 (2001), 357–74, esp. 362–3.

27 K. Cooper, *The Virgin and the Bride: Idealized Womanhood in Late Antiquity* (Cambridge, Mass., 1996), pp. 60–1.

28 Ibid., p. 74; *Decrees of the Ecumenical Councils*, ed. N. P. Tanner (London, 1990), Canon 3, p. 7.

29 Jerome, 'To Eustochium', in *The Letters of St. Jerome*, trans. C. C. Mierow (London, 1963), vol. 1, p. 85.

30 Pagels, *Adam, Eve, and the Serpent*, pp. 78–97.

31 Ibid., p. 82.

32 Brown, *The Body and Society*, p. 376.

33 Jerome, 'Against Jovinian', in *The Principal Works of St Jerome*, trans. W. H. Fremantle (Oxford, 1893), Select Library of Nicene and Post-Nicene Fathers, new series, vol. 6, p. 350.

34 For example see D. G. Hunter, 'Resistance to the virginal ideal in late fourth-century Rome: the case of Jovinian', *Theological Studies*, 48 (1987), 45–64; E. A. Clark, 'Anti-familial tendencies in ancient Christianity', *Journal of the History of Sexuality*, 5 (1995), 356–80 (esp. 371–8).

35 Augustine, *Confessions*, trans. R. S. Pine-Coffin (Harmondsworth, 1961). Manichaeism was a religion originating in third-century CE

Persia, positing a dualist theology of good and evil, light and dark, represented by God on one side and Satan on the other.

36 The three 'goods' of marriage were *proles* (offspring), *fides* (fidelity) and *sacramentum* (in its ancient sense of a bond or vow, referring here to marriage as symbolic of the unbreakable bind between Christ and the Church): Augustine, *The Good of Marriage*, trans. C. T. Wilcox, in R. J. Deferrari (ed.), *Saint Augustine, Treatises on Marriage and Other Subjects* (Washington, DC, 1955); explicated by Noonan, *Contraception*, pp. 126–31; Payer, *The Bridling of Desire*, pp. 69–70; and Kuefler, *The Manly Eunuch*, pp. 189–93. The idea that marriage was one of the 'seven sacraments' or signs of God's grace did not emerge until the twelfth century, most clearly in the work of Peter Lombard (*c.*1100–60): G. Duby, *The Knight, the Lady and the Priest: The Making of Modern Marriage in Medieval France*, trans. B. Bray (Harmondsworth, 1983), pp. 178–85.

37 Clement of Alexandria, *Stromateis: Books One to Three*, trans. J. Ferguson (Washington, DC, 1991), book 3, chs 49–53, pp. 286–9; Pagels, *Adam, Eve, and the Serpent*, pp. 21–2, 26–31, 'durable double standard' quote at p. 28.

38 Augustine, *Concerning the City of God, Against the Pagans*, trans. H. Bettenson (Harmondsworth, 1984), book 14, chs 10–26, pp. 566–92. Explained in Pagels, *Adam, Eve, and the Serpent*, pp. 109–12; Payer, *The Bridling of Desire*, ch. 2; J. E. Salisbury, 'The Latin doctors of the church on sexuality', *Journal of Medieval History*, 12 (1986), 279–89 (esp. 284–9); E. Sawyer, 'Celibate pleasures: masculinity, desire, and asceticism in Augustine', *Journal of the History of Sexuality*, 6 (1995), 1–29.

39 Clement, *Stromateis*, 3, 58, p. 292.

40 Augustine, *Concerning the City of God*, 14, 16, p. 577.

41 C. Leyser, 'Masculinity in flux: nocturnal emission and the limits of celibacy in the early middle ages', in D. M. Hadley (ed.), *Masculinity in Medieval Europe* (London, 1999), pp. 103–20; compare Foucault, 'Battle for chastity'.

42 Noonan, *Contraception*, pp. 150–1.

43 Brown, *The Body and Society*, p. 427.

44 K. Cooper and C. Leyser, 'The gender of grace: impotence, servitude and manliness in the fifth-century West', *Gender and History*, 12 (2000), 536–51, quote at 541.

45 Augustine, *Concerning the City of God*, 14, 24, p. 588, quoted in Cooper and Leyser, 'The gender of grace', 543.

46 Augustine, *Concerning the City of God*, 14, 16, p. 577.

47 Cooper and Leyser, 'The gender of grace', 541. Brown, however, also noted the significance of impotence in Augustine: *The Body and Society*, p. 417.

48 Cooper and Leyser, 'The gender of grace', 551, n. 33; also C. Leyser, *Authority and Asceticism from Augustine to Gregory the Great* (Oxford, 2000), pp. 3–32.

49 V. Burrus, *The Sex Lives of Saints: An Erotics of Ancient Hagiography* (Philadelphia, 2004).

50 Cooper and Leyser, 'The gender of grace', 537.
51 V. Burrus, *'Begotten, Not Made': Conceiving Manhood in Late Antiquity* (Stanford, 2000), p. 3.
52 Kuefler, *The Manly Eunuch*, pp. 6, 118–20.
53 Ibid., pp. 124, 181; also Sawyer, 'Celibate pleasures', 24–9.
54 Kuefler, *The Manly Eunuch*, p. 114.
55 Ibid., pp. 161–70, 187–94.
56 Ibid., pp. 221–82.
57 Cooper, *The Virgin and the Bride*, pp. 50, 63, 64.
58 Ibid., p. 76.
59 Ibid., esp. pp. 92–115; more fully developed in her *The Fall of the Roman Household* (Cambridge, 2007).
60 C. Atkinson, '"Precious balsam in a fragile glass": the ideology of virginity in the later middle ages', *Journal of Family History*, 8 (1983), 131–43; B. Newman, 'Flaws in the golden bowl: gender and spiritual formation in the twelfth century', *Traditio*, 45 (1989–90), 111–46; K. M. Phillips, 'Maidenhood as the perfect age of woman's life', in K. J. Lewis, N. James Menuge and K. M. Phillips (eds), *Young Medieval Women* (Stroud, 1999), pp. 1–24.
61 P. Schine Gold, *The Lady and the Virgin: Image, Attitude and Experience in Twelfth-Century France* (Chicago, 1985), pp. 43–75; M. Rubin, *Mother of God: A History of the Virgin Mary* (New Haven, 2009), pp. 121–88; J. de Voragine, *The Golden Legend: Readings on the Saints*, trans. W. Granger Ryan, 2 vols (Princeton, 1993), vol. 1, nos 4, 24, 39, 43, 66, 78, 93, 98; vol. 2, nos 139, 142, 158, 169, 172; K. A. Winstead, *Virgin Martyrs: Legends of Sainthood in Late Medieval England* (Ithaca, NY, 1997); K. J. Lewis, *The Cult of St Katherine in Late Medieval England* (Woodbridge, 2000); J. Wogan-Browne, *Saints' Lives and Women's Literary Culture c. 1150–1300: Virginity and Its Authorizations* (Oxford, 2001); S. Salih, *Versions of Virginity in Late Medieval England* (Cambridge, 2001).
62 J. Tibbetts Schulenberg, 'The heroics of virginity: brides of Christ and sacrificial mutilation', in M. B. Rose (ed.), *Women in the Middle Ages and Renaissance: Literary and Historical Perspectives* (Syracuse, NY, 1985), pp. 29–51.
63 J. H. Arnold, 'The labour of continence: masculinity and clerical virginity', in A. Bernau, R. Evans and S. Salih (eds), *Medieval Virginities* (Cardiff, 2003), pp. 102–18.
64 Generally speaking, by the early sixth century Ostrogoths prevailed in Italy, Visigoths in Spain, Vandals in North Africa, Burgundians in the Rhône valley, Franks in Gaul and Angles and Saxons in Britain, but P. J. Geary is one among scholars who have more recently emphasized the constructed and shifting meanings of these 'ethnic' categories: *The Myth of Nations: The Medieval Origins of Europe* (Princeton, 2002).
65 For greater elaboration of this paragraph see S. F. Wemple, *Women in Frankish Society: Marriage and the Cloister 500 to 900* (Philadelphia, 1981), part 1; J. A. Brundage, *Law, Sex, and Christian Society in Medieval*

Europe (Chicago, 1997), pp. 124–33; M. Rouche, 'The early middle ages in the West', in Veyne (ed.) *A History of Private Life*, vol. 1, pp. 465–79.

66 'Pactus Legis Salicae', *Laws of the Salian Franks*, ed. and trans. K. Fischer Drew (Philadelphia, 1991), p. 86; also pp. 104–6, 127, 147; Rouche, 'The early middle ages in the West', p. 460.

67 'Lex Salica Karolina', *Laws of the Salian Franks*, ed. and trans. Drew, pp. 184–5.

68 Saint Caesarius of Arles, *Sermons*, vol. 1 (1–80), trans. Sister M. M. Mueller (Washington DC, 1956), pp. 205, 206, 211, 212, 214, 215–16, 222, 224.

69 L. Bailey, '"These are not men": sex and drink in the sermons of Caesarius of Arles', *Journal of Early Christian Studies*, 15 (2007), 23–43. Leyser suggests that the image of a freewheeling and resistant lay congregation was part of Caesarius's own mythology of himself: *Authority and Asceticism*, pp. 93–7.

70 L. Bailey, 'Preaching and Pastoral Care in Late Antique Gaul: The Eusebius Gallicanus Sermon Collection' (PhD dissertation, Princeton University, 2004), p. 66. Sermons from this collection are found in 447 manuscripts mostly dating from the seventh to fifteenth century, which testifies to their widespread appeal and influence (pp. 36–7). See also Bailey, '"These are not men"', 40–1 for other fifth-century Gallic preachers who had little or nothing to say about sex.

71 L. Coon, '"What is the Word if not semen?": Priestly bodies in Carolingian exegesis', in L. Brubaker and J. M. H. Smith (eds), *Gender in the Early Medieval World: East and West, 300–900* (Cambridge, 2004), pp. 278–300.

72 M. Foucault, 'The end of the monarchy of sex' (1977), in S. Lotringer (ed.), *Foucault Live (Interviews, 1966–84)*, trans. J. Johnston (New York, 1989), pp. 137–8. See also M. Foucault, 'About the beginning of the hermeneutics of the self', in Carrette (ed.), *Religion and Culture: Michel Foucault*, esp. pp. 169–81.

73 A. Murray, 'Confession as a historical source in the thirteenth century', in R. H. C. Davis and J. M. Wallace-Hadrill (eds, with the assistance of R. J. A. I. Catto and M. H. Keen), *The Writing of History in the Middle Ages: Essays Presented to Richard William Southern* (Oxford, 1981), p. 279.

74 P. J. Payer, *Sex and the Penitentials: The Development of a Sexual Code 550–1100* (Toronto, 1984), pp. 7–10.

75 Ibid., pp. 52–3.

76 Ibid., pp. 19–54, and 117.

77 Ibid., p. 119 (also p. 12).

78 R. D. Fulk, 'Male homoeroticism in the Old English *Canons of Theodore*', in C. B. Pasternak and L. M. C. Weston (eds), *Sex and Sexuality in Anglo-Saxon England: Essays in Memory of Daniel Gillmore Calder* (Tempe, AZ, 2004), p. 7.

79 Murray, 'Confession as a historical source', pp. 279–80.

80 A. L. Barstow, *Married Priests and the Reforming Papacy: The Eleventh-Century Debates* (New York, 1982); C. N. L. Brooke, 'Gregorian reform in action: clerical marriage in England, 1050–1200', *Cambridge*

Historical Journal, 12 (1956), 1–21; M. Frasetto (ed.), *Medieval Purity and Piety: Essays on Medieval Clerical Celibacy and Religious Reform* (New York, 1998); R. Balzaretti, 'Men and sex in tenth-century Italy', in Hadley (ed.), *Masculinity in Medieval Europe*, pp. 143–59. Clergy of the lower orders (porter, lector, exorcist, acolyte) were never forbidden to marry; the rules on celibacy applied only to the higher orders (subdeacon, deacon and priest).

81 Brooke, 'Gregorian reform in action', p. 16; Barstow, *Married Priests*, p. 97.

82 Peter Damian, *Letters*, trans. O. J. Blum, 7 vols (Washington DC, 1989–2004), vol. 4. no. 112. L. K. Little, 'The personal development of Peter Damian', in W. C. Jordan, B. McNab and T. F. Ruiz (eds), *Order and Innovation in the Middle Ages: Essays in Honour of Joseph R. Strayer* (Princeton, 1976), pp. 317–41.

83 Damian, *Letters*, vol. 2, p. 39.

84 *The Exempla or Illustrative Stories from the Sermones Vulgares of Jacques de Vitry*, ed. T. F. Crane (London, 1890), p. 100, translation: p. 234.

85 For more detail on chronology see Brooke, 'Gregorian reform in action', 4–6.

86 J. A. McNamara, 'The *Herrenfrage*: the restructuring of the gender system, 1050–1150', in C. A. Lees (ed.), *Medieval Masculinities: Regarding Men in the Middle Ages* (Minneapolis, 1994), pp. 3–29, and 'Canossa and the ungendering of the public man', in S. P. Ramet and D. W. Treadgold (eds), *Render unto Caesar: The Religious Sphere in the World of Politics* (Washington, DC, 1995), pp. 131–50; D. Elliott, *Fallen Bodies: Pollution, Sexuality, and Demonology in the Middle Ages* (Philadelphia, 1999); M. S. Kuefler, 'Male friendship and the suspicion of sodomy in twelfth-century France', in S. Farmer and C. Braun Pasternak (eds), *Gender and Difference in the Middle Ages* (Minneapolis, 2003), pp. 145–81, esp. p. 162.

87 Elliott, *Fallen Bodies*, pp. 81–126.

88 Brooke, 'Gregorian reform in action', 15.

89 N. Partner, *Serious Entertainments: The Writing of History in Twelfth-Century England* (Chicago, 1977), p. 47; G. Tellenbach, *The Church in Western Europe from the Tenth to the Early Twelfth Century*, trans. T. Reuter (Cambridge, 1993), pp. 165–7.

90 *The Chronicle of Salimbene de Adam*, trans. J. L. Baird, G. Baglivi and J. R. Kane (Binghamton, NY, 1986), p. 430.

91 *The Register of Eudes of Rouen*, ed. J. F. O'Sullivan, trans. S. M. Brown (New York, 1964), e.g. pp. 13, 16, 20–1, 21–2, 22–3, 24–6, 27, 29–30, 43–4, 202, 234, 614–15.

92 Ibid., p. 24.

93 Ibid., p. 13.

94 Ibid., pp. 285, 383–4.

95 J. D. Thibodeaux, 'Man of the church, or man of the village? Gender and the parish clergy in medieval Normandy', *Gender and History*, 18 (2006), 380–99. See also R. N. Swanson, 'Angels incarnate: clergy and

masculinity from the Gregorian reform to the Reformation', and P. H. Cullum, 'Clergy, masculinity and transgression in late medieval England', both in Hadley (ed.), *Masculinity in Medieval Europe*, pp. 160–77, 178–96.

96 Payer, *Sex and the Penitentials*, pp. 37–8, quote at p. 37. In contrast, they pay a good deal of attention to same-sex practices, mostly among men, pp. 40–4.

97 P. J. Payer, 'Confession and the study of sex in the middle ages', in V. L. Bullough and J. A. Brundage (eds), *Handbook of Medieval Sexuality* (New York, 2000), p. 13.

98 To be treated further in chapter 5, below.

99 J. H. Arnold, *Belief and Unbelief in Medieval Europe* (London, 2005), pp. 29–30.

100 *The Life of Christina of Markyate: A Twelfth-Century Recluse*, ed. and trans. C. H. Talbot (Oxford, 1959), p. 61.

101 Caesarius of Heisterbach, *The Dialogue on Miracles*, trans. H. von E. Scott and C. C. Swinton Bland, 2 vols (London, 1929), ch. 40, pp. 179–80.

102 Translated in W. A. Christian, Jr, *Apparitions in Late Medieval and Renaissance Spain* (Princeton, 1981), pp. 153–6. See Caesarius, *The Dialogue on Miracles*, vol. 1, chs 45–6 for further tales of penitents who show ignorance of categories of sin and the role of confession. On later medieval efforts to improve the religious education of laypeople and their priests see Arnold, *Belief and Unbelief*, pp. 35–9.

103 J. F. Benton, *Self and Society in Medieval France: The Memoirs of Abbot Guibert of Nogent (1064?–c. 1115)* (New York, 1970), pp. 63–4.

104 'Hali Meiðhad (A Letter on Virginity)', in *Medieval English Prose for Women: Selections from the Katherine Group and Ancrene Wisse*, ed. B. Millett and J. Wogan-Browne, 2nd edn (Oxford, 1992), p. 31.

105 *The Life of Christina of Markyate*, pp. 45–67; Raymond of Capua, *The Life of St Catherine of Siena*, trans. G. Lamb (London, 1960), pp. 30–50; J. de Vitry, *The Life of Marie d'Oignies*, trans. M. H. King (Toronto, 1993), pp. 48–9; B. Gregersson and T. Gascoigne, *The Life of Saint Birgitta*, trans. J. Bolton Holloway (Toronto, 1991), pp. 15–20.

106 Raymond, *The Life of St Catherine*, pp. 91–2.

107 Gregersson and Gascoigne, *The Life of Saint Birgitta*, p. 16.

108 S. Stolpe, *Birgitta: på svenska, in English, auf deutsch* (Stockholm, 1973), p. 52.

109 *The Book of Margery Kempe*, trans. B. A. Windeatt (Harmondsworth, 1985), p. 46.

110 Noonan, *Contraception*, pp. 171–99, quotes from Huguccio at p. 197.

111 Ibid., pp. 292–5.

112 Ibid., pp. 303–40; also Tentler, *Sin and Confession*, pp. 224–6.

113 Noonan, *Contraception*, p. 374.

114 On sex and the Reformation see Brundage, *Law, Sex, and Christian Society*, pp. 551–75; L. Roper, *The Holy Household* (Oxford, 1989), pp. 64–9; J. F. Harrington, *Reordering Marriage and Society in Reformation Germany* (Cambridge, 1995), esp. pp. 61–71; I. Hull, *Sexuality, State, and Civil Society in Germany, 1700–1815* (Ithaca, NY, 1996), pp. 17–29;

M. Weisner-Hanks, *Christianity and Sexuality in the Early Modern World: Regulating Desire, Reforming Practice* (London, 2000), pp. 60–140.

115 A. I. Davidson, *The Emergence of Sexuality: Historical Epistemology and the Formation of Concepts* (Cambridge, MA, 2001), p. xiii.

CHAPTER 2 BEFORE HETEROSEXUALITY

1 E. K. Sedgwick, *Tendencies* (Durham, NC, 1994), p. 11.

2 A. J. Frantzen, *Before the Closet: Same-Sex Love from Beowulf to Angels in America* (Chicago, 1998); C. Dinshaw, *Getting Medieval: Sexualities and Communities, Pre- and Postmodern* (Durham, NC, 1999); these and similar studies are critiqued in J. A. Schultz, *Courtly Love, the Love of Courtliness, and the History of Sexuality* (Chicago, 2006), pp. 51–62.

3 L. M. Sylvester, *Medieval Romance and the Construction of Heterosexuality* (New York, 2008).

4 S. S. Lanser, '"Queer to queer": the sapphic body as transgressive text', in K. Kittredge (ed.), *Lewd & Notorious: Female Transgression in the Eighteenth Century* (Ann Arbor, Mich., 2003), ch. 1 (quotes from pp. 23, 34).

5 E. S. Wahl, *Invisible Relations: Representations of Female Intimacy in the Age of Enlightenment* (Stanford, 1999), pp. 7, 9.

6 Ibid., p. 18.

7 P. Hammond, *Figuring Sex between Men from Shakespeare to Rochester* (Oxford, 2002), p. 8.

8 Ibid., p. 11. This is not to criticize the book as a whole.

9 V. Nardizzi, S. Guy-Bray and W. Stockton (eds), *Queer Renaissance Historiography: Backward Gaze* (Farnham, 2009).

10 Ibid, ch. 11.

11 J. N. Katz, *The Invention of Heterosexuality* (New York, 1995), p. 34.

12 S. Wells, *Shakespeare, Sex & Love* (Oxford, 2010), pp. 25, 33, 39.

13 James Schultz has expressed this far more eloquently: Schultz, *Courtly Love*, ch. 4. See also J. A. Schultz, 'Heterosexuality as a threat to medieval studies', *Journal of the History of Sexuality*, 15 (2006), 14–29.

14 M. Camille, '"For our devotion and pleasure": The sexual objects of Jean, Duc de Berry', *Art History*, 24 (2001), 169–94.

15 *The Loving Virgin's Complaint*, circa 1626, in H. E. Rollins (ed.), *The Pepys Ballads*, 3 vols (Cambridge, Mass., 1929), vol. 2, p. 78.

16 J. A. Schultz, 'Bodies that don't matter: heterosexuality before heterosexuality in Gottfried's *Tristan*', in K. M. Phillips and B. Reay (eds), *Sexualities in History: A Reader* (New York, 2002), ch. 3. See also, Schultz, *Courtly Love*, chs 2–3.

17 K. Lochrie, *Heterosyncrasies: Female Sexuality When Normal Wasn't* (Minneapolis, 2005), p. xix.

18 R. A. Bach, *Shakespeare and Renaissance Literature before Heterosexuality* (New York, 2007), esp. 'Introduction: before heterosexuality'.

19   P. Simons, 'Homosociality and erotics in Italian Renaissance portrai-
     ture', in J. Woodhall (ed.), *Portraiture: Facing the Subject* (Manchester,
     1997), ch. 1 (quotes from p. 29).
20   Schultz, *Courtly Love*, p. xviii.
21   G. Duby, 'What do we know about love in twelfth-century France?' in
     his *Love and Marriage in the Middle Ages*, trans. Jane Dunnett (Chicago,
     1994), pp. 22–35; T. Adams, *Violent Passions: Managing Love in the Old
     French Verse Romance* (New York, 2005), p. 12.
22   The woman uses *amor* fifty-two times and *dilectio* forty-one times; the
     man uses *amor* forty-seven times and *dilectio* only ten times: C. J. Mews,
     *The Lost Love Letters of Heloise and Abelard: Perceptions of Dialogue
     in Twelfth-Century France* (New York, 2001), p. 136.
23   *The Letters of Heloise and Abelard: A Translation of Their Collected
     Correspondence and Related Writings*, ed. and trans. M. M. McLaughlin
     and B. Wheeler (New York, 2009), letters 2, 4.
24   Brilliantly surveyed down to 2001 in E. J. Burns, 'Courtly love: who
     needs it? Recent feminist work in the medieval French tradition',
     Signs, 27 (2001), 23–57.
25   Schultz, *Courtly Love*, esp. chs 2, 3 and 5, summarized pp. 170–1.
26   Ibid., pp. 94–8, quote at p. 96.
27   P. G. Walsh (ed.) and trans., *Andreas Capellanus on Love* (London,
     1982), p. 35.
28   S. Gaunt, *Love and Death in Medieval French and Occitan Courtly
     Literature: Martyrs to Love* (Oxford, 2006), pp. 191–203, quote at p. 198;
     also S. Huot, 'Love, race, and gender in medieval romance: Lancelot
     and the son of the giantess', *Journal of Medieval and Early Modern
     Studies*, 37 (2007), 373–91 among other recent studies.
29   Adams, *Violent Passions*, p. 20.
30   Ibid., pp. 23–36.
31   Ibid., p. 14, citing B. H. Rosenwein, 'Writing without fear about early
     medieval emotions', *Early Medieval Europe*, 10 (2001), 229–34, at 234.
32   *Andreas Capellanus on Love*, pp. 147–57; G. Paris, 'Lancelot du Lac, II:
     Conte de la Charette', *Romania*, 12 (1883), 459–534, at 518; C. S. Lewis,
     The Allegory of Love: A Study in Medieval Tradition (Oxford, 1936),
     ch. 1. On Paris's invention see D. F. Hult, 'Gaston Paris and the invention
     of courtly love', in R. H. Bloch and S. G. Nichols (eds), *Medievalism
     and the Modern Temper* (Baltimore, 1996), pp. 192–224.
33   Recently and in detail by Adams, *Violent Passions*, summarized pp.
     237–44, where she also gestures towards a more negative view of sexual
     desire in thirteenth-century courtly literature.
34   Sedgwick, *Tendencies*, pp. 10–11.
35   See the numerous instances in C. S. Mackay, *The Hammer of Witches:
     A Complete Translation of the Malleus Maleficarum* (Cambridge, 2009).
36   J. D'Emilio and E. B. Freedman, 'Family life and the regulation of
     deviance', in Phillips and Reay (eds), *Sexualities in History*, ch. 7 (quote
     from p. 142).
37   R. M. Karras, *Sexuality in Medieval Europe: Doing Unto Others* (New
     York, 2005).

38 K. Crawford, *European Sexualities, 1400–1800* (Cambridge, 2007), ch. 1 (quote at p. 48).

39 T. A. Foster, *Sex and the Eighteenth-Century Man: Massachusetts and the History of Sexuality in America* (Boston, 2006), ch. 1.

40 E. Behrend-Martínez, *Unfit for Marriage: Impotent Spouses on Trial in the Basque Region of Spain, 1650–1750* (Reno and Las Vegas, 2007), pp. x, xii.

41 Quoted in T. N. Tentler, *Sin and Confession on the Eve of the Reformation* (Princeton, 1977), pp. 171–2. The holy place would have to be subsequently re-consecrated, however.

42 M. M. Sheehan, '*Maritalis affectio* revisited', in R. R. Edwards and S. Spector (eds), *The Olde Daunce: Love, Friendship, Sex, and Marriage in the Medieval World* (Albany, NY, 1991), pp. 32–43.

43 R. H. Helmholz, *Marriage Litigation in Medieval England* (Cambridge, 1974), pp. 26–7; P. S. Gold, 'The marriage of Mary and Joseph in the medieval theology of marriage', in J. A. Brundage and V. L. Bullough (eds), *Sexual Practices and the Medieval Church* (Buffalo, 1982), pp. 102–17; J. A. Brundage, *Law, Sex, and Christian Society in Medieval Europe* (Chicago, 1987), pp. 236–7, 264–9.

44 D. Elliott, *Spiritual Marriage: Sexual Abstinence in Medieval Wedlock* (Princeton, 1993).

45 R. M. Wunderli, *London Church Courts and Society on the Eve of the Reformation* (Cambridge, Mass., 1981), pp. 81–102. Sexual crimes and defamation cases combined comprised between 80 and 90 per cent of cases in London Church courts of this period.

46 Taking data from the tables on cases before the London Church courts, 1471–1514, in ibid., pp. 144–7 (leaving out data from 1497 and 1498 which relate to two deaneries only), adultery made up on average around 25 per cent of cases and sometimes around one-third, fornication around 13 per cent, pimping around 12.5 per cent and prostitution almost 5 per cent.

47 A. J. Finch, 'Sexual morality and canon law: the evidence of the Rochester consistory court', *Journal of Medieval History*, 20 (1994), 261–75.

48 Wunderli found only one accusation of sodomy and one instance of imputed sodomitical slander from over 21,000 defendants between 1470 and 1516: *London Church Courts*, pp. 83–4; Ruth Mazo Karras found no clear accusations of lesbian acts in either the secular or ecclesiastical courts of fourteenth and fifteenth century London: *Common Women: Prostitution and Sexuality in Medieval England* (New York, 1996), p. 174, n. 67 and p. 185, n. 9; P. J. P Goldberg, who has undertaken extensive research in the fourteenth- and fifteenth-century York consistory court records, has not noticed any same-sex cases (personal communication).

49 M. Boone, 'State power and illicit sexuality: the persecution of sodomy in late medieval Bruges', *Journal of Medieval History*, 22 (1996), 135–53, 141–2; H. Puff, *Sodomy in Reformation Germany and Switzerland, 1400–1600* (Chicago, 2003), pp. 35–40.

50   Wunderli, *London Church Courts*, pp. 31–40.
51   S. Tarbin, 'Moral regulation and civic identity in London 1400–1530', in L. Rasmussen, V. Spear and D. Tillotson (eds), *Our Medieval Heritage: Essays in Honour of John Tillotson for his 60th Birthday* (Cardiff, 2002), pp. 126–36, at pp. 127–8.
52   L. Martines, *An Italian Renaissance Sextet: Six Tales in Historical Context* (Toronto, 2004), pp. 142, 162–3.
53   M. de Zayas, *The Enchantments of Love: Amorous and Exemplary Novels*, ed. and trans. H. P. Boyer (Berkeley and Los Angeles, 1990) (first published in 1637); and her *The Disenchantments of Love*, ed. and trans. H. P. Boyer (Albany, NY, 1997) (first published in 1647).
54   J. M. Ferraro, *Nefarious Crimes, Contested Justice: Illicit Sex and Infanticide in the Republic of Venice, 1557–1789* (Baltimore, 2008), p. 124.
55   Ibid., esp. ch. 5.
56   E. Foyster, 'A laughing matter? Marital discord and gender control in seventeenth-century England', *Rural History*, 4 (1993), 5–21.
57   D. M. Turner, *Fashioning Adultery: Gender, Sex and Civility in England, 1660–1740* (Cambridge, 2002), pp. 3, 8.
58   R. Brome, *The Antipodes*, ed. A. Haaker (London, 1967), p. 32–3. The play was first published in London in 1640.
59   M. Steggle, *Richard Brome: Place and Politics on the Caroline Stage* (Manchester, 2004), p. 143.
60   [R. Brome and A. Behn], *The Debauchee: Or the Credulous Cuckold, a Comedy* (London, 1677), p. 41.
61   F. Dabhoiwala, 'The pattern of sexual immorality in seventeenth- and eighteenth-century London', in P. Griffiths and M. S. R. Jenner (eds), *Londinopolis: Essays in the Cultural and Social History of Early Modern London* (Manchester, 2000), ch. 5.
62   B. K. Mudge (ed.), *When Flesh Becomes Word: An Anthology of Early Eighteenth-Century Libertine Literature* (New York, 2004), p. 56.
63   J. Hajnal, 'European marriage patterns in perspective', in D. V. Glass and D. E. C. Eversley (eds), *Population in History: Essays in Historical Demography* (London, 1965), pp. 101–43, argued this pattern prevailed from the sixteenth century. Medievalists have pushed his chronology back to the later fourteenth century: P. J. P. Goldberg, *Women, Work and Life Cycle in a Medieval Economy: Women in York and Yorkshire c.1300–1520* (Oxford, 1992), pp. 225–32; R. M. Smith, 'Geographical diversity in the resort to marriage in late medieval Europe: work, reputation and unmarried females in the household formation systems of northern and southern Europe', in P. J. P. Goldberg (ed.), *Women in Medieval English Society* (Stroud, 1997), pp. 16–59.
64   R. M. Trexler, 'La Prostitution Florentine au XVe siècle: patronages et clientèles', *Annales: ESC*, 36 (1981), 983–1015; J. Rossiaud, *Medieval Prostitution*, trans. L. G. Cochrane (Oxford, 1988); Crawford, *European Sexualities*. See also, M. Rocke, 'Gender and sexual culture in Renaissance Italy', in J. C. Brown and R. C. Davis (eds), *Gender and Society in Renaissance Italy* (London, 1998), ch. 7.

65 Crawford, *European Sexualities,* p. 24.
66 T. Hitchcock, *English Sexualities, 1700–1800* (New York, 1997), ch. 3.
67 See the tables in P. Laslett, K. Oosterveen and R. Smith (eds), *Bastardy and Its Comparative History: Studies in the History of Illegitimacy and Marital Nonconformism in Britain, France, Germany, Sweden, North America, Jamaica, and Japan* (Cambridge, Mass., 1980), pp. 23, 109; R. Adair, *Courtship, Illegitimacy and Marriage in Early Modern England* (Manchester, 1996), ch. 3.
68 S. McSheffrey, *Marriage, Sex, and Civic Culture in Late Medieval London* (Philadelphia, 2006), pp. 66–73; though she also finds cases where sexually active young women had no interest in marrying their partners.
69 A case from Cheshire, 1661, quoted by G. Walker, *Crime, Gender and Social Order in Early Modern England* (Cambridge, 2003), pp. 232–3.
70 P. J. P. Goldberg (ed.), *Women in England, c. 1275–1525: Documentary Sources* (Manchester, 1995), pp. 110–14.
71 A. J. Finch, 'Sexual relations and marriage in later medieval Normandy', *Journal of Ecclesiastical History*, 47 (1996), 236–56.
72 R. Barahona, *Sex Crimes, Honour, and the Law in Early Modern Spain: Vizcaya, 1528–1735* (Toronto, 2003).
73 Ibid., p. 7.
74 De Zayas, *Enchantments of Love*, p. 24.
75 Ibid., p. 52.
76 Ibid., p. 184.
77 Ibid., p. 187.
78 H. Abelove, 'Some speculations on the history of sexual intercourse during the long eighteenth century in England', *Genders*, 6 (1989), 125–30; T. Hitchcock, 'Redefining sex in eighteenth-century England', *History Workshop*, 41 (1996), 73–90; Hitchcock, *English Sexualities*, ch. 3.
79 K. M. Phillips, *Medieval Maidens: Young Women and Gender in England, 1270–1540* (New York, 2003), pp. 108–35; McSheffrey, *Marriage, Sex, and Civic Culture*, pp. 121–34; L. Gowing, '"The freedom of the streets": women and social space 1560–1640', in Griffiths and Jenner (eds), *Londinopolis*, pp. 130–51.
80 B. Reay, *Popular Cultures in England, 1550–1750* (London, 1998), ch. 1.
81 R. C. Davis, 'The geography of gender in the Renaissance', in Brown and Davis (eds), *Gender and Society in Renaissance Italy*, ch. 1; Crawford, *European Sexualities*, ch. 1; Ferraro, *Nefarious Crimes*.
82 D. M. Turner, 'Adulterous kisses and the meaning of familiarity in early modern Britain', in K. Harvey (ed.), *The Kiss in History* (Manchester, 2005), p. 82.
83 K. Thomas, 'Afterword', in ibid., pp. 193, 197.
84 Reay, *Popular Cultures*, ch. 1.
85 The best accounts for early modern England are M. Ingram, 'Ridings, rough music and the "reform of popular culture" in early modern England', *Past and Present*, 105 (1984), 79–113; M. Ingram, 'Ridings,

rough music and mocking rhymes in early modern England', in B. Reay (ed.), *Popular Culture in Seventeenth-Century England* (London, 1985), ch. 5; D. E. Underdown, 'The taming of the scold: the enforcement of patriarchal authority in early modern England', in A. Fletcher and J. Stevenson (eds), *Order and Disorder in Early Modern England* (Cambridge, 1985), ch. 4.

86   Ingram, 'Ridings, rough music and mocking rhymes', pp. 166–7.

87   These examples come from ibid., p. 166; and W. G. Day (ed.), *The Pepys Ballads*, 5 vols (Cambridge, 1987), vol. 4, p. 287. The word 'merkin' is probably 'murkin', as in dark, indicating the female private parts.

88   A. M. Froide, *Never Married: Singlewomen in Early Modern England* (Oxford, 2005), pp. 2–3.

89   For England, see F. Dabhoiwala, 'The construction of honour, reputation and status in late seventeenth- and early eighteenth-century England', *Transactions of the Royal Historical Society*, 6th series, 6 (1996), 201–13; G. Walker, 'Expanding the boundaries of female honour in early modern England', ibid., 235–45; B. Capp, 'The double standard revisited: plebeian women and male sexual reputation in early modern England', *Past and Present*, 162 (1999), 70–100; J. Bailey, *Unquiet Lives: Marriage and Marriage Breakdown in England, 1660–1800* (Cambridge, 2003), ch. 7. For Italy, see Rocke, 'Gender and sexual culture in Renaissance Italy'.

90   L. Gowing, 'Women, status, and the popular culture of dishonour', *Transactions of the Royal Historical Society*, 6th series, 6 (1996), 225.

91   Capp, 'The double standard revisited', 72.

92   L. Gowing, 'Gender and the language of insult in early modern London', *History Workshop*, 35 (1993), 1–21; L. Gowing, 'Language, power, and the law: women's slander litigation in early modern London', in J. Kermode and G. Walker (eds), *Women, Crime and the Courts in Early Modern England* (London, 1994), ch. 2; and L. Gowing, *Domestic Dangers: Women, Words, and Sex in Early Modern London* (Oxford, 1996).

93   Ingram, 'Ridings, rough music and the "reform of popular culture"'; Ingram, 'Ridings, rough music and mocking rhymes'; A. Fox, 'Ballads, libels and popular ridicule in Jacobean England', *Past and Present*, 145 (1994), 47–83. See also P. A. Brown, *Better a Shrew Than a Sheep: Women, Drama, and the Culture of Jest in Early Modern England* (Ithaca, NY, 2003), ch. 3.

94   T. Laqueur, *Making Sex: Body and Gender from the Greeks to Freud* (Cambridge, Mass., 1990), p. 8 (for quotes).

95   Ibid. See also, Laqueur's 'Orgasm, generation, and the politics of reproductive biology', in C. Gallagher and T. Laqueur (eds), *The Making of the Modern Body: Sexuality and Society in the Nineteenth Century* (Berkeley and Los Angeles, 1987), pp. 1–41.

96   Hitchcock, *English Sexualities*, ch. 4; K. Harvey, 'The substance of sexual difference: change and persistence in representations of the body in eighteenth-century England', *Gender and History*, 14 (2002), 202–23; M. Fissell, 'Gender and generation: representing reproduction

in early modern England', in Phillips and Reay (eds), _Sexualities in History_, ch. 5; M. E. Fissell, _Vernacular Bodies: The Politics of Reproduction in Early Modern England_ (Oxford, 2004), pp. 186–8, 198–202; C. M. Billing, _Masculinity, Corporality and the English Stage 1580–1635_ (Farnham, 2008), ch. 1.

97 J. Cadden, _Meanings of Sex Difference in the Middle Ages: Medicine, Science, and Culture_ (Cambridge, 1993), pp. 170–7, quotes at p. 171. See also I. McLean, _The Renaissance Notion of Woman: A Study in the Fortunes of Scholasticism and Medical Science in European Cultural Life_ (Cambridge, 1980), pp. 32–3; D. Jacquart and C. Thomasset, _Sexuality and Medicine in the Middle Ages_, trans. M. Adamson (Princeton, 1988), pp. 48–86.

98 Cadden, _Meanings of Sex Differences_, pp. 97–8.

99 Ibid., pp. 183–8; also her 'It takes all kinds: sexuality and gender differences in Hildegard of Bingen's "Book of Compound Medicine"', _Traditio_, 40 (1984), 149–74.

100 A. Barrett (ed.), _The Knowing of Woman's Kind in Childing: A Middle English Version of Material Derived from the 'Trotula' and Other Sources_ (Turnhout, 2001), p. 44; on 'Shape' see also Cadden, _Meanings of Sex Difference_, pp. 177–83. M. Green, 'Bodies, gender, health, disease: recent work on medieval women's medicine', in P. M. Soergel (ed.), _Studies in Medieval and Renaissance History_, 3rd series vol. 2: _Sexuality and Culture in Medieval and Renaissance Europe_ (New York, 2005), pp. 1–46, quote at p. 7. In the same volume, see also H. King, 'The mathematics of sex: one to two, or two to one', pp. 47–58, who argues that Laqueur's Galenic paradigm overlooks the Hippocratic tradition, which maintained some influence in the medieval era and Renaissance.

101 K. Harvey, _Reading Sex in the Eighteenth Century: Bodies and Gender in English Erotic Culture_ (Cambridge, 2004), chs 2–3.

102 Ibid., p. 81.

103 Ibid., p. 105.

104 S. D. Amussen, 'The gendering of popular culture in early modern England', in T. Harris (ed.), _Popular Culture in England, c. 1500–1850_ (London, 1995), p. 50; A. Fletcher, _Gender, Sex and Subordination in England 1500–1800_ (London, 1995), ch. 1: '_Prologue_: men's dilemmas'.

105 _Aristoteles [sic] Master-piece_ (1684), pp. 28–9.

106 Fletcher, _Gender, Sex and Subordination_, p. 5. Women's alleged sexual voracity has been the subject of vast scholarly literature, and of course we would not want to argue against observations of variety within and opposition to this theme within premodern discourse.

107 G. Walker, 'Rereading rape and sexual violence in early modern England', _Gender and History_, 10 (1998), 8.

108 K. Straub, _Domestic Affairs: Intimacy, Eroticism, and Violence between Servants and Masters in Eighteenth-Century Britain_ (Baltimore, 2009), p. 2.

109 Barahona, _Sex Crimes_, p. 81.

110 T. Meldrum, 'London domestic servants from depositional evidence, 1660–1750: servant–employer sexuality in the patriarchal household',

in T. Hitchcock, P. King and P. Sharpe (eds), *Chronicling Poverty: The Voices and Strategies of the English Poor, 1640–1840* (London, 1997), ch. 2; L. Gowing, 'The haunting of Susan Lay: servants and mistresses in seventeenth-century England', *Gender and History*, 14 (2002), 191 (for quote).

111 C. Fairchilds, 'Female sexual attitudes and the rise of illegitimacy: a case study', *Journal of Interdisciplinary History*, 8 (1978), 639.

112 Straub, *Domestic Affairs*, p. 36.

113 L. Gowing, *Common Bodies: Women, Touch and Power in Seventeenth-Century England* (London, 2003), ch. 3: 'Consent and desire'.

114 See R. Godbeer, 'William Byrd's "flourish": the sexual cosmos of a southern planter', in M. D. Smith (ed.), *Sex and Sexuality in Early America* (New York, 1998), ch. 6; and T. Burnard, 'The sexual life of an eighteenth-century Jamaican slave overseer', in ibid., ch. 7. See also S. D. Amussen, *Caribbean Exchanges: Slavery and the Transformation of English Society, 1640–1700* (Chapel Hill, NC, 2007), pp. 61, 99, 232–3.

115 Phillips, *Medieval Maidens*, pp. 83, 132; Karras, *Common Women*, pp. 57–61; B. Hanawalt, *Growing Up in Medieval London: The Experience of Childhood in History* (New York, 1993), pp. 122–3.

116 B. Capp, *When Gossips Meet: Women, Family, and Neighbourhood in Early Modern England* (Oxford, 2003).

117 S. Hindle, 'The shaming of Margaret Knowsley: gossip, gender and the experience of authority in early modern England', *Continuity and Change*, 9 (1994), 391–419.

118 Gowing, 'The haunting of Susan Lay', 194–5; Gowing, *Common Bodies*.

119 J. Wiltenburg, *Disorderly Women and Female Power in the Street Literature of Early Modern England and Germany* (Charlottesville, Va., 1992).

120 For cuckolds, see E. A. Foyster, *Manhood in Early Modern England: Honour, Sex and Marriage* (London, 1999), pp. 67–72, 104–17, 195–8.

121 Ibid., p. 136.

122 Schultz, *Courtly Love*, p. 53.

123 Crawford, *European Sexualities*, p. 46.

124 Schultz, *Courtly Love*, p. 53.

125 Ibid., pp. 55–6.

126 Ibid., pp. 60–1.

127 G. Ruggiero, *Machiavelli in Love: Sex, Self, and Society in the Italian Renaissance* (Baltimore, 2007), p. 31.

128 Ibid., ch. 1.

129 R. M. Karras and D. L. Boyd, '*Ut cum muliere*': a male transvestite prostitute in fourteenth-century London', in Phillips and Reay (eds), *Sexualities in History*, p. 92.

130 Ibid., transcript of case at pp. 100–1.

131 R. A. Bach, '(Re)placing John Donne in the history of sexuality', *ELH*, 72 (2005), pp. 259–89.

132 Ibid.

133 Thomas Newton [translator], *The Touchstone of Complexions* (London, 1576), p. 23v.

134 E. Keller, *Generating Bodies and Gendered Selves: The Rhetoric of Reproduction in Early Modern England* (Seattle, 2007), pp. 92–7.

135 L. Dawson, *Lovesickness and Gender in Early Modern English Literature* (Oxford, 2008), Introduction and ch. 1 (quote from p. 12). See also M. A. Wells, *The Secret Wound: Love-Melancholy and Early Modern Romance* (Stanford, 2007).

136 Dawson, *Lovesickness and Gender*, ch. 2.

137 E. Jorden, *A Briefe Discourse of a Disease Called the Suffocation of the Mother* (London, 1603), p. 22v.

138 Dawson, *Lovesickness and Gender*, p. 62.

CHAPTER 3 BETWEEN MEN

1 P. Hammond, *Figuring Sex Between Men from Shakespeare to Rochester* (Oxford, 2002), p. 14.

2 D. M. Halperin, *How to Do the History of Homosexuality* (Chicago, 2002), ch. 4.

3 G. W. Bredbeck, *Sodomy and Interpretation: Marlowe to Milton* (Ithaca, NY, 1991), p. 13.

4 The best short survey is by M. D. Jordan, 'Sodomy', in G. E. Haggerty (ed.), *Gay Histories and Cultures: An Encyclopedia* (New York, 2000), pp. 828–31. The remainder of this paragraph is indebted to his longer study, *The Invention of Sodomy in Christian Theology* (Chicago, 1997). On the story of Sodom in Genesis 19 and its interpretation as a sin against hospitality, see also D. S. Bailey, *Homosexuality and the Western Christian Tradition* (London, 1955), and J. Boswell, *Christianity, Social Tolerance and Homosexuality* (Chicago, 1980), pp. 93–7.

5 Jordan, 'Sodomy', p. 829.

6 Peter Damian, Letter 31 ('The Book of Gomorrah'), in *Letters*, trans. O. J. Blum, 3 vols (Washington, DC, 1989–92), vol. 2, pp. 46–7.

7 St Thomas Aquinas, *Summa Theologiae* (Blackfriars, 1963–), vol. 43, 2a2ae. 154, II, p. 245. The other forms of unnatural vice are 'by procuring pollution without any copulation', 'by copulation with a thing of undue species (bestiality)', and 'by not observing the natural manner of copulation, as to either undue means, or as to other monstrous and bestial manners of copulation'.

8 S. Wenzel (ed. and trans.), *Fasciculus Morum: A Fourteenth-Century Preacher's Handbook* (University Park, PA, 1989), pp. 686–9.

9 J. Merrick and B. T. Ragan (eds), *Homosexuality in Early Modern France: A Documentary Collection* (New York, 2001), p. 3.

10 C. Bingham, 'Seventeenth-century attitudes toward deviant sex', *Journal of Interdisciplinary History*, 1 (1971), 456.

11 J. Cadden, 'Sciences/silences: the natures and languages of sodomy in Peter of Abano's *Problemata* commentary', in K. Lochrie, P. McCracken and J. A. Schultz (eds), *Constructing Medieval Sexuality* (Minneapolis, 1997), p. 50.

12   K. Lochrie, 'Presumptive sodomy and its exclusions', *Textual Practice*, 13 (1999), 298.

13   G. Ruggiero, *The Boundaries of Eros: Sex Crime and Sexuality in Renaissance Venice* (New York, 1985), pp. 114–21.

14   Merrick and Ragan (eds), *Homosexuality in Early Modern France*, p. 24.

15   R. Godbeer, *Sexual Revolution in Early America* (Baltimore, 2002), p. 106.

16   Jordan, *Invention of Sodomy*, p. 126.

17   W. E. Burgwinkle, *Sodomy, Masculinity, and Law in Medieval Literature: France and England, 1050–1230* (New York, 2004), p. 1.

18   M. Goodich, *The Unmentionable Vice: Homosexuality in the Later Medieval Period* (Santa Barbara, 1979), pp. 7–10; H. Puff, *Sodomy in Reformation Germany and Switzerland, 1400–1600* (Chicago, 2003), p. 13.

19   See A. Bray, *Homosexuality in Renaissance England* (New York, 1995), ch. 1: 'Word and symbol'. First published in 1982. Although he uses the word 'homosexuality' rather than sodomy, it is a pioneering account of the issues. See, more recently, C. McFarlane, *The Sodomite in Fiction and Satire 1660–1750* (New York, 1997), ch. 1; T. Betteridge, 'The place of sodomy in the historical writings of John Bale and John Foxe', in T. Betteridge (ed.), *Sodomy in Early Modern Europe* (Manchester, 2002), ch. 1; D. Clarke, '"The sovereign's vice begets the subject's error": the Duke of Buckingham, "sodomy" and narratives of Edward II, 1622–28', in ibid., ch. 3.

20   Merrick and Ragan (eds), *Homosexuality in Early Modern France*, p. 4.

21   Boswell, *Christianity*, p. 270; J. A. Brundage, 'Review', *Catholic Historical Review*, 68:1 (1982), 62–4.

22   M. S. Kuefler, 'Male friendship and the suspicion of sodomy in twelfth-century France', in S. Farmer and C. B. Pasternak (eds), *Gender and Difference in the Middle Ages* (Minneapolis, 2003), pp. 145–81 (reprinted in Kuefler (ed.), *The Boswell Thesis: Essays on Christianity, Social Tolerance, and Homosexuality* (Chicago, 2006), pp. 179–212). He is influenced by R. I. Moore, *The Formation of a Persecuting Society: Power and Deviance in Western Europe, 950–1250* (Oxford, 1987), esp. pp. 91–4.

23   Quotes in Kuefler, 'Male friendship', pp. 165–6.

24   Burgwinkle, *Sodomy*, esp. pp. 1–23, quote at p. 2. Where Kuefler notes two possible drivers of sodomy's explosion in twelfth-century discourse, Burgwinkle suggests nine (ranging from a desire to reform morals in an era of supposed decline, to an attempt to attract men to service in the all-male arenas of the military, monastery or clergy through reassurances of institutional discipline and elitism), pp. 22–3.

25   Ibid., pp. 23–5, also 66–7. Arnaud's detailed trial records are translated in Goodich, *The Unmentionable Vice*, pp. 89–123, see pp. 113–14.

26   Jordan, *Invention of Sodomy*, p. 1; R. E. Zeikowitz, *Homoeroticism and Chivalry: Discourses of Male Same-Sex Desire in the Fourteenth Century*

(New York, 2003), pp. 102–6; J. A. Brundage, 'The politics of sodomy: Rex vs. Pons Hugh de Ampurias (1311)', in J. E. Salisbury (ed.), *Sex in the Middle Ages: A Book of Essays* (New York, 1991), pp. 239–46; Puff, *Sodomy*, pp. 17–30, 107–23, 124–39; Jordan, 'Sodomy', p. 828; W. Johansson and W. A. Percy, 'Homosexuality', in V. L. Bullough and J. A. Brundage (eds), *Handbook of Medieval Sexuality* (New York, 1996), p. 172.

27   Puff, *Sodomy*, pp. 110–11; also A. Gilmour-Bryson, 'Sodomy and the Knights Templar', *Journal of the History of Sexuality*, 7 (1996), 151–83; Zeikowitz, *Homoeroticism*, pp. 104–13.

28   On these examples see Goodich, *The Unmentionable Vice*, pp. 4–5; Burgwinkle, *Sodomy*, pp. 48–52 and 73–85; Zeikowitz, *Homoeroticism*, pp. 113–29; M. Hanrahan, 'Speaking of sodomy: Gower's advice to princes in the *Confessio Amantis*', *Exemplaria*, 14 (2002), 423–46; R. Mills, 'Male–male love and sex in the middle ages, 1000–1500', in M. Cook, H. G. Cocks, R. Mills and R. Trumbach, *A Gay History of Britain: Love and Sex between Men since the Middle Ages* (Oxford, 2007), pp. 1–43, at pp. 1–2, 6–8, 18–22.

29   On Italians, Puff, *Sodomy*, esp. pp. 117–18, 125–8; M. Boone, 'State power and illicit sexuality: the persecution of sodomy in late medieval Bruges', *Journal of Medieval History*, 22 (1996), 135–53, at 142; R. E. Zorach, 'The matter of Italy: sodomy and the scandal of style in sixteenth-century France', *Journal of Medieval and Early Modern Studies*, 28 (1998), 581–609; on the French, Burgwinkle, *Sodomy*, pp. 47–8; on Muslims, Boswell, *Christianity*, pp. 279–83; S. F. Kruger, 'Medieval (dis)identifications: Muslims and Jews in Guibert of Nogent', *New Literary History*, 28 (1997), 185–203; G. S. Hutcheson, 'The sodomitic Moor: queerness in the narrative of *Reconquista*', in G. Burger and S. F. Kruger (eds), *Queering the Middle Ages* (Minneapolis, 2001), pp. 99–121; on the New World, J. Goldberg, *Sodometries: Renaissance Texts, Modern Sexualities* (Stanford, 1992), chs 6 and 7; on Asia pre-1510, K. M. Phillips, '"They do not know the use of men": The absence of sodomy in medieval accounts of the Far East', in A. Harper and C. Proctor (eds), *Medieval Sexuality: A Casebook* (New York, 2008), pp. 189–208; on the Chinese from *c.* 1550, B. Hinsch, *Passions of the Cut Sleeve: The Male Homosexual Tradition in China* (Berkeley, 1990), pp. 1–2.

30   Puff, *Sodomy*, chs 6 and 7.

31   Burgwinkle, *Sodomy*, p. 33.

32   Puff, *Sodomy*, p. 17.

33   Ibid., pp. 90–1.

34   E. W. Monter, 'Sodomy and heresy in early modern Switzerland', *Journal of Homosexuality*, 6 (1980/1), 41–55, at 54–5 (originally published in French in 1974).

35   Ruggiero, *The Boundaries of Eros*, p. 128. The imbalance between eras may be partly accounted for by the incompleteness of the records up to 1425, but more importantly by the switch in jurisdictions from the *Signori di Notte* to the Council of Ten, pp. 127–9.

36   Boone, 'State power', quotes at 152, 153.
37   Ruggiero, *The Boundaries of Eros*, pp. 109–12, 135; some German cities gave the same reason: Puff, *Sodomy*, p. 26.
38   M. Rocke, *Forbidden Friendships: Homosexuality and Male Culture in Renaissance Florence* (New York, 1996), pp. 4, 50–2.
39   Ibid., p. 39.
40   *The Touchstone of Complexions*, trans. T. Newton (London, 1576), p. 23v.
41   Goodich, *The Unmentionable Vice*, pp. 93–123, esp. pp. 106, 120. A 'son' of Arnaud is mentioned (p. 97) and one deponent testifies that he and Arnaud had sex with a maid and another woman in Arnaud's house (p. 102).
42   R. Trumbach, 'The birth of the queen: sodomy and the emergence of gender equality in modern culture, 1660–1750', in M. B. Duberman, M. Vicinus and G. Chauncey (eds), *Hidden from History: Reclaiming the Gay and Lesbian Past* (London, 1991), pp. 129–40.
43   A. H. Nelson, *Monstrous Adversary: The Life of Edward de Vere, 17th Earl of Oxford* (Liverpool, 2003), pp. 213–18.
44   Ibid., p. 214.
45   Bingham, 'Seventeenth-century attitudes toward deviant sex', 447–68 (quote from 465).
46   Trumbach, 'The birth of the queen', p. 131.
47   Hammond, *Figuring Sex between Men*, pp. 241, 244, 245.
48   G. E. Haggerty, *Men in Love: Masculinity and Sexuality in the Eighteenth Century* (New York, 1999), pp. 6–11. Quote from p. 8. See also, McFarlane, *The Sodomite in Fiction*, p. 46.
49   Quoted in L. Crompton, *Byron and Greek Love: Homophobia in 19th-Century England* (London, 1985). Crompton sees Byron as bisexual, but his demonstrated interest in boys is probably more accurately described as libertinism.
50   F. MacCarthy, *Byron: Life and Legend* (New York, 2002), esp. pp. 40, 58–9, 76, 78, 80, 90, 126–9, 267, 340–1, 488–9.
51   R. Trumbach, 'Sodomitical assaults, gender role, and sexual development in eighteenth-century London', in K. Gerard and G. Hekma (eds), *The Pursuit of Sodomy: Male Homosexuality in Renaissance and Enlightenment Europe* (New York, 1989), pp. 407–29.
52   Goodich, *The Unmentionable Vice*, pp. 93–123.
53   Puff, *Sodomy*, pp. 77–8.
54   C. Berco, *Sexual Hierarchies, Public Status: Men, Sodomy, and Society in Spain's Golden Age* (Toronto, 2007), p. 45. See his ch. 2 for this breadth.
55   Observations based on forty cases involving alleged sodomy or attempted sodomy from 1721 to 1772 in the published *Proceedings of the Old Bailey, 1674–1834* in the online project directed by Tim Hitchcock and Robert Shoemaker (*http://www.oldbaileyonline.org*).
56   *Proceedings of the Old Bailey*, John Ashford, 6 September 1732.
57   Ibid., Emanuel Roze, 27 February 1760.
58   L. Martines, *An Italian Renaissance Sextet: Six Tales in Historical Context* (Toronto, 2004), p. 79.

59 G. R. Quaife, *Wanton Wenches and Wayward Wives: Peasants and Illicit Sex in Early Seventeenth-Century England* (London, 1979), p. 176.

60 A. N. Gilbert, 'Buggery and the British Navy', *Journal of Social History*, 10 (1976), 75.

61 See F. Dabhoiwala, 'The pattern of sexual immorality in seventeenth- and eighteenth-century London', in P. Griffiths and M. S. R. Jenner (eds), *Londinopolis: Essays in the Cultural and Social History of Early Modern London* (Manchester, 2000), ch. 5.

62 Compare the male–male case studies in Trumbach with the male–female cases in Quaife: Trumbach, 'Sodomitical assaults'; Quaife, *Wanton Wenches and Wayward Wives*. For the terrible violence against London women, see R. Trumbach, *Sex and the Gender Revolution* (Chicago, 1998).

63 *Proceedings of the Old Bailey*, James Williams, 7 December 1726.

64 Ibid., Richard Spencer, 5 July 1749.

65 Ibid., Henry Wolf, 22 May 1735.

66 Berco, *Sexual Hierarchies*, p. 29.

67 J. Merrick, 'Chaussons in the streets: sodomy in seventeenth-century Paris', *Journal of the History of Sexuality*, 15 (2006), 167–203.

68 Rocke, *Forbidden Friendships*, pp. 122–3.

69 A point also made by D. F. Greenberg, *The Construction of Homosexuality* (Chicago, 1990), p. 309.

70 Quoted in Burgwinkle, *Sodomy*, pp. xi–xii; see also Kuefler, 'Male friendship', pp. 151–2, 158.

71 See Kuefler, 'Male friendship', p. 159. However, the reason for Lanval's rejection of the queen is that he has fallen in love with a fairy lady.

72 J. Walters, '"No more than a boy": the shifting construction of masculinity from ancient Greece to the middle ages', *Gender and History*, 5 (1993), 24.

73 Rocke, *Forbidden Friendships*, pp. 39–40, 123–4, 128–30, 173–4.

74 Ibid., pp. 40, 128.

75 K. Boris (ed.), *Same-Sex Desire in the English Renaissance: A Sourcebook of Texts, 1470–1650* (New York, 2004), p. 42.

76 R. Godbeer, '"The Cry of Sodom": discourse, intercourse, and desire in colonial New England', in T. A. Foster (ed.), *Long before Stonewall: Histories of Same-Sex Sexuality in Early America* (New York, 2007), ch. 4; Godbeer, *Sexual Revolution in Early America*, pp. 45–50.

77 See M. R. Boes, 'On trial for sodomy in early modern Germany', in Betteridge (ed.), *Sodomy in Early Modern Europe*, ch. 2; W. Naphy, 'Sodomy in early modern Geneva: various definitions, diverse verdicts', in ibid., ch. 6.

78 Merrick, 'Chaussons in the streets'.

79 Merrick and Ragan (eds), *Homosexuality in Early Modern France*, p. 34.

80 F. G. Carvajal, *Butterflies Will Burn: Prosecuting Sodomites in Early Modern Spain and Mexico* (Austin, TX, 2003), pp. 131–2.

81 Berco, *Sexual Hierarchies*, p. 132.

82 D. J. Noordam, 'Sodomy in the Dutch Republic, 1600–1725', in Gerard and Hekma (eds), *The Pursuit of Sodomy*, pp. 219–21.

83   Godbeer, '"The Cry of Sodom"', p. 83. Godbeer sees something transcending a mere act.
84   T. Hitchcock, *English Sexualities, 1700–1800* (New York, 1997), pp. 61–2.
85   Bray, *Homosexuality in Renaissance England*, pp. 67–9, 75–7.
86   *Proceedings of the Old Bailey*, Charles Bradbury, 10 September 1755.
87   Ibid., George Duffus, 6 December 1721.
88   Ibid., William Brown, 11 July 1726.
89   Puff, *Sodomy*, pp. 11, 69, 91.
90   Halperin, *How to Do the History of Homosexuality*, pp. 113–17. As noted in our Introduction, J. Davidson has argued for much more diversity in Ancient Greek constructions of male same-sex erotics, for example in *The Greeks and Greek Love* (London, 2007), esp. pp. 466–92.
91   See Puff, *Sodomy*, p. 43.
92   Rocke, *Forbidden Friendships*, p. 96.
93   Ibid., chs. 3–4. Rocke has shown that in medieval Florence sodomy included oral sex and sex between the thighs, and that the sucker rather than the sucked was the active partner in oral sex.
94   Ibid., p. 105.
95   Berco, *Sexual Hierarchies*, p. 15.
96   Ibid., p. 25.
97   C. Berco, 'Producing patriarchy: male sodomy and gender in early modern Spain', *Journal of the History of Sexuality*, 17 (2008), 351–76.
98   Ibid., p. 363.
99   R. Trumbach, 'The heterosexual male in eighteenth-century London and his queer interactions', in K. O'Donnell and M. O'Rourke (eds), *Love, Sex, Intimacy and Friendship between Men, 1550–1800* (Houndmills, 2003), ch. 5.
100 S. Orgel, *Impersonations: The Performance of Gender in Shakespeare's England* (Cambridge, 1996), pp. 70–1.
101 M. Bly, *Queer Virgins and Virgin Queans on the Early Modern Stage* (Oxford, 2000), pp. 5, 17, 18, 23, 24, 25, for suggestions that the culture is outside the mainstream. (See p. 45 for the libidinal economy.)
102 For Barnfield, see B. R. Smith, *Homosexual Desire in Shakespeare's England: A Cultural Poetics* (Chicago, 1994), pp. 99–115 (quote from pp. 99–100).
103 Hammond, *Figuring Sex between Men*, pp. 49–52.
104 B. R. Burg, *Boys at Sea: Sodomy, Indecency, and Courts Martial in Nelson's Navy* (Houndmills, 2007), p. 104.
105 B. R. Burg, *An American Seafarer in the Age of Sail: The Erotic Diaries of Philip C. Van Buskirk 1851–1870* (New Haven, 1994), pp. xi, 74.
106 Ibid., ch. 7.
107 Puff, *Sodomy*, p. 92.
108 Ibid., p. 91.
109 A man alleged that another had got him drunk, engaged in mutual masturbation and then initiated oral and anal sex: 'he then turned round, and put his naked breech into my lap, and put his hand behind him, and put my y[ar]d in his body'. Despite the obvious forcefulness

of the penetrated, he was the sodomized in the indictment, and the passive penetrator was the sodomizer. See *Proceedings of the Old Bailey*, Robert Crook, Charles Gibson, 9 September 1772.

110 A. Bray, 'Homosexuality and the signs of male friendship in Elizabethan England', *History Workshop*, 29 (1990), 1–19. Reprinted in J. Goldberg (ed.), *Queering the Renaissance* (Durham, NC, 1994), pp. 40–61. See also Bray's *The Friend* (Chicago, 2003).

111 D. Clark, *Between Medieval Men: Male Friendship and Desire in Early Medieval English Literature* (Oxford, 2009), pp. 22–36. Further examples of homoerotic intimacy between men are discussed in A. J. Frantzen, *Before the Closet: Same-Sex Love from Beowulf to Angels in America* (Chicago, 1998), pp. 92–107.

112 R. Godbeer, *The Overflowing of Friendship: Love between Men and the Creation of the American Republic* (Baltimore, 2009), p. 5.

113 Bray, *The Friend*, p. 143; J. Masten, *Textual Intercourse: Collaboration, Authorship, and Sexualities in Renaissance Drama* (Cambridge, 1997), p. 32.

114 Bray, *The Friend*, pp. 13–41.

115 Ibid., pp. 126–34 and *passim*. Compare J. Boswell, *Same-Sex Unions in Premodern Europe* (New York, 1994).

116 Mills, 'Male–male love', pp. 5–8.

117 B. P. McGuire, *Friendship and Community: The Monastic Experience 350–1250* (Kalamazoo, Mich., 1988), pp. 296–338, quotes at pp. 298, 301. A less subtle account is Boswell, *Christianity*, pp. 221–6.

118 McGuire, *Friendship*, pp. 302–3.

119 Ibid., pp. 308, 327–8.

120 R. W. Southern, *Saint Anselm and His Biographer: A Study in Monastic Life and Thought c. 1059–c.1130* (Cambridge, 1963), pp. 67–76; Boswell, *Christianity*, pp. 218–19; McGuire, *Friendship*, pp. 210–27; J. P. Haseldine, 'Love, separation and male friendship: words and actions in Saint Anselm's letters to his friends', in D. M. Hadley (ed.), *Masculinity in Medieval Europe* (Harlow, 1999), pp. 238–55; S. N. Vaughn, 'Saint Anselm and his students writing about love: a theological foundation for the rise of romantic love in Europe', *Journal of the History of Sexuality*, 19 (2009), 54–73, quote at 58.

121 On monastic friendships and homoeroticism see also Burgwinkle, *Sodomy*, pp. 33–40.

122 For their relationship and correspondence, see D. M. Bergeron (ed.), *King James and Letters of Homoerotic Desire* (Iowa City, 1999), pp. 174–5, 179, 186, 199.

123 Bray, *The Friend*, pp. 96–104, 168–72.

124 Halperin, *How to Do the History of Homosexuality*, p. 121.

125 Clark, *Between Medieval Men*, p. 34 (on *freond* in Anglo-Saxon); Hammond, *Figuring Sex between Men*, pp. 18–21.

126 Quoted in Bergeron (ed.), *King James and Letters of Homoerotic Desire*, p. 141.

127 M. DiGangi, *The Homoerotics of Early Modern Drama* (Cambridge, 1997), p. 12.

128   Boris (ed.), *Same-Sex Desire in the English Renaissance*, pp. 288–9.
129   Haggerty, *Men in Love*; and his 'Male love and friendship in the eighteenth century', in O'Donnell and O'Rourke (eds), *Love, Sex, Intimacy*, p. 73.
130   Quoted in Bergeron (ed.), *King James and Letters of Homoerotic Desire*, p. 107.
131   Halperin, *How to Do the History of Homosexuality*, pp. 117–21.
132   Masten, *Textual Intercourse*, p. 34.
133   See Bergeron (ed.), *King James and Letters of Homoerotic Desire*, pp. 140, 180.
134   Bray, 'Homosexuality and the signs of male friendship' (Goldberg reprint), p. 56.
135   Rocke, *Forbidden Friendships*, ch. 5.
136   Bray, *The Friend*, esp. pp. 138–9, 164–72, quote at p. 306.
137   E. A. Foyster, *Manhood in Early Modern England: Honour, Sex, and Marriage* (New York, 1999), p. 56.
138   G. Ruggiero, *Machiavelli in Love: Sex, Self, and Society in the Italian Renaissance* (Baltimore, 2007), p. 149.
139   P. Rackin, 'Foreign country: the place of women and sexuality in Shakespeare's historical world', in R. Burt and J. M. Archer (eds), *Enclosure Acts: Sexuality, Property, and Culture in Early Modern England* (Ithaca, NY, 1994), ch. 4. See also the excellent discussion of *Romeo and Juliet* by N. F. Radel, 'Queer Romeo and Juliet: teaching early modern "sexuality" in Shakespeare's "heterosexual" tragedy', in M. Hunt (ed.), *Approaches to Teaching Shakespeare's Romeo and Juliet* (New York, 2000), pp. 91–7.
140   Frantzen, *Before the Closet*, p. 90.
141   L. Diggelmann, 'Of Grifons and tyrants: Anglo-Norman views of the Mediterranean world during the third crusade', in L. Bailey, L. Diggelmann and K. M. Phillips (eds), *Old Worlds, New Worlds: European Cultural Encounters, c. 1000–c.1750* (Turnhout, 2009), pp. 20–1.
142   See B. R. Smith, *Shakespeare and Masculinity* (Oxford, 2000); Ruggiero, *Machiavelli in Love*.
143   P. Carter, 'Men about town: representations of foppery and masculinity in early eighteenth-century urban society', in H. Barker and E. Chalus (eds), *Gender in Eighteenth-Century England: Roles, Representations and Responsibilities* (London, 1997), ch. 2.
144   Merrick and Ragan (eds), *Homosexuality in Early Modern France*, p. 2.
145   Ibid. Women, presumably because they are already effeminate, fade from the Frenchman's gloss almost as soon as they are mentioned.
146   Quoted in Mills, 'Male–male love', pp. 20–1.
147   T. Stehling, 'To love a medieval boy', *Journal of Homosexuality*, 8 (1983), 151–70, quote at 154. See also *Medieval Latin Poems of Male Love and Friendship*, trans. T. Stehling (New York, 1984), and (with caution) Boswell, *Christianity*, pp. 243–66.
148   M. Camille, 'The pose of the queer: Dante's gaze, Brunetto Latini's body', in Burger and Kruger (eds), *Queering the Middle Ages*, ch. 3.

149 C. Brown, 'Queer representations in the *Arçipreste de Talavera*, or the *Maldezir de mugures* is a drag', in J. Blackmore and G. S. Hutcheson (eds), *Queer Iberia: Sexualities, Cultures, and Crossings from the Middle Ages to the Renaissance* (Durham, NC, 1999), p. 86.

150 Cadden, 'Sciences/silences', pp. 45–9.

151 See K. Borris and G. Rousseau (eds), *The Sciences of Homosexuality in Early Modern Europe* (London, 2008), esp. chs 1 and 7 (by Borris).

152 T. Van der Meer, 'Sodomy and the pursuit of a third sex in the early modern period', in G. Herdt (ed.), *Third Sex, Third Gender: Beyond Sexual Dimorphism in Culture and History* (New York, 1996), p. 192.

153 Halperin, *How to Do the History of Homosexuality*, p. 127.

154 Bray, *Homosexuality in Renaissance England*, p. 103.

155 Hitchcock, *English Sexualities*, p. 70.

156 For example, Greenberg, *The Construction of Homosexuality*, pp. 333–7, 349, 389. See also, the entry in a respected gay historical enyclopedia: 'The mollies . . . were crucial to the formation of a modern homosexual identity. While the name *molly* has disappeared from the current gay male lexicon, related terms such as *Mary Ann*, *girlfriend*, and *sister* along with queeny camp behavior reflect cultural continuities across time': M. M. Holmes, 'Mollies', in Haggerty (ed.), *Gay Histories*, pp. 604–5.

157 For a critique of the source material, see McFarlane, *The Sodomite in Fiction*, pp. 60–8; and C. Patterson, 'The rage of Caliban: eighteenth-century molly houses and the twentieth-century search for sexual identity', in T. DiPiero and P. Gill (eds), *Illicit Sex: Identity Politics in Early Modern Culture* (Athens, Ga., 1997), pp. 256–69. The following observations are based on cases of alleged or attempted sodomy from *Proceedings of the Old Bailey*, many of which are from the 1720s, a period when the mollies were said to be active.

158 *Proceedings of the Old Bailey*, John Ashford, 6 September 1732.

159 Ibid., James Williams, 7 December 1726.

160 Ibid., Richard Manning, 17 January 1746.

161 Ibid., Charles Bradbury, 10 September 1755: for 'sodomite dog'. And this was from a Methodist preacher.

162 Ibid., Richard Manning, John Davis, 16 January 1745.

163 Ibid., John Painter, John Green, 30 August 1727.

164 Ibid., William Bailey, 21 October 1761.

165 Ibid., Thomas Rodin, 10 October 1722.

166 *A Faithful Narrative of the Proceedings in a Late Affair between the Rev. Mr. John Swinton and Mr. George Baker* (London, 1739), in A. Pettit and P. Spedding (eds), *Eighteenth-Century British Erotica*, 5 vols (London, 2002), vol. 5, pp. 355–90, quote from p. 375.

167 *Proceedings of the Old Bailey*, Charles Bradbury, 10 September 1755.

168 Ibid., John Dicks, 4 April 1722.

169 Ibid., Thomas Rodin, 10 October 1722; Richard Manning, John Davis, 16 January 1745.

170 Ibid., Richard Manning, John Davis, 16 January 1745.

171 Ibid., William Bailey, 21 October 1761.

172   Ibid., Charles Hitchin, 12 April 1727; George Kedear, 20 April 1726.
173   Ibid., Martin Mackintosh, 11 July 1726.
174   Ibid., Margaret Clap, 11 July 1726.
175   Burg, *Boys at Sea*, pp. 59–60.
176   M. Hunter (ed.), *Robert Boyle by Himself and His Friends* (London, 1994), pp. lxxvii, 20.
177   For defamation, see L. Gowing, *Domestic Dangers: Women, Words, and Sex in Early Modern London* (Oxford, 1996); see also the discussion in M. DiGangi, 'How queer was the Renaissance?', in O'Donnell and O'Rourke (eds), *Love, Sex, Intimacy*, ch.6.
178   Berco, *Sexual Hierarchies*, p. 39.
179   Hitchcock, *English Sexualities*, pp. 63–4.
180   Ruggiero, *Machiavelli in Love*, ch. 5.
181   See M. Rey, 'Parisian homosexuals create a lifestyle, 1700–1750: the police archives', in R. P. Maccubbin (ed.), *'Tis Nature's Fault: Unauthorized Sexuality during the Enlightenment* (Cambridge, 1987), pp. 179–91; Merrick and Ragan (eds), *Homosexuality in Early Modern France*, pp. 41–72.
182   Merrick and Ragan (eds), *Homosexuality in Early Modern France*, p. 59.
183   Ibid., p. 60.
184   Rey, 'Parisian homosexuals', p. 181.
185   J. Merrick, 'Commissioner Foucault, Inspector Noel, and the "pederasts" of Paris, 1780–3', *Journal of Social History*, 32 (1998), 287–307.
186   Van der Meer, 'Sodomy and the pursuit of a third sex in the early modern period', pp. 211–12.
187   See Merrick and Ragan (eds), *Homosexuality in Early Modern France*; Rey, 'Parisian homosexuals'; and M. Rey, 'Police and sodomy in eighteenth-century Paris', in Gerard and Hekma (eds), *The Pursuit of Sodomy*, pp. 129–46. Rey moves towards the subcultural thesis (see 'Parisian homosexuals', p. 189), but the content of his material does not really support this claim.
188   Merrick and Ragan (eds), *Homosexuality in Early Modern France*, p. 64.
189   See M. Sibalis, 'Male homosexuality in the age of Enlightenment and revolution, 1680–1850', in R. Aldrich (ed.), *Gay Life and Culture: A World History* (London, 2006), ch. 5. Note the section heading on p. 103: 'The homosexual subculture'.

CHAPTER 4   BETWEEN WOMEN

1   R. Jennings, *A Lesbian History of Britain: Love and Sex between Women since 1500* (Oxford, 2007).
2   Albio Cesare Cassio notes a tenth-century Greek text where *Lesbia* refers to tribades or *hetairistria*, though in classical Greek texts it usually designated a woman who performed fellatio: 'Post-Classical Λέσβια', *The Classical Quarterly*, n.s., 33:1 (1983), 296–7. Pierre de

Boudeille, Seigneur de Brantôme (d. 1614), used 'Lesbienne' to refer not only to inhabitants of Lesbos but also to women who enjoyed sex with other women, though for most 'this little exercise ... is nothing but an apprenticeship to come to the greater of men': *Vies des Dames Galantes* (Paris, n.d.), pp. 121–30, also M.-J. Bonnet, 'Sappho, or the importance of culture in the language of love: *Tribade, Lesbienne, Homosexuelle*', in A. Livia and K. Hall (eds), *Queerly Phrased: Language, Gender, and Sexuality* (New York, 1997), pp. 147–66, at p. 151. William King used 'lesbian' as an adjective in 1732 and noun in 1736 to refer to gender transgression, hermaphroditism and monstrosity as well as same-sex desires in editions of *The Toast*, a mock-epic poem attacking the Duchess of Newburgh: E. Donoghue, *Passions between Women: British Lesbian Culture 1668–1801* (New York, 1995), pp. 3, 54–7, 241, although Donoghue defends transhistorical use of the word.

3 For views at odds with ours, see M. Vicinus, 'Lesbian history: all theory and no facts or all facts and no theory', *Radical History Review*, 60 (1994), 57–75, at 60; B. Brooten, *Love between Women: Early Christian Responses to Female Homoeroticism* (Chicago, 1996), p. 5; M. R. Hunt, 'The sapphic strain: English lesbians in the long eighteenth century', in J. M. Bennett and A. M. Froide (eds), *Singlewomen in the European Past, 1250–1800* (Philadelphia, 1999), ch. 10; J. M. Bennett, '"Lesbian-like" and the social history of lesbianisms', *Journal of the History of Sexuality*, 9 (2000), 1–24, at 11–12; F. C. Sautman and P. Sheingorn, 'Introduction: charting the field', in F. C. Sautman and P. Sheingorn (eds), *Same Sex Love and Desire among Women in the Middle Ages* (New York, 2001), pp. 1–47, at p. 11. For a critique of Brooten's fusion of 'tribades' and 'viragines' (generally 'masculine, phallic women who desire and sexually penetrate other women and even boys') with modern concepts of lesbians as women with 'a long-term or even lifelong homoerotic orientation', see D. Halperin, 'Lesbian historiography before the name?', *GLQ*, 4 (1998), 559–78, at 564–5.

4 P. Crawford and S. Mendelson, 'Sexual identities in early modern England: the marriage of two women in 1680', *Gender and History*, 7 (1995), 362–77.

5 E. S. Wahl, *Invisible Relations: Representations of Female Intimacy in the Age of Enlightenment* (Stanford, 1999), pp. 6–7.

6 See V. Traub, 'The present future of lesbian historiography', in G. E. Haggerty and M. McGarry (eds), *A Companion to Lesbian, Gay, Bisexual, Transgender, and Queer Studies* (Oxford, 2007), ch. 7.

7 J. Boswell, *Christianity, Social Tolerance, and Homosexuality: Gay People in Western Europe from the Beginning of the Christian Era to the Fourteenth Century* (Chicago, 1980), p. xvii; S. Gaunt, 'Gay studies and feminism: a medievalist's perspective', Forum: Gay and Lesbian Concerns in Medieval Studies, *Medieval Feminist Newletter*, 13 (Spring, 1992), 3–7, at 4; B. Reay, *Popular Cultures in England, 1550–1750* (New York, 1998), p. 29; J. C. Brown, 'Lesbian sexuality in medieval and early modern Europe', in M. B. Duberman, M. Vicinus and G. Chauncey (eds), *Hidden from History: Reclaiming the Gay and*

Lesbian Past (New York, 1989), p. 75; Jennings, *A Lesbian History of Britain*, p. 1.

8   V. Traub, 'The renaissance of lesbianism in early modern England', *GLQ*, 7 (2001), 247.

9   The founding texts might be L. Crompton's 'The myth of lesbian impunity: capital laws from 1270 to 1791', *Journal of Homosexuality*, 6 (1981), 11–25, and L. Faderman, *Surpassing the Love of Men: Romantic Friendship and Love between Women from the Renaissance to the Present* (New York, 1981).

10   S. Schibanoff, 'Chaucer's lesbians: drawing blanks', *Medieval Feminist Newletter*, 13 (Spring 1992), 11–14, at 13.

11   Vicinus, 'Lesbian history', 58–9.

12   A. Rich, 'Compulsory heterosexuality and lesbian existence', *Signs*, 5 (1980), 631–60, quote at 635. She defines 'lesbian continuum' as 'woman-identified experience: not simply the fact that a woman has had or consciously desired genital sexual experience with another woman . . . [but also] many more forms of primary intensity between and among women, including the sharing of a rich inner life, the bonding against male tyranny, the giving and receiving of practical and political support', 648–9. Bennett's '"Lesbian-like"' revised the idea and located it within medieval history, esp. p. 15. Vicinus, 'Lesbian history', counsels moving on from its account of 'all-female bonding . . . as unproblematic nurturance and love', 58.

13   Sautman and Sheingorn, 'Introduction: charting the field', p. 29.

14   V. Traub, *The Renaissance of Lesbianism in Early Modern England* (Cambridge, 2002), pp. 6, 13.

15   C. Lansing, 'Donna con donna? A 1295 inquest into female sodomy', in P. M. Soergel (ed.), *Studies in Medieval and Renaissance History*, 3rd series, vol. 2, *Sexuality and Culture in Medieval and Renaissance Europe* (New York, 2005), pp. 109–22.

16   Ibid., p. 110, Latin text on p. 118.

17   Ibid., pp. 111, 114, 115.

18   Crompton, 'The myth of lesbian impunity', 15–16.

19   In 2000 Bennett counted twelve cases down to 1500, but Guercia's case has since come to light: '"Lesbian-like"', 3. For some premodern cases after 1500, see Crompton, 'The myth of lesbian impunity', 17–21; M. Boone, 'State power and illicit sexuality: the persecution of sodomy in late medieval Bruges', *Journal of Medieval History*, 22 (1996), 143; H. Puff, *Sodomy in Reformation Germany and Switzerland, 1400–1600* (Chicago, 2003), pp. 33–4.

20   M. Rocke, *Forbidden Friendships: Homosexuality and Male Culture in Renaissance Florence* (New York, 1996), p. 258, n. 23; G. Ruggiero, *The Boundaries of Eros: Sex Crime and Sexuality in Renaissance Venice* (New York, 1985), p. 189, n. 21; M. E. Perry, *Gender and Disorder in Early Modern Seville* (Princeton, 1990), p. 23.

21   H. Puff, 'Female sodomy: the trial of Katherina Hetzeldorfer (1477)', *Journal of Medieval and Early Modern Studies*, 30 (2000), 41–61.

22   Ibid., 58–61.

23 Ibid., 46–7.

24 Lansing, 'Donna con donna', p. 110.

25 Puff, 'Female sodomy', 43–6, quote at 44.

26 J. Cadden, *Meanings of Sex Difference in the Middle Ages: Medicine, Science, and Culture* (Cambridge, 1993), pp. 224–5; E. Benkov, 'The erased lesbian: sodomy and the legal tradition in medieval Europe', in Sautman and Sheingorn (eds), *Same Sex Love and Desire*, pp. 101–22, at pp. 111–14.

27 J. Murray, 'Twice marginal and twice invisible: lesbians in the Middle Ages', in V. L. Bullough and J. A. Brundage (eds), *Handbook of Medieval Sexuality* (New York, 1996), pp. 191–222, at p. 199. Also J. M. Brown, 'Lesbian sexuality in Renaissance Italy: the case of Sister Benedetta Carlini', *Signs*, 9 (1984), 754; Brooten, *Love between Women*, pp. 241, 307; Benkov, 'The erased lesbian'.

28 'The Penitential of Theodore' in J. T. McNeill and H. M. Gamer (eds and trans.), *Medieval Handbooks of Penance: A Translation of the Principal Libri Poenitentiales and Selections from Related Documents* (New York, 1938), p. 185. Male–male sex *in femoribus* and between boys was treated less seriously, but most sex acts between men merited between four and fifteen years' penance.

29 J. A. Brundage, *Law, Sex, and Christian Society in Medieval Europe* (Chicago, 1987), p. 167.

30 H. R. Lemay, 'William of Saliceto on human sexuality', *Viator*, 12 (1981), 165–81, at 178–80.

31 Brooten, *Love between Women*, pp. 49–50, 162–71; D. Jacquart and C. Thomasset, *Sexuality and Medicine in the Middle Ages*, trans. M. Adamson (Cambridge, 1988), pp. 45–7; K. Park, 'The rediscovery of the clitoris: French medicine and the tribade, 1570–1620', in D. Hillman and C. Mazzio (eds), *The Body in Parts: Fantasies of Corporeality in Early Modern Europe* (New York, 1997), pp. 171–93; Traub, *The Renaissance of Lesbianism*, pp. 87–93, 188–228.

32 Crompton, 'The myth of lesbian impunity', 13; Benkov, 'The erased lesbian', pp. 109–10.

33 S. Amer, 'Lesbian sex and the military: from the medieval Arabic tradition to French literature', in Sautman and Sheingorn (eds), *Same Sex Love and Desire*, pp. 179–98; text of poem in R. L. A. Clark, 'Jousting without a lance: the condemnation of female homoeroticism in the *Livre des Manières*', in the same volume, pp. 143–77, at 166–7; also Murray, 'Twice marginal', p. 210.

34 P. Simons, 'Lesbian (in)visibility in Italian Renaissance culture: Diana and other cases of *donna con donna*', *Journal of Homosexuality*, 27 (1994), 81–122.

35 Cited in U. Wiethaus, 'Female homoerotic discourse and religion in medieval Germanic culture', in S. Farmer and C. B. Pasternak (eds), *Gender and Difference in the Middle Ages* (Minneapolis, 2003), pp. 288–321, at p. 293.

36 J. C. Brown, *Immodest Acts: The Life of a Lesbian Nun in Renaissance Italy* (New York, 1986). Compare E. A. Matter's suggestion that

Benedetta Carlini's relationship with another nun was 'so bizarre as to defy our modern categories of sexual identity': 'Discourses of desire: sexuality and Christian women's visionary narratives', *Journal of Homosexuality*, 18 (1989), pp. 119–32, at pp. 122–3. Matter takes great care to read Benedetta's and other contemporary nuns' experiences within the context of women's spiritual *and* fleshly efforts at *imitatio Christi* and this as 'something more complicated than a repressed lesbian love story', 127. Although Benedetta belongs chronologically to the second part of this chapter, her alleged mystical experiences are congruent with those of medieval nuns.

37   Brown, *Immodest Acts*, pp. 151–5.
38   Ibid., p. 162.
39   Ibid., p. 162.
40   Ibid., p. 163.
41   Ibid., pp. 132–7.
42   Augustine, *Epistle* 211.14, cited in Brooten, *Love between Women*, pp. 350–1.
43   K. Lochrie, 'Between women', in C. Dinshaw and D. Wallace (eds), *The Cambridge Companion to Medieval Women's Writing* (Cambridge, 2003), pp. 70–88, at pp. 78–80; also C. Dinshaw, *Getting Medieval: Sexualities and Communities, Pre- and Postmodern* (Durham, NC, 1999), p. 88.
44   For example, Simons, 'Lesbian (in)visibility', 82.
45   Quoted in full in P. Dronke, *Medieval Latin and the Rise of the European Love-Lyric*, 2 vols (Oxford, 1968), vol. 2, pp. 480–1; Boswell, *Christianity*, pp. 220–1; often cited: see E. A. Matter, 'My sister, my spouse: woman-identified women in medieval Christianity', *Journal of Feminist Studies in Religion*, 2 (1986), 81–93, at 82–4.
46   Dronke, *Medieval Latin*, vol. 2, pp. 478–9; Boswell, *Christianity*, p. 220; Matter, 'My sister', 84; Murray, 'Twice marginal', pp. 207 and 211.
47   R. D. Hale, 'Brilliant constellations: history in the presence of the now', contribution to 'History's queer touch: a forum on Carolyn Dinshaw's *Getting Medieval: Sexualities and Communities, Pre- and Postmodern*', *Journal of the History of Sexuality*, 10 (2001), 167–72, at 169–70.
48   Wiethaus, 'Female homoerotic discourse', pp. 298–9. For a different perspective on the female homosociality of Helfta see R. Voaden, 'All girls together: community, gender and vision at Helfta', in D. Watt (ed.), *Medieval Women in their Communities* (Cardiff, 1997), pp. 72–91.
49   G. Leff, *Heresy in the Later Middle Ages*, 2 vols (Manchester, 1967), vol. 2, p. 721; M. Goodrich, 'Sodomy in medieval secular law', *Journal of Homosexuality*, 1 (1976), 295–302, at 296.
50   E. A. Petroff, *Consolation of the Blessed* (Millerton, NY, 1980), p. 34.
51   U. Wiethaus, 'In search of medieval women's friendships: Hildegard of Bingen's letters to her female contemporaries', in U. Wiethaus (ed.), *Maps of Flesh and Light: The Religious Experience of Medieval Women Mystics* (Syracuse, NY, 1993), pp. 93–111, quote at p. 105.
52   *The Life of Holy Hildegard*, in A. Silvas (ed. and trans.), *Jutta and Hildegard: The Biographical Sources* (University Park, PA, 1999), p. 165.

53 S. Schibanoff, 'Hildegard of Bingen and Richardis of Stade: the discourse of desire', in Sautman and Sheingorn (eds), *Same Sex Love and Desire*, pp. 49–83, at pp. 56–60.

54 Ibid., p. 55.

55 Ibid., pp. 67–8.

56 B. W. Holsinger, 'The flesh of the voice: embodiment and the homoerotics of devotion in the music of Hildegard of Bingen (1098–1179)', *Signs*, 19 (1993), 92–125, quotes at 117, 107. Holsinger insists, however, that 'lesbian' is an inappropriate word for Hildegard (119–20).

57 Acts 16: 1–3; 1 Timothy 1: 2.

58 Wiethaus, 'In search', pp. 105–10.

59 J. L. Baird (ed.), *The Personal Correspondence of Hildegard of Bingen* (Oxford, 2006), pp. 47–8. Hildegard's transferral of the mother role to Richardis and place of the daughter to herself may have a literal meaning (she elsewhere refers to Richardis as Mother – by implication Abbess – of Bassum), or (as Schibanoff suggests) may be a poetic expression of merging with Richardis, p. 62 and p. 78, n. 56. See also Wiethaus, 'In search', p. 107.

60 K. Lochrie, 'Mystical acts, queer tendencies', in K. Lochrie, P. McCracken and J. A. Schultz (eds), *Constructing Medieval Sexuality* (Minnesota, 1997), pp. 180–200, quote at p. 186.

61 S. Murk-Jansen, 'The use of gender and gender-related imagery in Hadewijch', in J. Chance (ed.), *Gender and Text in the Middle Ages* (Gainesville, 1996), pp. 52–68.

62 Wiethaus, 'Female homoerotic discourse', esp. pp. 300–10, quote at p. 309.

63 Matter, 'My sister', 84–6.

64 A. Rieger, 'Was Bieiris de Romans lesbian?', in W. D. Paden (ed.), *The Voice of the Trobairitz: Perspectives on the Women Troubadours* (Philadelphia, 1989), pp. 73–94. Also M. Bogin (ed. and trans.), *The Women Troubadours* (New York, 1980), p. 133; she also provides a summary of some earlier interpretations, pp. 176–7.

65 D. Watt, 'Read my lips: clippyng and kyssyng in the early sixteenth century', in Livia and Hall (eds), *Queerly Phrased*, pp. 167–77, at p. 175; D. Watt, 'Behaving like a man? Inccst, lesbian desire, and gender play in *Yde et Olive* and its adaptations', *Comparative Literature*, 50 (1998), 265–85; R. L. A. Clark, 'A heroine's sexual itinerary: incest, transvestism, and same-sex marriage in *Yde et Olyve*, in K. J. Taylor (ed.), *Gender Transgressions: Crossing the Normative Barrier in Old French Literature* (New York, 1998), pp. 889–905; K. M. Blumreich, 'Lesbian desire in the Old French "Roman de Silence"', *Arthuriana*, 7 (1997), 47–62.

66 H. E. Rollins (ed.), *The Pepys Ballads*, 3 vols (Cambridge, Mass., 1929), vol. 3, p. 142.

67 R. M. Dekker and L. C. van de Pol, *The Tradition of Female Transvestism in Early Modern Europe* (London, 1989); D. Dugaw, *Warrior Women and Popular Balladry, 1650–1850* (Cambridge, 1989).

68 *The Life of Long Meg of Westminster.* This book is in the library of Samuel Pepys at Magdalene College Library, Cambridge: Pepys Chapbooks, Penny Merriments Collection, vol. 2, no. 26.

69 F. Easton, 'Gender's two bodies: women warriors, female husbands and plebeian life', *Past and Present*, 180 (2003), 131–74.

70 Crawford and Mendelson, 'Sexual identities'.

71 Easton, 'Gender's two bodies', 135.

72 W. G. Day (ed.), *The Pepys Ballads*, 5 vols (Cambridge, 1987), vol. 5, p. 424.

73 [Henry Fielding], *The Female Husband or the Surprising History of Mrs Mary, alias Mr George Hamilton* (London, 1746), pp. 2, 11, 23; [John Cleland], *Historical and Physical Dissertation on the Case of Catherine Vizzani* (London, 1751), pp. 20, 34.

74 Fielding, *The Female Husband*, p. 15.

75 Ibid., p. 1.

76 Cleland, *Historical and Physical Dissertation*, pp. 41, 53.

77 T. Hitchcock, *English Sexualities, 1700–1800* (New York, 1997), p. 77.

78 Easton, 'Gender's two bodies', 157.

79 T. van der Meer, 'Tribades on trial: female same-sex offenders in late eighteenth-century Amsterdam', in J. C. Fout (ed.), *Forbidden History: The State, Society, and the Regulation of Sexuality in Modern Europe: Essays from the Journal of the History of Sexuality* (Chicago, 1992), pp. 189–210.

80 Ibid., p. 198.

81 Ibid., p. 197.

82 Crawford and Mendelson, 'Sexual identities', 373–4.

83 H. Whitbread (ed.), *No Priest But Love: Excerpts From the Diaries of Anne Lister, 1824–1826* (New York, 1992), p. 49.

84 Wahl, *Invisible Relations*, ch. 1; J. Merrick and B. T. Ragan (eds), *Homosexuality in Early Modern France: A Documentary Collection* (New York, 2001), pp. 26–8.

85 The author was Giles Jacob: [G. Jacob], *Tractatus de Hermaphroditis* (London, 1718), p. 17.

86 V. Traub, 'The psychomorphology of the clitoris, or, the reemergence of the *Tribade* in English culture', in V. Finucci and K. Brownlee (eds), *Generation and Degeneration: Tropes of Reproduction in Literature and History from Antiquity to Early Modern Europe* (Durham, NC, 2001), p. 169.

87 Traub, 'The renaissance of lesbianism', 253.

88 H. Andreadis, *Sappho in Early Modern England: Female Same-Sex Literary Erotics, 1550–1714* (Chicago, 2001), p. 3.

89 H. Andreadis, 'Sappho in early modern England: a study in sexual reputation', in E. Greene (ed.), *Re-Reading Sappho: Reception and Transmission* (Berkeley and Los Angeles, 1996), ch. 5 (quote from p. 112).

90 Ibid., pp. 107, 116.

91 J. DeJean, *Fictions of Sappho 1546–1937* (Chicago, 1989), p. 23.

92 Traub, *The Renaissance of Lesbianism*, pp. 1–5, 270–5 (quote on p. 3).

93 Simons, 'Lesbian (in)visibility', esp. 94–109.

94   M. Mourao, 'The representation of female desire in early modern pornographic texts, 1660–1745', *Signs*, 24 (1999), 589–94; J. G. Turner, *Schooling Sex: Libertine Literature and Erotic Education in Italy, France, and England 1534–1685* (Oxford, 2003), ch. 4.

95   *Tractatus de Hermaphroditis*, pp. 14–15, 16–17.

96   Ibid., p. 21.

97   Ibid., pp. 40–2.

98   Ibid., p. 45.

99   B. K. Mudge (ed.), *When Flesh Becomes Word: An Anthology of Early Eighteenth-Century Libertine Literature* (New York, 2004), p. 204.

100   S. Toulalan, *Imagining Sex: Pornography and Bodies in Seventeenth-Century England* (Oxford, 2007), ch. 4.

101   Mudge (ed.), *When Flesh Becomes Word*, p. 222.

102   Turner, *Schooling Sex*, pp. 194, 195, 197.

103   Merrick and Ragan (eds), *Homosexuality in Early Modern France*, p. 103. The edition used in this collection of documents is a modern translation of the French edition of 1858–95.

104   Ibid., pp. 103–4.

105   K. Boris (ed.), *Same-Sex Desire in the English Renaissance: A Sourcebook of Texts, 1470–1650* (New York, 2004), p. 303. This extract is from a 1934 English translation.

106   Exactly how it is rendered in the modern English translation of the nineteenth-century French version in Merrick and Ragan (eds), *Homosexuality in Early Modern France*, p. 103: 'the Lesbian dames' and 'the Lesbian women' become 'the ladies of Lesbos' and 'women of Lesbos'.

107   Ibid., pp. 104, 105.

108   Ibid., p. 105.

109   Ibid., pp. 214, 216.

110   See a similar observation by Traub, *The Renaissance of Lesbianism*, p. 299.

111   See the prominence of Phillips in Wahl, *Invisible Relations*, ch. 4; Andreadis, *Sappho in Early Modern England*, ch.3; Traub, *The Renaissance of Lesbianism*, pp. 295–325, 335–42.

112   Andreadis, *Sappho in Early Modern England*, pp. 67–8.

113   Wahl, *Invisible Relations*, p. 97.

114   Ibid., ch. 3.

115   N. Eustace, '"The Cornerstone of a Copious Work": love and power in eighteenth-century courtship', *Journal of Social History*, 34 (2001), 519.

116   S. Velasco, *Lesbians in Early Modern Spain* (Nashville, 2011), ch. 4. We are most grateful to the author for permitting us to read and cite her book before publication.

117   Ibid.

118   Ibid., 'Introduction'.

119   H. Whitbread (ed.), *I Know My Own Heart: The Diaries of Anne Lister 1791–1840* (New York, 1992), p. 10.

120   Ibid., pp. 121, 129, 145 (for quote), 154, 159.

121   Wahl, *Invisible Relations*, p. 113.

122   Ibid., pp. 118–19.
123   J. Farnsworth, 'Voicing female desire in "Poem XLIX"', *Studies in English Literature*, 36 (1996), 57–72; also Traub, *The Renaissance of Lesbianism*, pp. 288–90.
124   Whitbread (ed.), *I Know My Own Heart*, p. 262.
125   Ibid., p. 210.
126   Ibid., p. 273.
127   Ibid., pp. 273, 291.
128   Ibid., p. 291.
129   Whitbread (ed.), *No Priest But Love*, pp. 31–2.
130   Ibid., pp. 48–9.
131   Whitbread (ed.), *I Know My Own Heart*, p. 281.
132   Ibid; Whitbread (ed.), *No Priest But Love*.
133   For Lister's attempt to make sense of her desires, drawing on material in the unpublished as well as the printed journals, see A. Clark, 'Anne Lister's construction of lesbian identity', in K. M. Phillips and B. Reay (eds), *Sexualities in History: A Reader* (New York, 2002), ch. 12. As her chapter's title indicates, Clark assumes a lesbianism (albeit fractured) that we are here contesting.
134   Whitbread (ed.), *I Know My Own Heart*, p. 145.
135   A. Jagose, *Inconsequence: Lesbian Representation and the Logic of Sexual Sequence* (Ithaca, NY, 2002), pp. 13–24.
136   Ibid., p. 21.
137   Whitbread (ed.), *I Know My Own Heart*, p. 145.
138   Ibid., p. 267.
139   S. S. Lanser, '"Queer to queer": the sapphic body as transgressive text', in K. Kittredge (ed.), *Lewd & Notorious: Female Transgression in the Eighteenth Century* (Ann Arbor, Mich., 2003), p. 35.
140   Ibid., p. 34.
141   Ibid., p. 40.
142   Ibid.
143   Ibid., pp. 37–8.
144   Ibid., p. 41.
145   R. Brome, *The Antipodes*, ed. A. Haaker (London, 1967), p. 20. The play was first published in London in 1640.
146   Ibid.
147   Ibid.
148   M. de Zayas, *The Disenchantments of Love*, ed. and trans. H. P. Boyer (Albany, NY, 1997), p. 224. First published in 1647.
149   Velasco, *Lesbians in Early Modern Spain*, esp. Introduction.
150   Ibid., ch. 2.
151   Ibid.
152   Ibid.
153   Brantôme, *Vies des Dames Galantes*, p. 129, our translation.
154   Faderman, *Surpassing the Love of Men*, pp. 54–5.
155   B. Eriksson (ed. and trans.), 'A lesbian execution in Germany, 1721: the trial records', *Journal of the History of Homosexuality*, 6 (1981), 27–40, quotes at 31, 34.
156   Velasco, *Lesbians in Early Modern Spain*, ch. 2.

157 Vicinus, 'Lesbian history', 66, citing T. Castle, *The Apparitional Lesbian: Female Homosexuality and Modern Culture* (New York, 1993), p. 19.

158 Vicinus, 'Lesbian history': 'At the same time, we should not lose that sense of "dangerous love", so eloquently defended by Elizabeth Wilson a decade ago; risk-taking, romantic idealism, and passionate hedonism are not limited to a heterosexual imagination'; 'I am not making a case for lesbian history, but for the central place of lesbians in history. It is the presumed heterosexuality of women, past and present, which needs to be overcome', 66, 67; also Bennett, '"Lesbian-like"', 4–5.

CHAPTER 5 BEFORE PORNOGRAPHY

1 R. Darnton, 'Sex for thought', in K. M. Phillips and B. Reay (eds), *Sexualities in History: A Reader* (New York, 2002), ch. 10.

2 B. K. Mudge, *The Whore's Story: Women, Pornography, and the British Novel, 1684–1830* (Oxford, 2000), pp. 27–8.

3 L. Hunt, 'Introduction: obscenity and the origins of modernity, 1500–1800', in L. Hunt (ed.), *The Invention of Pornography: Obscenity and the Origins of Modernity, 1500–1800* (New York, 1993), p. 10.

4 I. F. Moulton, *Before Pornography: Erotic Writing in Early Modern England* (New York, 2000), p. 8.

5 A. Carter, *The Sadeian Woman: An Exercise in Cultural History* (London, 1979), p. 15.

6 Moulton, *Before Pornography*, pp. 5, 8: 'The word *pornographoi* appears only once in classical Greek writing, in the *Deipnosophistae* of the second-century complier Athenaeus. . . . [T]he term *pornographoi* would seem to refer to artists who painted pictures of whores or courtesans' (p. 8).

7 Ibid., p. 8; Hunt, 'Introduction', p. 13. A French treatise on prostitution, *Le Pornographe* (1769), traded on ancient meanings of the word, while by the 1830s and 1840s *pornographique, pornographe* and *pornographie* started to refer to sexually obscene writing and imagery.

8 L. M. Bitel, *Land of Women: Tales of Sex and Gender from Early Ireland* (Ithaca, NY, 1996), pp. 204–5.

9 J. Goldberg, 'John Skathelok's dick: voyeurism and "pornography" in late medieval England', in N. McDonald (ed.), *Medieval Obscenities* (Woodbridge, 2006), pp. 105–23. It is puzzling to find some experts in medieval linguistics slipping between 'pornography' and 'obscenity' in their objections to Hunt's chronology: e.g. J. Ziolkowski, 'Introduction' and L. Dunton-Downer, 'Poetic language and the obscene', in J. Ziolkowski (ed.), *Obscenity: Social Control and Artistic Creation in the European Middle Ages* (Leiden, 1998), pp. 5, 22–3.

10 J. A. Brundage, 'Obscene and lascivious: behavioral obscenity in canon law', in Ziolkowski (ed.), *Obscenity*, pp. 247–59.

11 F. Mormando, *The Preacher's Demons: Bernadino of Siena and the Social Underworld of Early Renaissance Italy* (Chicago, 1999), pp. 154–5.

12   McDonald, 'Introduction', in McDonald (ed.), *Medieval Obscenities*, pp. 3, 7.

13   M. Jones, *The Secret Middle Ages* (Stroud, 2002), pp. 249–50; also M. Jones, 'The late-medieval Dutch pilgrim badges', in T. Hyman and R. Malbert (eds), *Carnivalesque* (London, 2000), pp. 98–101; M. Mitchener, *Medieval Pilgrim and Secular Badges* (London, 1986), p. 126.

14   J. Koldeweij, '"Shameless and naked images": obscene badges as parodies of popular devotion', in S. Blick and R. Tekippe (eds), *Art and Architecture of Late Medieval Pilgrimage in Northern Europe and the British Isles* (Leiden, 2005), p. 493. Among his other essays on the badges see 'Lifting the veil on pilgrimage badges', in J. Stopford (ed.), *Pilgrimage Explored* (York, 1999), pp. 161–88.

15   K. Lochrie, 'Queer souvenirs', unpublished paper delivered at the 'Medieval Sexuality' conference, Center for Medieval and Renaissance Studies, UCLA, 6–7 March 2009.

16   A. M. Rasmussen, 'Wanderlust: obscenity and the meanings of mobility', unpublished paper delivered at the 'Medieval Sexuality' conference, Center for Medieval and Renaissance Studies, UCLA, 6–7 March 2009.

17   McDonald, 'Introduction', in McDonald (ed.), *Medieval Obscenities*, pp. 10–11.

18   Koldeweij, '"Shameless and naked images"', pp. 503–4.

19   For discussion and examples see M. Grant and A. Mulas, *Eros in Pompeii: The Secret Rooms of the National Museum of Naples* (New York, 1975); E. Keuls, *The Reign of the Phallus: Sexual Politics in Ancient Athens* (New York, 1985).

20   A. Weir and J. Jermin, *Images of Lust: Sexual Carvings on Medieval Churches* (London, 1986), pp. 147–8

21   M. Camille, 'Dr Witkowski's anus: French doctors, German homosexuals and the obscene in medieval church art', in McDonald (ed.), *Medieval Obscenities*, quote at p. 33.

22   The contributors to two recent essay collections, Ziolkowski (ed.), *Obscenity* and McDonald (ed.), *Medieval Obscenities*, resist any singular definition of 'obscenity' as it applies to medieval culture and question whether sexually frank material would have been 'obscene' to medieval audiences. On medieval meanings of 'obscene' see especially E. Dillon, 'Representing obscene sound', and A. Minnis, 'From *coilles* to *bel chose*: discourses of obscenity in Jean de Meun and Chaucer', in McDonald (ed.), *Medieval Obscenities*, pp. 60–2 and 156.

23   There are 167 extant or recorded sheelas in the British Isles: see B. Freitag, *Sheela-na-Gigs: Unravelling an Enigma* (New York, 2004), pp. 121–58.

24   Ibid., pp. 1–11 surveys the sheelas' most common physical attributes.

25   Ibid., pp. 52–67.

26   The main theories are surveyed in ibid., pp. 20–51.

27   J. Dor, 'The sheela-na-gig: an incongruous sign of sexual purity?', in A. Bernau, R. Evans and S. Salih (eds), *Medieval Virginities* (Cardiff, 2003), pp. 33–55.

28   J. Andersen, *The Witch on the Wall: Medieval Erotic Sculpture in the British Isles* (Copenhagen, 1977); Weir and Jermin, *Images of Lust*, pp. 15–17.

29   Although see Bitel, *Land of Women*, pp. 204–5, 233.

30   Freitag, *Sheela-na-Gigs*, p. 69.

31   Ibid., pp. 68–118.

32   Weir and Jermin, *Images of Lust*, p. 7, plate 1, and p. 23. The Romanesque carving has been inserted into the church tower but its original position is unclear.

33   Camille, 'Dr Witkowski's anus', p. 36; Andersen, *The Witch on the Wall*, pp. 27–31.

34   M. Camille, 'Obscenity under erasure: censorship in medieval illuminated manuscripts', in Ziolkowski (ed.), *Obscenity*, esp pp. 150–4.

35   More than twenty references to 'taboo' are listed in the volume's index: Ziolkowski (ed.), *Obscenity*, p. 357.

36   *OED*, s.v. 'taboo'.

37   M. Caputi, *Voluptuous Yearnings: A Feminist Theory of the Obscene* (Lanham, Md, 1994), p. 12. For examples see essays by Caviness and Ford in Ziolkowski (ed.), *Obscenity*, pp. 156, 178.

38   T. Heffernan, *Sacred Biography: Saints and Their Biographers in the Middle Ages* (Oxford, 1988), pp. 267–86; K. Gravdal, *Ravishing Maidens: Writing Rape in Medieval French Law and Literature* (Philadelphia, 1991), ch. 1; S. Gaunt, *Gender and Genre in Medieval French Literature* (Cambridge, 1995), pp. 194–8.

39   *The Golden Legend: Readings on the Saints*, trans. W. Granger Ryan, 2 vols (Princeton, 1993), vol. 1, pp. 369, 155. Each of the virgin's lives was slightly different, and not all contained the elements mentioned here; we generalize in the interests of brevity.

40   *The Belles Heures of Jean de France, Duc de Berry*, The Metropolitan Museum of Art, New York, The Cloisters Collection, Purchase, 1954, fols 17r, 17v, 179, 180 (T. B. Husband, *The Art of Illumination: The Limbourg Brothers and the Belles Heures of Jean de France, Duc de Berry* (New York, 2008), pp. 99, 101, 213, 214); J. Wogan-Browne, 'Saints' lives and the female reader', *Forum for Modern Language Studies*, 37 (1991), 314–32.

41   For example, K. J. Lewis, '"Lete me suffer": reading the torture of St Margaret of Antioch in late medieval England', in J. Wogan-Browne, R. Voaden, A. Diamond, A. Hutchinson, C. Meale and L. Johnson (eds), *Medieval Women: Texts and Contexts in Late Medieval Britain: Essays for Felicity Riddy* (Turnhout, 2000), pp. 69–82; S. Salih, *Versions of Virginity in Late Medieval England* (Cambridge, 2001), pp. 74–106.

42   P. Bailey, 'Parasexuality and glamour: the Victorian barmaid as cultural prototype', in Phillips and Reay (eds), *Sexualities in History*, pp. 222–3.

43   This argument is developed in K. M. Phillips, 'Desiring virgins: maidens, martyrs and femininity in late medieval England', in P. J. P. Goldberg and F. Riddy (eds), *Youth in the Middle Ages* (Woodbridge, 2004), pp. 45–59.

44 D. Johnston, 'Erotica and satire in medieval Welsh poetry', in Ziolkowski (ed.), *Obscenity*, quotes at pp. 65, 69, 70–1.

45 G. Boccaccio, *The Decameron*, trans. M. Musa and P. Bondanella (New York, 1982).

46 Gravdal, *Ravishing Maidens*; G. L. Smith, *The Medieval French Pastourelle Tradition: Poetic Motivations and Generic Transformations* (Gainesville, Fla., 2009).

47 Helpful overviews include C. Muscatine, *The Old French Fabliaux* (New Haven, 1986) and N. J. Lacy, *Reading Fabliaux* (New York, 1993), but readers should expect to find scholarly disagreement pervading these and every study of fabliaux.

48 Boccaccio, *The Decameron*, pp. 581–5; G. Chaucer, *The Riverside Chaucer*, ed. L. D. Benson, 3rd edn (Oxford, 1988), pp. 78–84.

49 Chaucer, *The Riverside Chaucer*, pp. 68–77.

50 Muscatine, *The Old French Fabliaux*, pp. 24–46.

51 Lacy, *Reading Fabliaux*, pp. 14, 16, 18 and 60–77, quote at p. 18.

52 Ibid., p. 41.

53 Ibid., pp. 37–8. Compare Muscatine, who contends fabliaux have their own ethical system 'usually ignoring conventional morality': *The Old French Fabliaux*, p. 93.

54 R. H. Bloch, 'Modest maids and modified nouns: obscenity in the fabliaux', in Ziolkowski (ed.), *Obscenity*, p. 293.

55 Lacy, *Reading Fabliaux*, p. 14, n. 13.

56 Cited in Bloch, 'Modest maids', p. 296.

57 Alastair Minnis notes both satiric and respectable medieval uses of cunt ('cunte' or 'count') – the latter evident in some late medieval English medical texts. The Wife of Bath's *bel chose*, in contrast, could have had improper connotations: Minnis, 'From *coilles* to *bel chose*', pp. 172–5.

58 Examples from Muscatine, *The Old French Fabliaux*, pp. 112–14.

59 Lacy, *Reading Fabliaux*, pp. 78–95, esp. pp. 94–5.

60 M. Camille, *Image on the Edge: Margins of Medieval Art* (London, 1992), p. 160.

61 For the ballad's performative aspects (not just sexual), see N. Wurzbach, *The Rise of the English Street Ballad, 1550–1650* (Cambridge, 1990), chs 1–3.

62 W. G. Day (ed.), *The Pepys Ballads*, 5 vols (Cambridge, 1987), vol. 3, p. 306.

63 Ibid., vol. 5, p. 161.

64 Ibid., vol. 3, p. 6.

65 Ibid., p. 87.

66 Ibid., p. 190.

67 Ibid., p. 3.

68 For example, ibid., vol. 1, pp. 264–5, 354–5, 360–1, vol. 3, pp. 3, 35, 139.

69 Ibid., vol. 3, pp. 78, 132, vol. 4, p. 20.

70 Ibid., vol. 5, p. 21.

71 Quoted by V. A. C. Gatrell, *The Hanging Tree: Execution and the English People 1770–1868* (Oxford, 1994), p. 137.

72 Ibid., pp. 138, 152–3.
73 L. Gowing, *Domestic Dangers: Women, Words, and Sex in Early Modern London* (Oxford, 1996), pp. 42–4, 52–8, 232–62. The quote comes from p. 58.
74 Somerset Record Office, Q/SR 95 ii/41: Somerset Quarter Sessions Rolls, 1657. G. R. Quaife first drew attention to this document in his *Wanton Wenches and Wayward Wives: Peasants and Illicit Sex in Early Seventeenth-Century England* (London, 1979), pp. 156–7.
75 P. Findlen, 'Humanism, politics and pornography in Renaissance Italy', in Hunt (ed.), *The Invention of Pornography*, ch. 1; Moulton, *Before Pornography*, ch. 3.
76 Moulton, *Before Pornography*, p. 128.
77 S. Toulalan, *Imagining Sex: Pornography and Bodies in Seventeenth-Century England* (Oxford, 2007), pp. 22–3.
78 R. Porter, 'The literature of sexual advice before 1800', in R. Porter and M. Teich (eds), *Sexual Knowledge, Sexual Science: The History of Attitudes to Sexuality* (Cambridge, 1994), p. 150.
79 T. Hitchcock, *English Sexualities, 1700–1800* (New York, 1997), p. 14; T. W. Laqueur, *Solitary Sex: A Cultural History of Masturbation* (New York, 2003), p. 335.
80 Hunt, 'Introduction', p. 31; R. Weil, 'Sometimes a scepter is only a scepter: pornography and politics in Restoration England', in Hunt (ed.), *The Invention of Pornography*, ch. 3.
81 J. G. Turner, *Libertines and Radicals in Early Modern London: Sexuality, Politics and Literary Culture, 1630–1685* (Cambridge, 2002), pp. xiv–xv.
82 V. Gatrell, *City of Laughter: Sex and Satire in Eighteenth-Century London* (London, 2006), pp. 2–5, 323–8.
83 Hunt, 'Introduction', p. 10.
84 Darnton, 'Sex for thought', p. 207.
85 Quoted in M. Jacob, 'The materialist world of pornography', in Hunt (ed.), *The Invention of Pornography*, p. 180.
86 W. Kendrick, *The Secret Museum: Pornography in Modern Culture* (Berkeley and Los Angeles, 1996), an influential history of pornography first published in 1987.
87 J. G. Turner, *Schooling Sex: Libertine Literature and Erotic Education in Italy, France, and England, 1534–1685* (Oxford, 2003), pp. xi, 6.
88 M. V. Vicente, 'Pornography and the Spanish Inquisition: the reading of a "forbidden best seller"', unpublished essay, 2010. We are very grateful to Dr Vicente for allowing us to quote from her forthcoming work.
89 J. Cleland, *Fanny Hill or Memoirs of a Woman of Pleasure*, ed. P. Wagner (Harmondsworth, 1985), pp. 49–50. First published in London, 1748–9.
90 Toulalan makes a similar point about seventeenth-century erotic literature: *Imagining Sex*, pp. 137, 148–9, 275.
91 Cleland, *Fanny Hill*, p. 62.
92 Ibid., p. 109.
93 Ibid., pp. 81–2.
94 Ibid., p. 72.

95   Ibid., p. 81.
96   That is, in the sense of desire rather than gender.
97   Cleland, *Fanny Hill*, pp. 48–50.
98   Ibid., p. 80.
99   A. Jagose, '"Critical extasy": orgasm and sensibility in *Memoirs of a Woman of Pleasure*', *Signs*, 32 (2007), 459–82.
100 M. Mourao, 'The representation of female desire in early modern pornographic texts, 1660–1745', *Signs*, 24 (1999), 573–602.
101 B. K. Mudge (ed.), *When Flesh Becomes Word: An Anthology of Early Eighteenth-Century Libertine Literature* (New York, 2004), pp. 12, 26.
102 Moulton, *Before Pornography*, pp. 12, 15.
103 Jagose, "Critical extasy", p. 475.
104 L. Z. Sigel (ed.), *International Exposure: Perspectives on Modern European Pornography, 1800–2000* (New Brunswick, NJ, 2005).
105 E. Borenstein, 'Stripping the nation bare: Russian pornography and the insistence on meaning', in ibid., p. 235.
106 L. Williams, 'Epilogue', in her *Hard Core: Power, Pleasure, and the 'Frenzy of the Visible'* (Berkeley and Los Angeles, 1999), pp. 280–315; and L. Williams, 'Porn studies: proliferating pornographies on/scene: an introduction', in L. Williams (ed.), *Porn Studies* (Durham, NC, 2004), pp. 1–23.
107 Williams, 'Porn studies', pp. 1–3.
108 Hitchcock, *English Sexualities*, ch. 2, esp. p. 16.
109 Goldberg, 'John Skathelok's dick', pp. 118–19.
110 P. Darmon, *Trial by Impotence: Virility and Marriage in Pre-Revolutionary France*, trans. P. Keegan (London, 1985).
111 A. Robert [L. Severin], *Quatre Livres des Arrests et Choses Jugées par la Cour* (Paris, 1627), quoted in ibid., p. 171.
112 Darmon, *Trial by Impotence*, p. 180.
113 Ibid., p. 183.

EPILOGUE: SEX AT SEA?

1   L. Wallace, *Sexual Encounters: Pacific Texts, Modern Sexualities* (Ithaca, NY, 2003). See also K. Wilson, *The Island Race: Englishness, Empire and Gender in the Eighteenth Century* (London, 2003), ch. 5: 'Breasts, sodomy and the lash: masculinity and Enlightenment aboard the Cook voyages'.
2   G. Dening, *Performances* (Melbourne, 1996), p. 137.
3   G. Robertson, *The Discovery of Tahiti: A Journal of the Second Voyage of H. M. S. Dolphin Round the World*, ed. H. Carrington (London, 1948), pp. 184–5, 207, 208; J. C. Beaglehole (ed.), *The Journals of Captain James Cook on His Voyages of Discovery: The Voyage of the Resolution and Discovery 1776–1780* (Cambridge, 1967), vol. 3, pt 2, p. 1164.
4   R. Porter, 'The exotic as erotic: Captain Cook at Tahiti', in G. S. Rousseau and R. Porter (eds), *Exoticism in the Enlightenment* (Manchester, 1990), p. 125.

5   L.-A. de Bougainville, *The Pacific Journal of Louis-Antoine de Bougainville, 1767–1768*, ed. J. Dunmore (London, 2002), p. 63.
6   Ibid., p. 66.
7   Ibid., p. 74.
8   G. Forster, *A Voyage Round the World*, ed. N. Thomas and O. Berghof (Honolulu, 2000), vol. 1, p. 121.
9   Ibid., p. 311.
10 Ibid., p. 315 and p. 464, n. 36.
11 Ibid., pp. 148–9, 351.
12 Beaglehole (ed.), *The Journals of Captain James Cook*, vol. 3, pt 2, p. 1015.
13 Ibid., p. 1044.
14 Ibid., pp. 1045–7.
15 Ibid., p. 1084.
16 Ibid., p. 1095.
17 Ibid., p. 1124.
18 Ibid., p. 1151.
19 Ibid., pp. 1154, 1159.
20 Ibid., pp. 1204, 1216, 1229.
21 W. Bligh, *The Log of the Bounty*, 2 vols (London, 1937), vol. 2, p. 123.
22 Wilson, *The Island Race*, p. 184.
23 D. A. Chappell, 'Shipboard relations between Pacific Island women and Euroamerican men 1767–1887', *Journal of Pacific History*, 27 (1992), 131–49.
24 Beaglehole (ed.), *The Journals of Captain James Cook*, vol. 3, pt 2, p. 1044.
25 Bligh, *The Log of the Bounty*, vol. 1, pp. 373, 375 (for quote), 434.
26 G. H. von Langsdorff, *Voyages and Travels in Various Parts of the World During the Years 1803, 1804, 1805, 1806, and 1807*, 2 vols (London, 1813; reprint: Amsterdam, 1968), vol. 1, pp. 93–5.
27 D. Porter, *Journal of a Cruise Made to the Pacific Ocean*, 2 vols (New York, 1822; reprint: Upper Saddle River, NJ, 1970), vol. 2, pp. 59–61.
28 J. Damousi, *Depraved and Disorderly: Female Convicts, Sexuality and Gender in Colonial Australia* (Cambridge, 1997), chs 1–2.
29 *The Journal and Letters of Lt Ralph Clark 1787–1792*, ed. P. G. Fidlon and R. J. Ryan (Sydney, 1981), p. 12.
30 Ibid., pp. 19, 20.
31 Ibid., p. 97.
32 Damousi, *Depraved and Disorderly*, pp. 40–2, 52.
33 Dening, *Performances*, pp. 149–61.
34 Porter, *Journal of a Cruise*, vol. 1, pp. xl–xli.
35 C. S. Stewart, *A Visit to the South Seas* (London, 1832), pp. 167–8.
36 W. Ellis, *Polynesian Researches, During a Residence of Nearly Six Years in the South Sea Islands*, 2 vols (London, 1829; reprint: London, 1967), vol. 1, p. 325.
37 This is the theme of Wallace, *Sexual Encounters*.
38 R. Edmond, *Representing the South Pacific: Colonial Discourse from Cook to Gauguin* (Cambridge, 1997), p. 69.

39 Damousi, *Depraved and Disorderly*, pp. 48–9, 70–1.
40 Forster, *A Voyage Round the World*, vol .1, pp. 196, 197, 331.
41 Beaglehole (ed.), *The Journals of Captain James Cook*, vol. 3, pt 2, pp. 1171–2, 1226.
42 Bligh, *The Log of the Bounty*, vol. 2, p. 35.
43 Ibid., pp. 16–17 (square brackets in original).
44 Ibid., pp. 124–6.
45 Porter, 'The exotic as erotic', p. 135, p. 143, n. 92; Beaglehole (ed.), *The Journals of Captain James Cook*, vol. 3, pt 2, p. 1373.
46 Porter, *Journal of a Cruise*, vol. 2, p. 59.
47 Langsdorff, *Voyages and Travels*, vol. 1, p. 108.
48 Ibid., p. 109.
49 Ibid., pp. 109–10.
50 Ibid., pp. 134–5.
51 Wallace, *Sexual Encounters*, ch. 3.
52 Langsdorff, *Voyages and Travels*, vol. 2, pp. 47–8.
53 Ibid., p. 64.
54 J. Lamb, V. Smith and N. Thomas (eds), *Exploration & Exchange: A South Seas Anthology, 1680–1900* (Chicago, 2000), p. xvi.
55 S. Tcherkézoff, *'First Contacts' in Polynesia: The Samoan Case (1722–1848). Western Misunderstandings about Sexuality and Divinity* (Canberra, 2004), p. 42.
56 A. Salmond, *Aphrodite's Island: The European Discovery of Tahiti* (Auckland, 2009), p. 101.
57 Ibid., pp. 51, 54, 64, 95, 100, 101, 353, 463.
58 'The journal of Nassau-Siegen', in *The Pacific Journal of Louis-Antoine de Bougainville*, ed. Dunmore, p. 283.
59 Ibid.
60 'The journal of Fesche', in *The Pacific Journal of Louis-Antoine de Bougainville*, ed. Dunmore, p. 257.
61 Wallace, *Sexual Encounters*, pp. 8, 19.
62 Wilson, *The Island Race*, esp. p. 200, is more aware of the 'instabilities' and 'indeterminacies' in British sexual culture.
63 Wallace, *Sexual Encounters*, pp. 14–16.
64 *The Pacific Journal of Louis-Antoine de Bougainville*, ed. Dunmore, pp. xli–xliii, 97, 228–30.
65 C. L. Lyons, 'Mapping an Atlantic sexual culture: homoeroticism in eighteenth-century Philadelphia', *William and Mary Quarterly*, 60 (2003), 119–54.
66 J. F. Chuchiak, 'The sins of the fathers: Franciscan friars, parish priests, and the sexual conquest of the Yucatec Maya, 1548–1808', *Ethnohistory*, 54 (2007), 69–127; K. Gauderman, 'It happened on the way to the *Temascal* and other stories: desiring the illicit in colonial Spanish America', *Ethnohistory*, 54 (2007), 177–86.
67 P. Sigal, 'Queer Nahuatl: Sahagún's faggots and sodomites, lesbians and hermaphrodites', *Ethnohistory*, 54 (2007), 9–34.
68 W. Stavig, 'Political "abomination" and private reservation: the nefarious sin, homosexuality, and cultural values in colonial Peru', in

P. Sigal (ed.), *Infamous Desire: Male Homosexuality in Colonial Latin America* (Chicago, 2003), ch. 4.

69 R. A. Gutiérrez, 'Warfare, homosexuality, and gender status among American Indian men in the southwest', in T. A. Foster (ed.), *Long Before Stonewall: Histories of Same-Sex Sexuality in Early America* (New York, 2007), p. 20.

70 Quoted by B. T. McCormack, 'Conjugal violence, sex, sin, and murder in the mission communities of Alta California', *Journal of the History of Sexuality*, 16 (2007), 399. See also A. Hurtado, 'Sexuality in California's Franciscan missions: cultural perceptions and historical realities', in K. M. Phillips and B. Reay (eds), *Sexualities in History: A Reader* (New York, 2002), ch. 8.

71 Bligh, *The Log of the Bounty*, vol. 2, pp. 16–17.

72 Langsdorff, *Voyages and Travels*, vol. 2, pp. 64–5.

73 Quoted in Wallace, *Sexual Encounters*, p. 95.

74 C. Brickell, *Mates & Lovers: A History of Gay New Zealand* (Auckland, 2008), pp. 23–30.

Index